*50 Historical
Secrets to Becom*

Steal from the Greats

J. D. Maxwell

Published by J. D. Maxwell, 2024.

While every precaution has been taken in the preparation of this book, the publisher assumes no responsibility for errors or omissions, or for damages resulting from the use of the information contained herein.

STEAL FROM THE GREATS

First edition. October 7, 2024.

Copyright © 2024 J. D. Maxwell.

ISBN: 979-8224594023

Written by J. D. Maxwell.

What if you could unlock the secrets of greatness from the most influential people in history? **"Steal from the Greats"** distills the lives of 50 extraordinary figures—from warriors and philosophers to inventors and revolutionaries—into actionable lessons for self-improvement. Discover how Alexander the Great's bold leadership, Marie Curie's relentless pursuit of knowledge, and Marcus Aurelius' wisdom in adversity can guide you to success in your own life.

But this isn't just a history book. It's a blueprint for how you can take the best from these figures and apply their principles to your everyday challenges. Whether you're striving to develop mental toughness, sharpen your leadership skills, or find the drive to overcome obstacles, the timeless lessons in this book will provide you with practical, real-life applications to transform yourself.

With direct, no-nonsense advice, this book shows how the truths, struggles, and victories of history's icons can help you build a life of purpose, freedom, and power. **Learn from the best. Become your best.**

About the Author

J.D. Maxwell is an avid historian, philosopher, and self-improvement enthusiast who has spent the last decade studying the lives of extraordinary individuals. With a background in psychology and a passion for understanding human potential, Maxwell has dedicated his career to uncovering the timeless principles that have guided history's most influential figures.

Maxwell's writing is known for its engaging blend of historical storytelling and practical, no-nonsense advice, aimed at helping readers apply the lessons of the past to their own lives. Drawing on his extensive research, Maxwell weaves together history and personal development in a way that empowers individuals to think deeply, act decisively, and pursue greatness in their own unique ways.

When he's not diving into historical archives or crafting his next book, Maxwell can be found hiking, practicing martial arts, or exploring ancient ruins in search of inspiration. His belief in the power of resilience, truth, and hard work is not just something he writes about—it's a philosophy he lives by.

J.D. Maxwell is a firm believer that the greatest achievements in life are built on the shoulders of those who came before, and through his work, he strives to guide others to realize their own potential by learning from the best history has to offer.

Introduction

There's a reason history fascinates us. It's not just the epic battles, the groundbreaking discoveries, or the inspiring leadership. It's something deeper. We sense that those who came before us have left behind valuable lessons, and if we can tap into that wisdom, we can learn to navigate our own lives with greater purpose and power. Greatness is not a mystery. It leaves clues. The people who achieved it—whether through brilliance, courage, or relentless determination—show us the way forward. This book is about finding those clues and using them to become the best version of yourself.

But here's the twist: this book isn't about hero worship. It's about **stealing** from the greats. That's right—stealing. Taking the most valuable lessons from the lives of history's most iconic figures and applying those lessons to your own life. You see, greatness isn't something reserved for a few legendary individuals. It's a set of principles, strategies, and mindsets that anyone can use. Whether you want to become a stronger leader, a sharper thinker, or someone who can weather life's storms, these men and women have already charted the course. All you have to do is follow it.

Think about it. We often admire figures like Alexander the Great or Abraham Lincoln from a distance, as if they existed in a world we can never touch. But the truth is, they were human beings just like us. They faced doubt, hardship, and failure. They made mistakes. And yet, they found a way to rise above all of that. They mastered themselves and their circumstances. That's what this book is about—learning how to master yourself by learning from the masters of history.

The lessons these historical figures offer aren't abstract or theoretical. They are grounded in hard-earned wisdom, the kind you can apply immediately to your life. We're not here for feel-good inspiration that fades as soon as you put the book down. We're here for practical, real-world advice that will make a tangible difference. Men like you, driven to improve, need more than just motivation. You need strategies that work. You need the truth, laid out in simple, no-nonsense terms. You want power, freedom, and the discipline to achieve what you set out to do. The figures in these pages—whether they were inventors, conquerors, philosophers, or revolutionaries—possessed these qualities. They mastered their environments and bent the world to their will. You can do the same.

Now, let's talk about the approach of this book. Each chapter will introduce you to a new historical figure. We'll begin by diving into who they were—their struggles, their triumphs, and their defining moments. You'll get a glimpse into their mindset and the challenges they faced. But we won't stop there. The true value comes from extracting the lessons they left behind. I'll show you exactly how to apply those lessons to your own life. You won't just be reading about history—you'll be learning how to *use* history to build a better future for yourself.

Consider Thomas Edison, who revolutionized the world with his inventions. His story isn't just about the lightbulb or the phonograph—it's about the relentless drive to keep going despite thousands of failures. What can you learn from that? How can you adopt his persistence and turn it into fuel for your own goals? Or take Marcus Aurelius, the Stoic Roman emperor who ruled one of the most powerful empires in history. His philosophy of staying calm in the face of chaos is just as relevant now as it was two thousand years ago. How can you develop that mental toughness to handle whatever life throws your way?

These figures didn't succeed because they were lucky or special—they succeeded because they mastered certain principles. They understood the importance of truth, hard work, and the freedom to carve their own path. And those same principles are available to you. No matter where you are in life, the tools are here, waiting to be picked up.

One thing to keep in mind as you read: this book isn't just a history lesson. It's a blueprint. You're not here to admire from afar—you're here to take what these greats did right and **make it your own**. You're going to steal their best ideas, their mindset, and their habits and use them to build yourself into someone who is unstoppable. The men and women in these pages faced real struggles, just like you. They weren't perfect. But they found ways to rise above, and so can you. You'll learn from their victories and their mistakes. You'll find out what made them tick, and you'll use that to fuel your own growth.

But why steal from history? Because history is honest. It shows us what works. It strips away the fluff and gives us the raw truth about what it takes to succeed. The people we'll study didn't have shortcuts—they had grit, vision, and the courage to keep going when others would have quit. In today's world, where distractions are endless and excuses are easy to come by, we need these lessons more than ever.

By the time you finish this book, you won't just know about 50 historical figures. You'll have a toolkit full of strategies and mindsets you can use to conquer your own challenges. Whether it's building resilience, developing focus, or becoming a more decisive leader, you'll find the lessons that resonate with you—and you'll apply them in ways that matter. This is your journey. These are your tools. History has laid out the blueprint. Now it's time for you to take it, make it your own, and build the life you've always wanted.

So, get ready. This is more than a book—it's a roadmap to greatness, built on the wisdom of the people who've been there before. **Learn from the best. Become your best.** Let's begin.

Visionaries and Innovators

Leonardo da Vinci

Imagine being able to master not just one field, but many—painting, engineering, anatomy, architecture, and even flight. Few people have ever come close to the level of genius that **Leonardo da Vinci** achieved in his lifetime. He's not just a historical figure we admire; he's someone who **broke the boundaries of what a human being can accomplish**. Leonardo lived at the intersection of art and science, blending creativity with intense curiosity and relentless hard work. He's a reminder that **you don't have to be limited by one path**. His life shows us that the more we stretch our minds, the more capable we become.

Da Vinci wasn't born into privilege. He wasn't given the tools to succeed on a silver platter. He made himself into the genius we know today through curiosity, persistence, and relentless exploration. And that's where the lessons for us begin. You don't have to be extraordinary to achieve extraordinary things. But you do have to be willing to **push beyond what's comfortable**. Da Vinci's life shows us exactly how to do that.

Let's dive into his story—one of a man who refused to settle for mediocrity, who sought to understand everything, and who, through sheer curiosity and obsession with improvement, left behind a legacy that still impacts us centuries later.

Autobiography

Leonardo was born in 1452, the illegitimate son of a Florentine notary and a peasant woman. Because of his illegitimacy, he was denied formal education, but that didn't stop him from learning. As a young boy, he displayed an unusual talent for drawing, and by age 14, his father apprenticed him to the famous painter Andrea del Verrocchio. It was here that Leonardo's love for art blossomed, but it was also where he began to understand the power of **observation** and **curiosity**. Verrocchio's workshop wasn't just about painting—it was a hub of creative and scientific inquiry. It combined art with the mechanics of the world around it. This was Leonardo's first exposure to **thinking beyond the canvas**, and he soaked it up like a sponge.

What made Leonardo truly special was his insatiable curiosity. He didn't just paint a bird—he wanted to know **how it flew**. He didn't just draw the human body—he dissected cadavers to understand how muscles, bones, and organs worked together. In an era where specialization wasn't just encouraged but expected, Leonardo refused to be boxed in. He became a **polymath**, someone who excelled in multiple fields, driven by his obsessive desire to know more.

Throughout his life, Leonardo worked on projects that spanned multiple disciplines. His artistic masterpieces like the *Mona Lisa* and *The Last Supper* are known worldwide, but he was equally dedicated to his work in engineering, anatomy, and mechanics. He designed early prototypes of flying machines, sketched intricate diagrams of human anatomy, and conceived city plans that were centuries ahead of their time. Yet, despite all his successes, Leonardo was also known for leaving many of his projects unfinished. His notebooks—filled with sketches, observations, and inventions—are a testament to his mind constantly racing ahead, never content to stay in one place.

Leonardo's greatest gift wasn't his genius—it was his ability to **see the world differently**. He didn't accept things as they were; he questioned everything. And that questioning led to the breakthroughs that continue to inspire us today.

Lessons and Applications

So, how can you apply the lessons of Leonardo da Vinci's life to your own journey? How can his boundless curiosity and passion for exploration translate into your self-improvement? Here are three crucial takeaways from Leonardo's life that you can start using right now to level up in every area of your life.

1. Cultivate Relentless Curiosity

If there's one thing Leonardo da Vinci mastered, it was the art of **asking questions**. He didn't just accept what was in front of him; he dug deeper, constantly challenging the status quo. Curiosity was at the core of his genius, and it's something we can all develop.

You might not be dissecting cadavers or designing flying machines, but think about your own life. How often do you question the things you encounter every day? How often do you seek to truly understand why things work the way they do? Most people go through life on autopilot, accepting things as they are. But if you want to achieve greatness, you've got to flip that switch. You have to **train your mind to stay curious**.

Start by cultivating a habit of asking "why." It sounds simple, but most people don't do it. Why do you do what you do every day? Why do you follow certain routines? Why do certain systems in your work or personal life function the way they do? When you start asking "why," you begin to unravel new insights and see opportunities for improvement that most people overlook.

In practical terms, this could mean picking up new skills or studying areas outside your comfort zone. Leonardo didn't stick to just one field—he mastered many. You don't have to be limited by your current job or career. Start learning about things that interest you, even if they don't seem directly related to your goals right now. Curiosity opens doors. The more you know, the more connections your brain can make, and the more innovative solutions you'll find in all aspects of your life.

2. Embrace the Process of Mastery

One of the most striking things about Leonardo's life was his **dedication to the process**. He wasn't just focused on the end result—he was obsessed with the craft itself. Whether he was painting or studying anatomy, he poured himself into the work, fully immersing himself in the pursuit of mastery. This wasn't about quick wins; it was about long-term growth and development.

We live in a world that prizes instant gratification. But if you want to follow in Leonardo's footsteps, you need to shift your mindset. It's not about getting rich or successful quickly. It's about dedicating yourself to the process and the work itself. The results will come, but only if you're willing to fall in love with the grind.

Mastery isn't achieved overnight. Leonardo didn't become a genius by accident. He spent **decades** honing his skills, constantly pushing himself to improve. You need to adopt that same mindset. Whether you're working on a career goal, a fitness goal, or improving your relationships, you must focus on the process, not the outcome. The daily work, the small steps forward—that's where the real growth happens.

Leonardo's process involved **constant iteration**. He was known for reworking his paintings, revisiting designs, and tweaking ideas over and over again. Take this lesson to heart. Don't be afraid of the grind. Fall in love with the process of getting better every day. Mastery comes from consistent, deliberate practice. If you're willing to put in the work, the results will follow.

3. Think Beyond Limitations

Leonardo da Vinci didn't believe in limits. His life was a testament to the idea that you don't have to be defined by your circumstances or even your field of study. He was an artist, an engineer, a scientist, an inventor. He didn't allow society to box him in, and you shouldn't either.

Too often, we let our environment, our past, or our perceived skillsets dictate what we can and can't do. Maybe you've been told you're only good at one thing, or maybe you've convinced yourself that certain goals are out of reach. Leonardo would have scoffed at those limitations. He saw potential everywhere and in everything. You need to develop that same mindset.

This doesn't mean you have to become an expert in multiple fields, but it does mean **expanding your horizons**. Don't be afraid to venture into new territories. If you're an entrepreneur, study psychology to understand your customers better. If you're in a corporate job, learn design principles to enhance your creativity. Break out of the narrow view that says you can only excel at one thing.

Leonardo's greatest innovations came from cross-pollinating his knowledge in different fields. His studies of anatomy informed his art. His understanding of mechanics influenced his inventions. You can do the same by applying knowledge from one area of your life to another. Think bigger. Challenge yourself to pursue things that seem outside your expertise. The truth is, limitations only exist if you let them. Leonardo didn't, and neither should you.

Thomas Edison

Think about the devices and comforts you enjoy today—your lightbulbs, your music players, even some of the tools you use for work. Now, realize that **Thomas Edison**, one of history's greatest inventors, had a hand in laying the foundation for much of the modern world. He wasn't just an inventor, though; Edison was the living embodiment of persistence. He wasn't handed success. In fact, he faced thousands of failures, setbacks, and obstacles. But what separated Edison from everyone else wasn't his intelligence or his ideas—it was his ability to keep going when others quit.

Edison once famously said, "I have not failed. I've just found 10,000 ways that won't work." That right there is the mindset of a man who understood the value of **relentless persistence**. He didn't see failure as a wall; he saw it as a stepping stone. And that's a lesson every one of us can take to heart. Edison teaches us that **persistence, not talent, is the real key to success**. You don't have to be the smartest guy in the room, but if you're the one who keeps pushing forward when everyone else has thrown in the towel, you will win.

Edison's life gives us a blueprint on how to handle adversity, how to keep going in the face of failure, and how to turn setbacks into stepping stones for greatness. This chapter will walk you through his life and show you how to apply the principles of persistence and hard work to your own life.

Autobiography

Thomas Alva Edison was born on February 11, 1847, in Milan, Ohio. He came from humble beginnings, the youngest of seven children in a middle-class family. His father, Samuel Edison, was a jack-of-all-trades, dabbling in everything from farming to real estate. His mother, Nancy Matthews Elliott, was a schoolteacher, and her influence was pivotal in Edison's early education. Due to illness and hyperactivity, Edison was home-schooled by his mother, which turned out to be one of the best things that could have happened to him. This gave him the freedom to explore and learn at his own pace, often indulging in his deep curiosity for how things worked.

By the time he was 12, Edison had developed a love for tinkering and experimentation, often conducting chemical experiments in a makeshift lab at home. His curiosity wasn't just confined to books or ideas—he had a passion for **applying knowledge**. This was evident when, as a teenager, he worked as a telegraph operator. It wasn't enough for him to just do the job; he wanted to improve the equipment. This desire to innovate became a driving force throughout his life.

But it wasn't all smooth sailing. Edison's early ventures were fraught with failure. In 1870, at the age of 23, he invented an automatic vote recorder, which he believed would revolutionize the voting process. But it was a complete flop; nobody wanted it. Many people would have been discouraged by this, especially so early in their career, but not Edison. He shrugged it off and moved on to the next idea. That's where his resilience really began to show.

In 1877, Edison invented the phonograph, a device that could record and reproduce sound—a world-changing invention. But this was just the beginning. By 1879, after countless experiments and failures, Edison developed the first practical incandescent lightbulb, a breakthrough that would make him a household name. The process wasn't easy. Edison and his team tested over 6,000 different materials to find the right filament for the bulb. It took hundreds of failed attempts, but he refused to give up.

Edison went on to hold over **1,000 patents** in his lifetime, contributing to the invention of the motion picture camera, electric power distribution, and many other technologies that transformed society. But perhaps his greatest invention wasn't a device—it was his mindset. Edison proved that the secret to success isn't avoiding failure, but **using failure as fuel to keep moving forward.**

Lessons and Applications

Edison's story is inspiring, but it's not just about looking back and admiring his persistence. His life provides concrete lessons that you can apply to your own goals and ambitions. Here are three powerful takeaways from Edison's life that, when applied, will help you achieve more and break through obstacles.

1. Redefine Failure as Part of the Process

The first thing you can learn from Thomas Edison is to **completely redefine your relationship with failure.** For most people, failure is something to be feared or avoided. It's seen as a sign that you're not cut out for something or that you should give up. Edison, however, flipped this thinking on its head. He viewed failure not as a dead end but as **valuable feedback.** When one experiment failed, he didn't see it as wasted effort—he saw it as eliminating one more possibility that didn't work, bringing him closer to the solution.

Think about that. What would change in your life if you no longer saw failure as a negative? Instead of feeling defeated after a setback, imagine feeling energized because you've just gained new information. Failure stops being something to fear and becomes part of your process for success.

In practical terms, this means embracing failure in whatever you're pursuing. Whether you're building a business, working on a fitness goal, or trying to improve a relationship, understand that failure is not only inevitable—it's essential. You're going to stumble, and that's okay. The key is to **extract the lessons from each failure** and keep moving forward.

Let's say you're working on a business idea, and you hit a roadblock—maybe a deal falls through, or your product doesn't sell as expected. Rather than seeing this as a sign to quit, you need to **analyze the failure**. What went wrong? What can you learn from it? How can you adjust your approach and move forward smarter? Edison tested thousands of materials for his lightbulb filament before finding one that worked. He didn't stop after 10 or even 100 failures. He **kept going until he got it right**. And that's the mindset you need to adopt.

Start redefining failure as **part of the journey**. Each misstep gets you one step closer to where you want to be. The key is not to give up at the first sign of difficulty. Just like Edison, you need to keep testing, keep trying, and keep moving forward.

2. Persistence Overcomes Talent Every Time

Edison wasn't the most intelligent or naturally gifted inventor of his time. In fact, he was often ridiculed for his lack of formal education. But what he lacked in traditional intelligence, he made up for in sheer **persistence**. He outworked everyone else. When others gave up after a few failures, he doubled down and kept pushing. This is one of the most critical lessons you can take from Edison: **Persistence will take you farther than talent ever could**.

Many men get discouraged because they think they aren't talented enough to succeed in their chosen field. They believe that success is reserved for the gifted or the lucky. But Edison's life shows us the opposite is true. Persistence is the great equalizer. You don't have to be the smartest or the most skilled. If you're willing to outwork everyone else, you'll succeed where others fail.

Think about a goal you've set for yourself—whether it's in your career, your health, or your personal life. Now ask yourself this: Are you willing to persist through the inevitable challenges? Are you willing to keep going when you don't feel like it? If you adopt

Edison's approach, you'll realize that the willingness to **push through obstacles** is far more important than natural ability.

In your daily life, persistence can look like small, consistent actions. If you're working on getting in shape, it's about showing up to the gym day after day, even when you don't see immediate results. If you're building a business, it's about continuing to work, even when success seems a long way off. Persistence means **staying in the game** long enough for your efforts to pay off.

Edison once said, "Many of life's failures are people who did not realize how close they were to success when they gave up." That's the essence of persistence—you don't quit because you're closer than you think. Success often comes to those who simply **refuse to stop**.

3. Focus on Practical Solutions, Not Theories

Edison was not a man of lofty theories. He didn't waste his time debating abstract concepts. He was focused on **practical results**. When he set out to create the lightbulb, his goal wasn't to understand the nature of light—it was to create a reliable, affordable source of it that people could use in their daily lives. His obsession with **practicality** is one of the most important lessons you can take away from his life.

Too often, we get caught up in overthinking. We spend so much time theorizing about what might work or trying to perfect our plan that we never actually take action. Edison was the opposite. He believed in **experimenting, failing fast, and refining along the way**. Instead of waiting for the perfect moment or the perfect plan, he took action. He built things, tested them, and improved them as he went.

If you want to achieve big things, you have to adopt a **bias toward action**. Stop waiting for the perfect conditions. Stop theorizing and start doing. You don't need to have everything figured out to make progress. Whether you're starting a new project, tackling a fitness goal, or trying to improve a relationship, the key is to **get started**. You'll learn and improve as you go, just like Edison did.

Let's say you've got an idea for a business or a personal project, but you're hesitating because you feel like you're not ready. Maybe you don't have all the resources or the perfect plan. The truth is, if you wait until everything is perfect, you'll never start. Edison didn't wait for perfection. He started with what he had, took action, and adjusted along the way.

Take the lightbulb as an example. He didn't hit a home run on his first try. In fact, his early prototypes failed spectacularly. But that's because he was **focused on practical experimentation**, not on crafting a flawless theory. Edison believed in getting his hands dirty, working through the problem, and finding solutions that worked in the real world, not just on paper. That's what you need to do.

In practical terms, this means adopting a "test-and-learn" approach to your goals. Don't get stuck in analysis paralysis. Take action, even if you don't feel 100% ready. Start the business. Begin the workout plan. Reach out to that mentor. Whatever your goal is, **take the first step**, and adjust as you go. This approach allows you to learn faster and make real progress, rather than spinning your wheels thinking about what might go wrong.

Remember, Edison wasn't successful because he had the best ideas from the start. He was successful because he put his ideas into practice, failed, and improved them over time. The key takeaway here is this: **stop waiting for the perfect plan and start taking imperfect action**. You'll figure things out faster, gain valuable experience, and make progress where others are still waiting for ideal conditions.

Nikola Tesla

When you think of the name **Nikola Tesla**, you might picture lightning, electric currents, or massive inventions that changed the world. You'd be right, but Tesla was more than an inventor. He was a man whose vision transcended his time, a man driven by an obsession with ideas that others thought impossible. Tesla didn't just push boundaries; he **smashed** through them. He saw the world not as it was but as it **could be**—and then worked relentlessly to turn his vision into reality.

Tesla's genius wasn't just in his ability to innovate; it was in his **unwavering belief** in his own vision. Even when the world doubted him—when he was labeled a dreamer, eccentric, or worse—Tesla stuck to his path. His life serves as a stark reminder that **the only limits we have are the ones we accept.** He teaches us that when you have a vision, when you believe in something so strongly that you're willing to sacrifice everything for it, you become unstoppable.

This chapter will walk you through Tesla's remarkable life, his boundless imagination, and his relentless work ethic. But more importantly, it will show you how to take these lessons and **apply them directly to your own life**. Tesla may have been a genius, but his core principles—vision, persistence, and belief—are traits that any of us can develop and use to fuel our own success.

Autobiography

Nikola Tesla was born on July 10, 1856, in the village of Smiljan, in modern-day Croatia. The son of an Eastern Orthodox priest and a mother who was deeply inventive herself, Tesla was exposed to both spirituality and creativity from a young age. His mother, who had a gift for crafting and inventing small household devices, undoubtedly influenced his curiosity and love for creation.

From a young age, Tesla exhibited signs of brilliance. He had an astonishing memory and could visualize complex machinery in his mind, a trait that would serve him well throughout his career. After studying engineering at the Austrian Polytechnic in Graz, Tesla moved to the United States in 1884, seeking greater opportunities. He arrived in New York with nothing but four cents in his pocket and a head full of ideas that would later revolutionize the world.

In the U.S., Tesla initially worked for Thomas Edison, but their relationship quickly soured due to fundamental differences in how they viewed electricity. While Edison was focused on direct current (DC) electricity, Tesla championed the use of alternating current (AC), a more efficient system that could transmit electricity over long distances. The **War of Currents** between Edison and Tesla is now legendary, and though Tesla ultimately won, his victory wasn't without hardship. He was often ridiculed and discredited, even as his inventions proved their superiority.

Despite his successes, Tesla faced financial challenges throughout his life. He wasn't interested in wealth for its own sake; instead, he was focused on his **vision** of a world powered by free, renewable energy. Tesla imagined wireless energy transmission, a global network of communication (something remarkably like the internet), and even machines capable of harnessing the energy of the Earth itself. Unfortunately, much of this vision went unrealized during his lifetime, as financial backers pulled out and he was often overshadowed by more commercially successful inventors.

Tesla died in 1943, impoverished and largely forgotten by the mainstream, but his influence lives on in nearly every aspect of modern life. From the electricity we use today to wireless communication, Tesla's ideas have shaped the world in ways few could have predicted. His legacy is not just one of invention but of **uncompromising belief** in his vision, even when the world didn't understand it.

Lessons and Applications

Tesla's life offers us powerful lessons—not just in invention, but in how to turn our own visions into reality. His brilliance came from his relentless focus, his ability to imagine the future, and his belief that no obstacle was insurmountable. Here are three key lessons we can take from Tesla's life and **apply directly to our own journey**.

1. Develop a Bold Vision and Stick to It—No Matter the Doubts

Tesla was a visionary in the truest sense. He saw possibilities that others couldn't even dream of. His vision for alternating current wasn't just a technical improvement; it was a **revolutionary shift** in how the world would use electricity. While others ridiculed him and clung to the old way of doing things, Tesla stayed committed to his vision, knowing that it was superior. He didn't let the doubts of others sway him, and that's something we can all learn from.

In your own life, it's critical to have a **bold vision**—something that drives you forward, even when the world around you doesn't understand it. This could be a career goal, a business idea, or even a personal transformation you want to achieve. The important part is that your vision **challenges the status quo**. If your dream is easily understood or accepted by everyone, it's probably not big enough. Tesla teaches us that **the greater the vision, the greater the resistance**—and that's a good thing. Resistance means you're doing something that matters.

But having a bold vision is only half the battle. You have to **stick to it**, especially when the road gets tough. Tesla could have given up when Edison's DC system was dominating the electrical world. He could have abandoned his ideas when financiers like J.P. Morgan pulled their backing for his wireless energy transmission project. But he didn't. He stayed true to his vision because he believed in it with everything he had. That's the mindset you need to adopt.

In practical terms, this means **doubling down on your vision when others doubt you.** Don't let naysayers, failures, or setbacks make you question your path. If you truly believe in your goal, you must be willing to endure the hardships that come with it. Surround yourself with people who share your vision, and don't be afraid to cut out the voices that try to drag you down. **Your belief in your vision must be stronger than anyone's doubts**—even your own.

2. Obsession Is a Tool, Not a Flaw

Tesla wasn't just passionate about his work—he was **obsessed**. He famously worked for days on end without sleep, driven by the need to bring his ideas to life. This kind of obsession can often be seen as unhealthy or unbalanced, but Tesla's life shows us that when harnessed correctly, **obsession is a tool for greatness.**

If you look at anyone who has achieved extraordinary success, whether in business, sports, or art, you'll find that they all share one thing: **a deep, almost irrational obsession** with what they do. This isn't about balance. It's about **immersion**. Tesla lived and breathed his inventions. He didn't have a backup plan because he didn't need one. His focus was so intense that he couldn't see failure as an option. That's what allowed him to push boundaries and make breakthroughs that others couldn't.

In your own life, you need to **embrace obsession** when it comes to your goals. Forget the idea that you need to have everything balanced and in moderation. If you want to achieve something truly great, you have to be willing to throw yourself into it fully. This doesn't mean burning out or neglecting other aspects of your life, but it does mean dedicating yourself to your vision with **unrelenting focus.**

Think about the goals you've set for yourself. Are you obsessed with achieving them, or are you just interested? There's a big difference. Interest fades when things get difficult. Obsession, on the other hand, drives you through the tough times. It keeps you up late working on your business when everyone else has gone to bed. It pushes you to go to the gym even when you're tired. It makes you study harder, learn more, and keep improving long after others have given up.

To harness obsession, you need to **immerse yourself in your work**. Block out distractions and create an environment where your focus can thrive. Tesla didn't just tinker with ideas when it was convenient—he lived them. For you, this might mean setting strict routines, cutting out activities that don't serve your goal, and dedicating your mental and physical energy toward progress. When you do this, you'll find that your obsession becomes a powerful force that drives you to achieve things you never thought possible.

3. Don't Let Money Be Your Master—Focus on Legacy

One of the most remarkable things about Tesla is that he wasn't driven by money. In fact, he often sacrificed financial success for the sake of his inventions. Tesla's focus was always on the **legacy** he could leave behind—the ways in which his inventions would transform humanity. While others, like his rival Edison, pursued profit, Tesla was willing to walk away from financial gain if it meant staying true to his vision.

This is an incredibly important lesson, especially in today's world where success is often measured by wealth. Tesla's life shows us that **true fulfillment comes not from financial gain, but from creating something that outlasts us.** Money is a tool, but it shouldn't be your master. When you focus on building a legacy—something that will positively impact others—you create deeper meaning in your life and your work.

In practical terms, this means **aligning your goals with a purpose larger than yourself**. What kind of impact do you want to leave behind? What can you create or contribute that will outlast you? Whether you're building a business, pursuing a career, or working on personal growth, keep your focus on the long-term impact. Tesla didn't care about becoming the richest man alive; he cared about changing the world.

This mindset frees you from the constant pressure to chase money and status. Instead, you can direct your energy toward **creating something meaningful**. When you focus on legacy, your decisions become clearer, and you're less likely to be swayed by short-term rewards. Tesla walked away from lucrative deals because they didn't align with his vision. He was willing to sacrifice immediate gains for the sake of his long-term goals. You can do the same by staying focused on your purpose, rather than getting distracted by temporary success.

Steve Jobs

When you think about innovation in the modern world, **Steve Jobs** stands out as one of the most iconic and influential figures. He didn't just create products—he created experiences that changed the way we interact with technology. Jobs wasn't just a businessman; he was a visionary, a creator, and a master of focus. He understood that to build something truly revolutionary, you need to think differently, push boundaries, and sometimes go against the grain. Jobs' legacy is proof that when you combine relentless innovation with an uncompromising vision, you can change the world.

From founding Apple in a garage to revolutionizing multiple industries—computers, music, phones, even animation—Jobs showed us what's possible when you demand excellence from yourself and your team. He was obsessed with **perfection**, with **simplicity**, and with delivering products that not only worked but inspired. His life offers us profound lessons on **pursuing bold visions**, **cutting through the noise**, and **focusing on what really matters**. The path to greatness, as Jobs proved, isn't about doing more—it's about doing the right things with unyielding intensity.

This chapter explores Jobs' life and the lessons he left behind, showing how his drive for innovation, focus, and simplicity can be directly applied to your life and help you achieve your own form of success.

Autobiography

Steve Jobs was born on February 24, 1955, in San Francisco, California. He was adopted by Paul and Clara Jobs, who raised him in Silicon Valley, a hotbed for the budding tech industry at the time. From an early age, Jobs showed a curiosity for electronics and machinery. He spent much of his childhood tinkering with devices in his garage and attended talks at Hewlett-Packard, where he met his future business partner, Steve Wozniak.

In 1972, Jobs enrolled at Reed College in Portland, Oregon, but dropped out after just one semester. Although he left school, he stayed on campus for a while, attending classes that interested him, including calligraphy—a course that would later influence the design and typography of Apple's products. Jobs then traveled to India in search of spiritual enlightenment before returning to the U.S., where he found his true calling: **entrepreneurship and innovation**.

In 1976, Jobs co-founded Apple with Wozniak and Ronald Wayne in Jobs' parents' garage. They created the **Apple I**, a personal computer that was a hit among tech enthusiasts. But it was the **Apple II**, released in 1977, that really put Apple on the map. It was one of the first personal computers to appeal to a mass audience, making technology accessible to the average person.

Jobs' journey wasn't without setbacks. In 1985, he was ousted from Apple after a power struggle with then-CEO John Sculley. For many, this would have been the end of the story. But for Jobs, it was a **beginning**. After leaving Apple, he founded **NeXT**, a computer platform development company, and acquired **Pixar**, which he turned into one of the most successful animation studios in history. During this period, Jobs learned valuable lessons about leadership, innovation, and resilience.

In 1997, Jobs returned to Apple, a company that was on the brink of bankruptcy. Over the next decade, he transformed it into one of the most valuable companies in the world. Under his leadership, Apple introduced groundbreaking products like the iMac, iPod, iPhone, and iPad, each one disrupting industries and setting new standards for innovation.

Jobs was a perfectionist, obsessed with design and user experience. His philosophy of focusing on **simplicity and elegance** guided everything Apple created. But Jobs wasn't just about making things look good—he demanded that they work flawlessly, too. His commitment to excellence and his **unwavering vision** shaped Apple's culture and influenced millions of lives around the world.

Jobs passed away in 2011, but his legacy lives on. He left behind more than just a company—he left a blueprint for how to pursue excellence with relentless focus. He showed the world that vision, simplicity, and a refusal to compromise can lead to extraordinary success.

Lessons and Applications

Steve Jobs' life offers a wealth of lessons on how to achieve greatness, but perhaps the most important are his focus, vision, and pursuit of simplicity. These traits didn't just make Apple a success; they can make **you** a success as well. Here are three powerful, actionable lessons from Jobs that you can apply directly to your life.

1. Focus on What Really Matters—Cut Out the Noise

One of the most important lessons from Steve Jobs is the power of **focus**. Jobs was famous for saying, "People think focus means saying yes to the thing you've got to focus on. But that's not what it means at all. It means saying no to the hundred other good ideas that there are. You have to pick carefully." This was a guiding principle in his life and career. When he returned to Apple in 1997, the company was spread thin, with too many products and not enough direction. Jobs cut 70% of the product line, focusing the company on just a few key products—the iMac, the iPod, and eventually the iPhone. This **laser-focused approach** allowed Apple to excel where others floundered.

In your life, you need to apply the same principle. **You can't do everything.** You're going to be bombarded with opportunities, distractions, and seemingly good ideas. But the truth is, spreading yourself too thin will lead to mediocrity. The key is to focus on the few things that really matter—the things that will move the needle in your life and your goals.

So, how do you know what to focus on? Start by identifying your **core priorities**. What are the 2 or 3 things that will make the biggest impact in your life right now? Maybe it's building a business, improving your fitness, or developing a new skill. Whatever it is, once you've identified your core priorities, **cut out everything else**. This may mean saying no to projects, social obligations, or even hobbies that don't align with your main focus. It's not easy, but as Jobs showed, **the power of focus** is undeniable.

In practical terms, this means creating a daily routine that revolves around your most important goals. Block out time for deep work, eliminate distractions, and be ruthless about where you spend your energy. The fewer things you try to do, the more successful you'll be at the things that really matter.

2. Think Different—Embrace Bold, Unconventional Ideas

Steve Jobs didn't just invent products—he **challenged the status quo**. The slogan "Think Different" wasn't just a marketing phrase for Apple; it was a mantra for how Jobs approached everything in his life. He didn't want to create slightly better products than his competitors; he wanted to **revolutionize entire industries**. When everyone else was focused on improving existing products, Jobs was focused on creating something entirely new. He didn't believe in small, incremental changes—he believed in bold, **game-changing innovations**.

This mindset is something we can all learn from. Too often, we play it safe in life. We follow the path laid out by others, or we aim for minor improvements instead of massive breakthroughs. But if you want to achieve something truly great, you have to be willing to

think differently. You have to embrace bold ideas, even if they seem impossible or unconventional.

In your own life, this means questioning assumptions and **breaking out of traditional thinking**. Don't just settle for improving what's already there—look for opportunities to create something entirely new. Whether you're starting a business, advancing your career, or working on a personal project, ask yourself: How can I **approach this differently**? What are the rules that everyone is following, and how can I break them in a way that gives me an advantage?

Jobs didn't just follow trends—he created them. The iPhone wasn't just a better phone; it was a **completely new way** of thinking about mobile devices. That's the level of innovation you should aim for in your own life. Whether you're working on a project, a business, or personal growth, don't be afraid to **push boundaries** and take risks. Bold, unconventional thinking is what leads to breakthroughs.

3. Pursue Simplicity and Excellence—Don't Settle for Mediocrity

Perhaps the most defining characteristic of Steve Jobs was his obsession with **simplicity and excellence**. He believed that great design wasn't just about how something looked—it was about how it worked. Jobs was relentless in his pursuit of perfection, famously demanding that even the insides of Apple products—the parts users would never see—be beautifully designed. His attention to detail and his refusal to settle for anything less than excellence set Apple apart from its competitors.

The lesson here is clear: **Don't settle for mediocrity**. Whether you're working on a project, building a career, or pursuing a personal goal, you should aim for **excellence in everything you do**. This doesn't mean being a perfectionist or delaying action until everything is perfect, but it does mean having high standards and refusing to cut corners.

In practical terms, this means paying attention to the **details**. When you're working on something, whether it's a presentation, a product, or a personal goal, ask yourself: How can I make this better? What can I improve to create something truly excellent? Don't just do the minimum required—go the extra mile to ensure that what you're producing is the best it can be.

But it's not just about striving for excellence—it's about **simplicity**. Jobs understood that simplicity is powerful. He once said, "Simple can be harder than complex. You have to work hard to get your thinking clean to make it simple." This is a crucial lesson for all of us. Complexity can be overwhelming, and it often leads to confusion and failure. When you simplify your approach—whether in work, life, or personal goals—you can **focus on what truly matters** and achieve better results.

In your life, this might mean simplifying your schedule, eliminating unnecessary tasks, or focusing on just a few key goals instead of trying to do everything. Remember, simplicity is a form of excellence. It allows you to focus on what's important and **do it incredibly well**.

Marie Curie

Imagine being the first person—man or woman—to win not just one, but **two** Nobel Prizes. Now, picture doing this in a time when women weren't even expected to attend universities, let alone lead groundbreaking scientific discoveries. **Marie Curie** did just that. She wasn't just a pioneer in science—she was a trailblazer for women and an embodiment of what it means to be utterly committed to your work. Curie's life story teaches us that when you combine an unrelenting passion with sheer perseverance, even the most daunting barriers can be broken.

Marie Curie wasn't handed her success. She fought for it, worked for it, and endured challenges that would have broken most people. She proved that **true strength lies not just in intellect but in resilience**. From humble beginnings in Poland to the forefront of science in France, Curie's journey is one of dedication, sacrifice, and an unwavering belief in her purpose. Her life offers profound lessons on pushing past limitations, staying committed to your passions, and embracing hard work even when the odds seem insurmountable.

This chapter will dive deep into Curie's remarkable life and legacy, offering powerful lessons that you can apply to your own journey—whether you're pursuing a career, personal growth, or overcoming life's challenges.

Autobiography

Marie Skłodowska Curie was born on November 7, 1867, in Warsaw, Poland, then part of the Russian Empire. Raised in a family of teachers, Curie's passion for learning was ignited early on, despite the limited opportunities available to women at the time. Poland was under Russian control, and Polish education was heavily restricted.

But Curie's family encouraged her intellectual curiosity, teaching her the value of perseverance in the face of oppression.

At a young age, Curie faced tragedy when her mother died of tuberculosis and her eldest sister passed away from typhus. These early losses left a profound impact on her and strengthened her resolve to pursue her goals, despite any personal hardships. After completing her secondary education, Curie longed to continue her studies, but the University of Warsaw did not accept women. Unwilling to let this limitation dictate her future, Curie joined an underground institution known as the **Flying University**, where women were allowed to study in secret.

In 1891, Curie moved to Paris to pursue her dream of higher education at the **University of Paris (Sorbonne)**. There, she earned degrees in both physics and mathematics, often studying by candlelight in a small, cold apartment, enduring poverty and hunger to reach her goals. During this time, she met Pierre Curie, a brilliant physicist, who became her partner in both marriage and scientific discovery.

Together, Marie and Pierre embarked on groundbreaking research on radioactivity, a term that **Marie Curie herself coined**. They discovered two new elements—polonium, named after her homeland, and radium. Their work revolutionized the field of science, but it was not without its dangers. Marie often worked with radioactive materials without proper safety protocols, unknowingly putting her health at great risk. Nonetheless, her dedication never wavered.

In 1903, the couple was awarded the **Nobel Prize in Physics**, shared with Henri Becquerel. Curie became the first woman to win a Nobel Prize. But tragedy struck again in 1906 when Pierre was killed in a tragic accident. Devastated, but not broken, Curie continued their work, taking over Pierre's position at the University of Paris and becoming the first female professor in the institution's history.

In 1911, Curie won her **second Nobel Prize**, this time in chemistry, for her work on radium and polonium, making her the only person to win Nobel Prizes in two different scientific fields. Her contributions laid the foundation for modern atomic science and paved the way for future generations of women in science. Despite facing prejudice, personal loss, and physical danger, Curie never gave up. Her life was a testament to the power of perseverance, passion, and the pursuit of knowledge.

Lessons and Applications

Marie Curie's journey offers invaluable lessons on how to push past limitations, embrace hard work, and stay committed to your passion, no matter the challenges. Let's explore three actionable takeaways from her life that you can apply to your own.

1. Embrace Hard Work and Perseverance—It's Not About Talent, It's About Grit

Marie Curie's success didn't come from natural talent alone—it came from **relentless hard work** and an unwavering commitment to her goals. In a time when women were discouraged from pursuing higher education and faced systemic barriers at every turn, Curie pushed forward, driven by her passion for science. She worked long hours in poor conditions, often sacrificing her health and personal well-being to continue her research. Curie's story is a powerful reminder that **success is not a matter of talent, but of perseverance**.

Too often, people believe that success comes easily to those who are naturally gifted. But if Curie's life teaches us anything, it's that success is about **showing up every day, no matter the obstacles**. It's about putting in the hours, staying focused, and refusing to quit when things get hard.

In your own life, this means adopting a mindset that values grit over talent. Whether you're working on a professional goal, improving your fitness, or learning a new skill, recognize that **hard work will always beat talent when talent doesn't work hard.** Don't rely on short bursts of inspiration or expect quick results. Success is built over time through **consistent effort.** Embrace the grind, knowing that every hour you put in brings you one step closer to your goals.

When you face setbacks, remember Curie's story. She didn't let obstacles stop her—she worked through them. When doors were closed to her, she found another way. **Perseverance isn't about never facing failure—it's about pushing through failure until you find success.** Whatever challenge you're facing right now, commit to seeing it through. Show up every day, put in the work, and trust that your persistence will pay off.

2. Stay Committed to Your Passion, Even When the World Doubts You

Marie Curie's life was filled with skepticism and doubt from the outside world. As a woman in science, she faced prejudice, with many in the academic and scientific communities questioning her abilities. But Curie's passion for her work was **stronger than the doubts of others.** She stayed committed to her research, not because she wanted recognition or approval, but because she believed in the importance of her work.

Curie's commitment to her passion is a lesson we can all learn from. **The world will often doubt you.** Whether it's your career choice, a business venture, or a personal goal, there will always be people who question your abilities or your choices. The key is to stay focused on your passion and your purpose. **Don't let external doubt become internal doubt.** When you know what you're working toward is important, stay committed, even when others don't understand.

In practical terms, this means being clear about why you're pursuing your goal. What drives you? What's the deeper purpose behind what you're doing? When you have a clear sense of purpose, it becomes easier to stay focused when obstacles arise. Just like Curie, who was driven by her love for science and discovery, you need to have a **purpose that fuels your persistence**.

Surround yourself with people who support your vision, but don't rely on the validation of others to keep you going. **Your passion has to come from within**. When external recognition or success seems far away, remind yourself why you started in the first place. Stay committed, and don't let the doubts of others throw you off course.

3. Break Barriers and Push Beyond Expectations—Don't Let Your Circumstances Define You

Marie Curie faced countless barriers throughout her life. As a woman in a male-dominated field, she was constantly underestimated and excluded from opportunities. Yet, she didn't let her circumstances define her. She didn't accept society's limitations, nor did she allow her gender to determine her destiny. Curie **broke through every barrier placed in front of her**, creating her own path and setting new standards for what women—and scientists—could achieve.

This lesson is perhaps the most powerful takeaway from Curie's life: **don't let your circumstances dictate your potential**. Whether it's societal expectations, personal setbacks, or even internal doubts, it's easy to believe that the obstacles in front of you are immovable. But Curie's life proves that no barrier is too high if you're willing to keep pushing.

In your own life, this means **refusing to be boxed in** by limitations—whether they're external or self-imposed. If you've been told that you can't achieve something because of where you come from, your background, your education, or any other factor, challenge that belief. Recognize that **you have the power to define your own path**. Curie didn't let the limitations of her time hold her back, and neither should you.

Breaking barriers requires courage, but it also requires a mindset that **sees obstacles as opportunities for growth**. Don't shy away from challenges—embrace them. Every barrier you break through is a testament to your strength and resilience. Instead of asking, "Why me?" when faced with a challenge, ask yourself, "How can I rise above this?" By adopting this mindset, you'll find that the barriers in your life become stepping stones to your success.

Wright Brothers

Imagine standing on the edge of history, staring at the sky, and wondering if it's possible for humans to fly. For centuries, the idea of human flight was dismissed as fantasy—something reserved for birds, not men. But in 1903, two brothers from Ohio did the unthinkable. **Wilbur and Orville Wright** didn't just dream of flying—they made it a reality. They built the first successful airplane and forever changed the course of history. But what's even more remarkable than their invention is **how they did it**. The Wright brothers didn't have advanced degrees, wealthy backers, or cutting-edge technology. They had something much more powerful: **an unshakable belief in their vision, relentless perseverance, and the ability to work together as a team.**

The Wright brothers didn't just build an airplane—they built a blueprint for how to tackle the impossible. They faced ridicule, setbacks, and failures, yet they never gave up. Their story is a testament to what can be accomplished through innovation, collaboration, and perseverance. They remind us that **no dream is too big** if you're willing to work for it. The lessons from their journey to flight are timeless and relevant to anyone aiming to defy the odds, break through limitations, and achieve greatness.

This chapter explores how the Wright brothers turned a wild dream into reality and what their story can teach us about **turning our own impossible goals into achievable successes.**

Autobiography

Wilbur Wright was born in 1867, and Orville Wright followed four years later in 1871. They were raised in a household that encouraged curiosity and learning. Their father, Milton Wright, was a bishop in the United Brethren Church and had a strong intellectual influence on the boys, often bringing home books and gadgets that sparked their imagination. Their mother, Susan, also had a mechanical mind and encouraged her sons to build and tinker from a young age.

Wilbur and Orville weren't born into wealth or privilege, but what they lacked in financial resources, they made up for with curiosity and determination. As boys, they were fascinated by flight, building kites and tinkering with simple machines. This fascination grew when their father brought home a rubber-band-powered toy helicopter, which ignited their lifelong obsession with flight. But flying wasn't something anyone took seriously back then—it was a fanciful idea, more suited for fiction than reality. Yet, the Wright brothers refused to let the opinions of others dictate their path.

As young men, they opened a bicycle repair and manufacturing shop, where they honed their mechanical skills. But their true passion was still human flight. The late 1800s and early 1900s were a time of scientific experimentation with gliders and attempts at heavier-than-air flight, but no one had successfully solved the problem. The Wright brothers dove into the challenge with the same analytical approach they had used in their bicycle business—testing, experimenting, and learning from every failure.

They didn't have formal engineering training, but they educated themselves by studying the work of pioneers like Otto Lilienthal and Samuel Langley. They knew that controlled flight was the key to success, so they spent years experimenting with gliders in the windy dunes of Kitty Hawk, North Carolina. After countless failures and revisions, they finally made a breakthrough in wing design and control mechanisms. They developed a technique called **wing warping**, which allowed the pilot to control the aircraft's movement, a revolutionary concept at the time.

On December 17, 1903, the Wright brothers made history. Their airplane, the **Wright Flyer**, flew for 12 seconds over the dunes of Kitty Hawk, covering a distance of 120 feet. It wasn't a long flight, but it was the first time a heavier-than-air machine had flown under its own power with a pilot aboard. They had done it. Human flight was no longer a dream—it was a reality.

But the Wright brothers didn't stop there. They continued to refine their designs, improving both flight duration and control. They knew that one successful flight wasn't enough. They were determined to make aviation a practical reality. Despite facing skepticism and competition, they patented their invention and went on to sell their airplanes to governments and militaries around the world, forever changing the landscape of transportation and warfare.

The Wright brothers' story isn't just about inventing the airplane—it's about **overcoming impossible odds**. They were ordinary men who, through perseverance, innovation, and teamwork, achieved something extraordinary. And their journey offers powerful lessons for anyone striving to reach their own ambitious goals.

Lessons and Applications

The story of the Wright brothers is a masterclass in perseverance, innovation, and teamwork. These are qualities that anyone can apply to their own life, no matter what field they're in or what goal they're pursuing. Let's break down three actionable lessons from their journey and explore how you can use them to achieve your own success.

1. Break the Impossible into Small, Achievable Steps

The Wright brothers weren't trying to build a perfect airplane on their first attempt. They knew that if they aimed for perfection right out of the gate, they'd be paralyzed by the enormity of the task. Instead, they broke the problem of flight into smaller, manageable pieces. First, they studied existing attempts at gliders and learned from the failures of others. Then they focused on developing control mechanisms with their wing-warping design. After mastering control, they tackled the challenge of propulsion, building their own lightweight engine to power their flyer.

This incremental approach allowed them to make consistent progress, even in the face of setbacks. By **breaking the impossible into small, achievable steps**, they were able to tackle one problem at a time, building on each success and learning from each failure.

In your own life, the same principle applies. **Big goals can be overwhelming.** If you focus solely on the end result, you may feel paralyzed by the scale of the challenge. Instead, break your goal down into smaller, more manageable tasks. If your goal is to start a business, don't focus on becoming the next Steve Jobs overnight. Focus on one step at a time—validating your idea, creating a prototype, getting feedback, and so on. Each small step moves you closer to your goal, and with each success, you build momentum.

In practical terms, this means creating a **roadmap** for your goals. Start with the big picture—your ultimate goal—and then break it down into smaller milestones. What can you accomplish this week? This month? This year? By setting small, achievable goals, you keep yourself motivated and prevent the overwhelming feeling that often leads to giving up.

Just like the Wright brothers didn't invent the perfect airplane in one go, you don't need to solve all your problems at once. Take it step by step, and with each small victory, you'll find yourself closer to achieving what once seemed impossible.

2. Learn from Every Failure and Use It to Improve

One of the most defining traits of the Wright brothers was their ability to **learn from failure**. Every time one of their gliders crashed or a test flight failed, they didn't see it as the end of the road—they saw it as a lesson. They meticulously recorded data from each flight, analyzed what went wrong, and made adjustments for the next attempt. It's this willingness to embrace failure and **learn from every mistake** that ultimately led to their success.

The Wright brothers were relentless in their testing. They built a wind tunnel to test different wing shapes, experimenting with designs long before they ever tried to fly again. This methodical approach allowed them to turn every failure into an opportunity for improvement. They understood that **failure isn't the opposite of success—it's part of the process.**

In your own life, failure is inevitable. Whether you're starting a new business, learning a new skill, or working toward a personal goal, you're going to face setbacks. But like the Wright brothers, you have to **shift your mindset**. Instead of seeing failure as a sign that you should quit, view it as an opportunity to learn. Ask yourself: What went wrong? What can I do better next time? How can I improve?

In practical terms, this means adopting a **growth mindset**. When you fail, don't give up or feel defeated. Take the time to analyze what happened and find the lessons in it. Maybe you missed a step in your planning, or perhaps you need to adjust your strategy. Whatever the case, **failure isn't a dead end—it's a stepping stone** to success. The key is to keep moving forward, adjusting and improving with each attempt.

Remember, the Wright brothers didn't succeed on their first try, or their second, or their hundredth. They succeeded because they **refused to give up**, and they used every failure as fuel for their next breakthrough. You can do the same in your own life. Keep pushing, keep learning, and you'll find that each failure brings you one step closer to success.

3. Collaborate and Leverage the Power of Teamwork

One of the most overlooked aspects of the Wright brothers' success is the fact that they **worked together as a team**. Wilbur and Orville had different strengths—Wilbur was more analytical and methodical, while Orville was more practical and hands-on. By combining their skills, they were able to tackle problems from multiple angles and find solutions that neither of them could have achieved alone. Their collaboration was built on trust, mutual respect, and a shared vision of success.

The lesson here is clear: **you don't have to do it all alone.** Collaboration and teamwork can amplify your strengths and help you achieve goals that would be impossible on your own. Whether it's working with a partner on a business venture, seeking mentorship, or surrounding yourself with like-minded individuals, **the right people can accelerate your success.**

In your own life, think about how you can **leverage teamwork** to achieve your goals. Who can you partner with to bring out the best in each other? What mentors or advisors can you learn from? Surround yourself with people who share your vision and can offer complementary skills. Working together, you can tackle bigger challenges and make faster progress than you ever could alone.

In practical terms, this means actively seeking out collaboration. Don't isolate yourself or assume you need to have all the answers. Whether you're building a business, pursuing a fitness goal, or working on personal development, **find people who can support and challenge you.** The Wright brothers' success wasn't just the result of their individual talents—it was the product of their teamwork and the ability to combine their strengths to solve complex problems.

Elon Musk

Few figures in the modern world embody ambition, innovation, and sheer audacity quite like **Elon Musk**. Musk isn't just a tech entrepreneur—he's a man who has set out to reshape industries, redefine the future of energy, and even explore the boundaries of human existence in space. He's the driving force behind companies like **Tesla**, **SpaceX**, **Neuralink**, and **The Boring Company**—ventures that would be monumental on their own, but combined, they reveal a vision that's nothing short of revolutionary. Musk is the kind of figure that makes you rethink what's possible.

But Musk's greatness doesn't lie solely in his ability to innovate or build companies. What sets him apart is his **willingness to dream on a scale that seems impossible**—and then execute on that vision with relentless focus and determination. His story is one of bold ambition, risk-taking, and pushing through setbacks that would cripple most people. Musk's life teaches us that **success doesn't just come from having a good idea—it comes from the willingness to take massive risks and endure hardships to bring that idea to life**.

This chapter will dive into Musk's journey, exploring how he became one of the most influential people in the world and what lessons we can take from his relentless pursuit of turning the impossible into reality. Whether you're building a business, pursuing a bold vision, or simply looking to level up in your own life, Musk's story offers profound lessons in how to **think big, take risks, and persevere through challenges**.

Autobiography

Elon Musk was born on June 28, 1971, in Pretoria, South Africa. His early life was marked by a love for reading, particularly in science fiction and technology. While his childhood wasn't easy—he was often bullied and had a distant relationship with his father—Musk found solace in books, dreaming of a future that seemed limitless. At age 12, he taught himself how to program, and by 1984, he had sold the source code for a video game he created called *Blastar* for $500.

Musk's early ambition was evident, but he knew that South Africa wasn't the place to achieve his grand visions. At 17, he moved to Canada to attend Queen's University and later transferred to the University of Pennsylvania in the United States, where he earned degrees in both economics and physics. From the beginning, Musk was interested in solving large, complex problems—ones that could impact humanity on a global scale.

In 1995, Musk dropped out of a Ph.D. program at Stanford University after just two days to pursue business ventures in the emerging internet sector. His first startup, **Zip2**, was an online city guide for newspapers. The company was sold for nearly $300 million, and Musk, who was in his mid-20s, was already a millionaire. But rather than retire comfortably, Musk doubled down. He used the proceeds from the sale to co-found **X.com**, which later became **PayPal**, revolutionizing online payments before being sold to eBay for $1.5 billion in 2002.

With two successful companies under his belt, Musk could have easily retired. But instead, he aimed even higher. He turned his focus to three industries he believed were critical to the future: space exploration, clean energy, and artificial intelligence. In 2002, he founded **SpaceX**, with the goal of reducing the cost of space travel and making life multi-planetary. Two years later, he joined **Tesla**, an electric car company that was on the verge of bankruptcy, and transformed it into a global leader in sustainable energy and electric vehicles.

Musk's ventures were far from guaranteed successes. SpaceX experienced multiple rocket failures before successfully launching into orbit, and Tesla came close to collapse multiple times. But

Musk's **resilience and refusal to accept failure** kept these ventures alive. He famously poured his personal fortune into SpaceX and Tesla, even borrowing money for rent when both companies were on the brink of bankruptcy. But his perseverance paid off. SpaceX became the first privately funded company to send a spacecraft to the International Space Station, and Tesla revolutionized the automotive industry with electric vehicles that became not just environmentally friendly, but desirable.

Today, Musk continues to push boundaries, with his eyes set on colonizing Mars, transforming the global energy grid, and even developing brain-computer interfaces through **Neuralink**. His ability to dream big, take massive risks, and execute with intensity offers a roadmap for anyone with the ambition to challenge the status quo.

Lessons and Applications

Elon Musk's journey offers profound lessons in ambition, risk, and execution—qualities that can be applied to any area of life. Let's break down three key takeaways from Musk's life that you can put into action.

1. Think Bigger Than Everyone Else—Bold Vision Creates Bold Results

One of the most powerful lessons from Musk's life is the importance of **thinking bigger** than everyone else. While most entrepreneurs or business leaders focus on incremental improvements, Musk is driven by **moonshot goals**. He doesn't just want to make a better car—he wants to **end the world's reliance on fossil fuels**. He doesn't just want to reduce the cost of space travel—he wants to make humans a **multi-planetary species**.

Musk's approach teaches us that if you want to achieve something extraordinary, you have to **dream on a scale that others find absurd.** The reason Musk has been able to revolutionize so many industries is because his vision isn't constrained by what's currently possible—he's focused on **what could be.** This ability to think beyond limits is what separates those who make small changes from those who change the world.

In your own life, ask yourself: **Are you thinking big enough?** It's easy to get caught up in setting safe, achievable goals, but Musk's life shows us that **bold vision creates bold results.** Whether you're starting a business, pursuing a personal project, or setting long-term goals, don't just aim for modest improvements—**aim for something that challenges the status quo.**

For practical application, take time to write down your biggest, boldest goals. What's the one thing you'd pursue if you knew you couldn't fail? What would you aim for if you weren't afraid of the risks or the critics? Once you've identified that vision, commit to it. Just like Musk, who faced constant skepticism for his ambitions to colonize Mars, you need to stay focused on the larger goal, no matter how impossible it may seem to others.

Thinking bigger also means surrounding yourself with people who share your vision and aren't afraid to **challenge the conventional.** Don't settle for what's comfortable—dare to push beyond what others believe is possible. If you want to achieve extraordinary results, you need to start by **thinking at an extraordinary level.**

2. Take Risks Others Aren't Willing to Take—Embrace Uncertainty

Elon Musk's life is a masterclass in risk-taking. Whether it's putting his entire fortune on the line to keep Tesla and SpaceX afloat or building companies in industries that were considered impossible to break into, Musk has always been willing to **take risks others wouldn't dare to**. And that's one of the biggest reasons for his success. He's not afraid to bet on himself, even when the stakes are sky-high.

The truth is, most people are risk-averse. They want security, certainty, and a clear path to success. But the problem with playing it safe is that it often leads to **mediocre results**. Musk's success comes from his willingness to embrace uncertainty and take risks that others shy away from. He understands that **great rewards require great risks**.

In your own life, you need to ask yourself: **Are you willing to take risks to achieve your goals?** Whether you're starting a business, making a career change, or pursuing a bold idea, there will always be uncertainty. But if you wait for the perfect moment, the perfect conditions, or the guarantee of success, you'll never take action. Musk didn't wait for certainty—he took calculated risks, knowing that **failure was a possibility** but also understanding that **the bigger risk was doing nothing at all**.

For practical application, start by identifying the **risks you've been avoiding**. What's the one bold move you could make right now that would bring you closer to your goals? Maybe it's quitting your job to pursue your business full-time, or maybe it's investing in something you believe in. Whatever it is, don't let fear paralyze you. Take inspiration from Musk, who risked his entire fortune to fund his vision, and be willing to step into uncertainty.

Taking risks also means being willing to **fail**. Musk's ventures have had their fair share of failures, from rocket explosions to product delays. But he never let those setbacks stop him from moving forward. He viewed failure as **part of the process**. If you want to achieve something great, you need to develop the same mindset—be willing to take risks, fail, learn, and keep moving forward.

3. Relentless Execution—Ideas Are Worthless Without Action

While Elon Musk is known for his bold vision, what truly sets him apart is his **relentless execution**. Ideas are worthless without action, and Musk is a prime example of someone who **doesn't just talk—he executes at a level few can match**. He famously works 80 to 100 hours a week across multiple companies, driving each one forward with unyielding focus and energy. It's not enough to have a big idea; you have to put in the work, day after day, to make that idea a reality.

Musk's work ethic and ability to execute are what have turned his dreams into tangible successes. He's involved in the minutiae of his companies, from design decisions at Tesla to the technical details of SpaceX's rockets. His approach shows us that while vision is important, it's **relentless action** that turns vision into reality.

In your own life, this means asking yourself: **Are you executing at the level you need to be?** It's easy to get caught up in ideas, brainstorming, and planning, but at some point, you need to take action. Whether it's starting that project you've been putting off, making a tough decision, or simply putting in more focused work, execution is what will separate you from the rest.

For practical application, start by setting clear, actionable goals. Break down your big ideas into **daily tasks** that move you closer to your objective. Make a commitment to put in the work consistently, even when it's difficult or when progress seems slow. Musk's success didn't happen overnight—it was the result of years of intense focus, long hours, and a willingness to **push through obstacles**.

Execution also means being **willing to do the hard work**. Musk didn't delegate his most important tasks—he was in the trenches, leading by example. You need to be willing to do the same. Whether it's making tough decisions, working long hours, or tackling the most challenging aspects of your goals, relentless execution is the key to achieving extraordinary success.

Leaders and Strategists

Alexander the Great

Picture this: by the time he was 30 years old, **Alexander the Great** had created one of the largest empires the world had ever seen, stretching from Greece to Egypt, and all the way to the edges of India. This was a man who conquered more territory than anyone in history by that age, and he did it with a combination of **fearless leadership**, **unrelenting ambition**, and **military brilliance**. Alexander wasn't just a king—he was a commander whose vision extended beyond what anyone believed was possible. He took a small, united kingdom and transformed it into a colossal empire, shaping the course of history and leaving a legacy that still resonates today.

But Alexander's greatness wasn't just about the battles he fought or the lands he conquered. It was about **how he led, how he inspired loyalty**, and **how he set ambitious goals that no one thought could be achieved**. His story is a testament to what can be accomplished through **visionary leadership, strategic thinking, and the courage to pursue monumental goals**.

In this chapter, we'll explore Alexander's extraordinary life and extract powerful lessons on how you can apply his principles to your own ambitions. Alexander's legacy is filled with lessons on how to lead others, how to think strategically, and how to pursue greatness relentlessly.

Autobiography

Alexander III of Macedon, more famously known as **Alexander the Great**, was born in 356 BCE in Pella, the ancient capital of Macedonia. From a young age, Alexander was surrounded by power and greatness. His father, King Philip II of Macedonia, was a brilliant military commander who had united the Greek city-states under Macedonian rule. His mother, Olympias, was fiercely ambitious and instilled in Alexander the belief that he was destined for greatness. According to legend, she even told Alexander that he was the son of Zeus, the king of the gods, which only strengthened his sense of destiny.

As a child, Alexander was tutored by none other than **Aristotle**, the great philosopher, who shaped his thinking and fostered his interest in science, philosophy, and strategy. This education would prove crucial later in Alexander's campaigns, where his strategic mind would be as valuable as his battlefield skills. But even as a boy, Alexander was fearless and fiercely independent. One famous story tells of how, at the age of 12, he tamed a wild horse named Bucephalus, which no one else had been able to control. That horse would become his companion throughout his conquests, a symbol of Alexander's untamable spirit.

At the age of 20, after the assassination of his father, Alexander ascended to the throne of Macedonia. Many doubted that this young king could hold the vast empire his father had built, let alone expand it. But Alexander was determined to not only maintain the empire but to surpass it. His ambition knew no bounds, and he immediately set his sights on conquering the **Persian Empire**, the largest and most powerful empire of the time.

In 334 BCE, Alexander led his army into Asia Minor, beginning a series of campaigns that would change the course of history. Over the next decade, Alexander fought and won a string of battles that are still studied in military academies today. His most famous victory came at the **Battle of Gaugamela** in 331 BCE, where, despite being vastly outnumbered, Alexander's strategic brilliance and bold tactics led to the defeat of King Darius III of Persia, effectively marking the end of the Persian Empire.

But Alexander wasn't content with just Persia. His ambition drove him further east, into India, where he fought the legendary

Battle of the Hydaspes against King Porus. Although his army was exhausted from years of campaigning, Alexander's leadership and determination carried them through. By the time he was 30, he had conquered much of the known world.

Yet Alexander's empire wasn't built on brute force alone. He was a visionary leader who sought to unify the cultures he conquered, marrying Persian nobles and encouraging his men to do the same. He founded over 20 cities, most famously **Alexandria** in Egypt, which became a center of learning and culture for centuries. His ambition wasn't just to conquer lands but to create a legacy that would endure long after his death.

However, like many great leaders, Alexander's relentless drive ultimately took a toll. In 323 BCE, at the age of 32, Alexander died under mysterious circumstances in Babylon, just as he was planning further conquests. His empire, which had been built on his unique leadership and vision, quickly fractured after his death, but his legacy as one of the greatest military leaders in history remains intact.

Lessons and Applications

Alexander's life is filled with lessons that extend far beyond the battlefield. He was a man of **bold vision**, **unrelenting ambition**, and **strategic genius**, all of which can be applied to your own life. Whether you're leading a team, pursuing a personal goal, or aiming to achieve something monumental, Alexander's principles offer a powerful guide.

1. Lead by Example—Inspire Through Action, Not Just Words

One of the most powerful aspects of Alexander's leadership was his ability to **inspire loyalty and courage** in his men. He wasn't the kind of leader who directed battles from a safe distance. Instead,

Alexander **led from the front**, often charging into battle alongside his soldiers. This fearless attitude earned him the loyalty of his men and created an unbreakable bond between leader and follower. His soldiers didn't just follow him out of duty—they followed him because they believed in him and were inspired by his example.

This kind of leadership is incredibly powerful in any context. Whether you're leading a team at work, in the military, or even in your personal life, people are far more likely to follow you if they see you living the values you espouse. **Leadership isn't about giving orders—it's about showing people what's possible through your actions.**

In practical terms, this means being the first to take on challenges, staying engaged when things get tough, and showing your team that you're willing to work just as hard (if not harder) than they are. If you want people to push themselves beyond their limits, you have to be willing to do the same. The people around you will notice, and they'll be inspired by your commitment.

For example, if you're leading a business and expect your team to stay late to meet deadlines, don't just issue directives—**be there with them**. Show them that you're not afraid to put in the extra hours and effort. This kind of leadership fosters trust and loyalty, which will pay dividends when you face challenges.

Alexander didn't win battles simply because of his strategic genius—he won because his men **believed in him**. They were willing to follow him into the most dangerous situations because they knew he would be right there with them, facing the same risks. By leading by example, you can inspire the same level of dedication and commitment in those around you.

2. Be Relentless in Pursuing Your Vision—Ambition Knows No Boundaries

One of Alexander's defining characteristics was his **unrelenting ambition**. He wasn't satisfied with small victories or incremental progress—he wanted to conquer the world. While most leaders would have been content with ruling Macedonia or perhaps expanding into neighboring territories, Alexander set his sights on the vast Persian Empire, and even after achieving that, he continued to push eastward into India.

This level of ambition can seem intimidating, but it holds a crucial lesson: **don't limit yourself by what others believe is possible**. Too often, we set goals based on what we think we can achieve within our current circumstances, rather than dreaming big and pushing ourselves to our full potential. Alexander's life shows us that **there are no boundaries except those we impose on ourselves**.

In your own life, ask yourself: Are you aiming high enough? Are your goals bold and ambitious, or are you playing it safe? Just like Alexander didn't limit his conquests to what was considered "achievable," you shouldn't limit your goals based on what seems realistic. **Dream bigger**. Push yourself beyond your comfort zone. Set goals that challenge you, that force you to grow, and that might even scare you a little.

This doesn't mean being reckless—Alexander's conquests were carefully planned and strategically executed. But it does mean being **willing to take risks** and aim for something that feels just out of reach. Ambition is a powerful force, and when combined with relentless execution, it can lead to extraordinary achievements.

For practical application, start by **reassessing your goals**. Are you aiming for something that truly excites you, or are you settling for what's comfortable? Set a bold vision for yourself, one that pushes you to stretch beyond what you think is possible. Then, make a plan to pursue that vision with the same intensity and determination that Alexander pursued his conquests. Ambition without action is just a dream, but ambition backed by relentless execution can change the world.

3. Think Strategically—Know When to Push Forward and When to Hold Back

While Alexander is often remembered for his boldness, what truly set him apart as a military leader was his **strategic genius**. He didn't rush into battles blindly or rely solely on brute force. Instead, he meticulously planned his campaigns, carefully analyzing his enemies, terrain, and resources before making his move. Alexander's ability to think several steps ahead of his opponents allowed him to win battles even when he was vastly outnumbered.

This principle applies to any challenge in life. Whether you're running a business, managing a project, or pursuing a personal goal, success doesn't come from sheer effort alone—it comes from **strategic thinking**. You need to be able to assess the landscape, understand the challenges you're facing, and devise a plan that maximizes your strengths while minimizing your weaknesses.

In practical terms, this means taking the time to **analyze your situation** before diving in. Don't just rely on brute force or hard work—think strategically about how to achieve your goals. What are the key obstacles in your way? What resources do you have at your disposal? How can you outmaneuver challenges rather than confront them head-on?

For example, if you're trying to grow a business, don't just throw more money or effort at the problem. Take a step back and analyze the market, your competitors, and your customers. Identify opportunities where you can gain an advantage, and devise a strategy that leverages your strengths while avoiding unnecessary risks. This kind of strategic thinking allows you to **win battles even when the odds are against you**, just like Alexander did.

At the same time, recognize that **strategic thinking also means knowing when to hold back**. Alexander didn't win every battle by charging headfirst into the enemy—sometimes, he waited for the perfect moment to strike. In your own life, patience and timing can be just as important as effort. Know when to push forward, and know when to step back and wait for the right opportunity. The key is to always be thinking ahead, anticipating challenges and planning your next move.

Julius Caesar

Few names in history command the same respect and awe as **Julius Caesar**. He wasn't just a brilliant military commander or a skilled politician—Caesar was a visionary leader who fundamentally transformed the Roman Republic and laid the foundations for the Roman Empire. His ambition, strategic genius, and ability to make decisive, bold moves in the face of uncertainty set him apart from others in his time. From his swift and calculated crossing of the Rubicon to his transformation of Rome's political system, Caesar embodied what it means to **seize opportunity, lead with conviction, and act decisively**.

Caesar's greatness wasn't just about his victories on the battlefield—it was about his ability to **see opportunities where others saw obstacles** and to take risks when others hesitated. He knew that greatness isn't handed to you—it's seized. His life offers powerful lessons on **how to think strategically, how to make bold decisions, and how to turn setbacks into stepping stones for success**. If there's one thing Caesar can teach us, it's that **fortune favors the brave**.

This chapter will explore Julius Caesar's extraordinary life, examining the boldness of his leadership and the calculated risks he took to shape his destiny. Most importantly, we'll break down how you can take these lessons from Caesar's life and apply them to your own journey—whether you're leading a team, making tough decisions, or pursuing a personal goal.

Autobiography

Gaius Julius Caesar was born in 100 BCE to an aristocratic family in Rome, though they weren't particularly wealthy or influential at the time. Caesar's early years were marked by political instability and civil unrest within the Roman Republic. Despite these challenges, Caesar displayed early signs of ambition, intelligence, and leadership. He was well-educated, studying rhetoric, law, and military strategy, and developed a love for oratory that would serve him well in his later political career.

By the age of 16, Caesar's family had aligned with the populist faction in Rome, which sought to limit the power of the aristocratic Senate and empower the common people. This political affiliation would shape much of Caesar's career, as he continuously positioned himself as a champion of the people, even while navigating the complexities of Roman power structures.

In his early military career, Caesar distinguished himself as a talented and charismatic leader, quickly rising through the ranks. But it was his command in **Gaul** (modern-day France) that truly solidified his reputation. Over the course of nearly a decade, from 58 BCE to 50 BCE, Caesar led the Roman legions in a series of campaigns that expanded Roman territory, subdued hostile tribes, and brought immense wealth back to Rome. His conquest of Gaul was one of the most impressive military feats in Roman history, showcasing his tactical brilliance and his ability to inspire loyalty in his soldiers.

But Caesar wasn't content with military glory alone—he had his eyes on political power. Rome, at this time, was divided between two factions: the Senate, dominated by conservative elites, and the populists, who sought to empower the common people. Caesar's growing influence and popularity with the people made him a threat to the Senate. In 49 BCE, faced with the prospect of losing everything, Caesar made one of the most famous decisions in history: he **crossed the Rubicon**, a small river that marked the boundary between his province and Rome, effectively declaring war on the Roman Senate.

"**Alea iacta est**"—"The die is cast," Caesar famously declared as he crossed the Rubicon, knowing that there was no turning back. This bold, decisive move sparked a civil war that would ultimately lead to Caesar's triumph. Within a year, Caesar had defeated his rivals and taken control of Rome as its dictator.

As dictator, Caesar initiated a series of reforms that would reshape Roman society. He introduced policies to alleviate debt, reformed the calendar (creating the **Julian calendar**), and expanded citizenship to more people in the provinces. But Caesar's consolidation of power made him many enemies among the Senate's elite. In 44 BCE, just as he was on the verge of declaring himself king, Caesar was assassinated by a group of senators who feared his growing power.

Though his life was cut short, Caesar's legacy endured. His actions paved the way for the rise of the Roman Empire under his adopted heir, Augustus, and his name became synonymous with power and leadership. **Caesar** is not just a title but a symbol of authority that would be used by rulers for centuries, from the Kaisers of Germany to the Czars of Russia.

Lessons and Applications

Julius Caesar's life offers profound lessons in leadership, bold decision-making, and strategic thinking. Whether you're facing a critical decision in your career, leading a team through a difficult challenge, or pursuing a personal goal, Caesar's example provides a powerful blueprint for success. Let's break down three key lessons from Caesar's life and explore how you can apply them to your own journey.

1. Seize the Moment—Bold Decisions Lead to Bold Results

One of the most defining moments in Caesar's life was his decision to **cross the Rubicon**. This wasn't a rash, impulsive act—it was a calculated risk, taken with the understanding that there was no turning back. By crossing the Rubicon, Caesar knew he was committing to a path that would either lead to greatness or destruction. But that's exactly what sets Caesar apart from others: he was willing to **seize the moment**, to make a bold decision when the opportunity presented itself.

In life, we often face moments where we stand at a crossroads, uncertain of which path to take. These are the moments that define us, the moments where we have to choose whether to play it safe or take a calculated risk. Caesar's life teaches us that **bold decisions lead to bold results**. Playing it safe might keep you comfortable, but it rarely leads to greatness.

In your own life, when you're faced with a tough decision, don't shy away from taking bold action. Ask yourself: **What's the bigger risk—taking the leap or staying where you are?** More often than not, staying in your comfort zone is the real danger. Just like Caesar, who recognized that not crossing the Rubicon would mean losing his influence and power, you need to recognize that sometimes the greatest opportunities come from taking risks.

But bold decision-making isn't about being reckless—it's about making **calculated risks**. Caesar didn't cross the Rubicon on a whim; he weighed his options, assessed the political landscape, and made a move when the time was right. You can apply this same strategic thinking to your own decisions. Don't be afraid to take risks, but make sure those risks are **calculated and informed**. Once you commit, go all in. Caesar didn't hesitate, and neither should you.

2. Think Strategically—Plan Several Steps Ahead

Caesar's success wasn't just about his boldness—it was about his **strategic brilliance**. On the battlefield, Caesar was known for his ability to outthink his enemies, often turning seemingly hopeless situations into stunning victories. In his political career, he was equally strategic, aligning himself with the right people, making calculated moves to secure power, and always thinking several steps ahead of his opponents.

This lesson is incredibly relevant to anyone pursuing success in today's fast-paced, competitive world. It's not enough to work hard—you need to **think strategically**. Whether you're leading a business, managing a career, or pursuing personal goals, the ability to plan ahead, anticipate challenges, and adapt to changing circumstances is crucial.

In practical terms, this means **always having a plan**, but being flexible enough to adjust that plan when needed. Caesar didn't just react to events—he shaped them. He anticipated his enemies' moves, positioned his forces strategically, and always had a backup plan. You can apply this to your own life by constantly evaluating your goals and the steps you need to take to achieve them. What challenges might arise? What opportunities can you create or capitalize on?

For example, if you're building a business, don't just focus on short-term goals—think about where you want to be in five or ten years. What steps can you take now to position yourself for future success? What potential obstacles do you need to plan for, and how can you navigate them strategically? This kind of long-term thinking is what separates successful people from those who get stuck reacting to immediate challenges.

Caesar's ability to think several steps ahead allowed him to win battles, secure political alliances, and ultimately reshape Rome. In your own life, adopting a **strategic mindset** can help you not only achieve your goals but also turn setbacks into opportunities for growth.

3. Turn Setbacks Into Opportunities—Failure Is a Stepping Stone to Success

Julius Caesar's life was filled with setbacks, but what made him truly great was his ability to **turn those setbacks into opportunities.** Early in his career, Caesar was captured by pirates, but instead of being defeated by the experience, he used it to his advantage. He promised his captors that he would return and punish them—a promise he kept, turning a humiliating situation into a demonstration of his power and determination. Throughout his life, Caesar faced political opposition, military challenges, and personal betrayals, but each time, he emerged stronger.

This lesson is invaluable for anyone facing challenges in their own life. **Setbacks are inevitable**, but how you respond to them defines your future. Caesar understood that failure wasn't the end—it was a stepping stone to success. Every defeat, every obstacle, every betrayal was an opportunity to learn, adapt, and come back stronger.

In your own life, you will face setbacks—whether it's a failed project, a lost opportunity, or a personal challenge. The key is not to let those setbacks define you, but to use them as fuel for growth. Ask yourself: **What can I learn from this experience? How can I turn this situation to my advantage?** Just like Caesar, who used his defeats to regroup and come back even stronger, you can turn every setback into an opportunity for growth.

For practical application, develop a mindset that views failure as part of the process. When you encounter a setback, don't dwell on it—analyze it. Identify what went wrong, adjust your strategy, and move forward with renewed determination. This kind of resilience is what will separate you from those who give up at the first sign of failure.

Caesar didn't let setbacks stop him from achieving greatness, and neither should you. **Learn from your failures, adapt, and use them as fuel to propel you forward.**

Abraham Lincoln

When you think of leadership in its purest form, one name stands out among the giants of history—**Abraham Lincoln**. He wasn't born into privilege, nor did he rise to prominence on a wave of popularity. Instead, Lincoln's greatness was forged through personal hardship, relentless resilience, and an unwavering commitment to doing what was right, even when it seemed impossible. As the 16th president of the United States, Lincoln led the country through its most divisive and brutal conflict—the **American Civil War**—and brought about the end of slavery. His life is a testament to the power of **integrity, courage in adversity, and the ability to unite people in the face of overwhelming odds.**

Lincoln wasn't perfect, and he wasn't infallible, but what made him extraordinary was his ability to stand firm in his principles while navigating one of the most tumultuous periods in American history. He didn't seek power for its own sake but used it to **preserve the union and bring about justice**. His story isn't just one of political mastery—it's a story of personal growth, overcoming failure, and the **power of resilience**. Lincoln's life offers timeless lessons on how to lead with compassion, handle criticism with grace, and stay true to your values in moments of crisis.

In this chapter, we'll explore Abraham Lincoln's incredible journey, the challenges he faced, and the lessons we can draw from his leadership that will help you in your own life—whether you're leading a team, overcoming obstacles, or striving to live with purpose and integrity.

Autobiography

Abraham Lincoln was born on February 12, 1809, in a one-room log cabin in Hardin County, Kentucky. His family was poor, and

Lincoln's childhood was marked by hardship and loss. When he was only nine years old, his mother, Nancy Hanks Lincoln, died, leaving him and his sister in the care of their father, Thomas Lincoln, who later remarried. Lincoln's early years were spent working on the family farm and teaching himself to read and write by the light of the fireplace. Though he received little formal education, Lincoln had a voracious appetite for learning and devoured any books he could find, including the Bible, Shakespeare, and legal texts.

At the age of 21, Lincoln struck out on his own, settling in New Salem, Illinois, where he worked a series of odd jobs, from rail-splitting to storekeeping. But Lincoln wasn't content with manual labor. His mind was set on **self-improvement and public service**. He began studying law and developed a reputation as an eloquent speaker and debater. In 1834, Lincoln won a seat in the Illinois state legislature, marking the beginning of his political career.

But Lincoln's rise to prominence wasn't a straight line. He faced numerous setbacks, including failed business ventures, a broken engagement, and multiple electoral defeats. Yet, through every failure, Lincoln's **resilience and determination** kept him moving forward. He became known for his honesty, earning the nickname "Honest Abe," and his ability to communicate complex ideas in simple, powerful terms.

Lincoln's life took a dramatic turn in 1858 when he challenged **Stephen A. Douglas** for a seat in the U.S. Senate. Though Lincoln lost the election, the series of debates between him and Douglas catapulted him onto the national stage. His opposition to the expansion of slavery, framed in moral terms, resonated with many Northerners and earned him the Republican nomination for president in 1860.

Lincoln's presidency, however, was not an easy one. Upon his election, the country was already on the brink of civil war, and by the time he took office in March 1861, the Southern states had seceded from the Union. Over the next four years, Lincoln would lead the nation through the bloodiest conflict in its history—the **American Civil War**. His primary goal was to **preserve the Union**, but as the war progressed, he came to see the abolition of slavery as both a moral and strategic necessity. In 1863, Lincoln issued the **Emancipation Proclamation**, freeing slaves in the Confederate states and turning the war into a fight for human freedom.

Lincoln's ability to navigate the complexities of war, his patience in dealing with a divided nation, and his steadfast commitment to his principles ultimately led to the Union's victory in 1865. But just days after the war ended, Lincoln's life was cut short when he was assassinated by John Wilkes Booth at Ford's Theatre. Despite his tragic death, Lincoln's legacy endures as one of America's greatest presidents, a leader who united a fractured nation and helped set the course toward freedom and equality.

Lessons and Applications

Abraham Lincoln's life offers powerful lessons in **resilience, integrity, and leadership in the face of adversity**. Whether you're facing personal challenges, navigating difficult decisions, or leading others through tough times, Lincoln's example provides a road map for success. Let's explore three key lessons from Lincoln's life and how you can apply them to your own journey.

1. Resilience in the Face of Setbacks—The Power of Persistence

One of the most remarkable qualities of Abraham Lincoln was his **unbreakable resilience**. Throughout his life, Lincoln faced numerous failures—both personal and professional—but he never let these setbacks define him. From failed business ventures and election losses to the death of his first love and the devastating toll of the Civil War, Lincoln endured hardships that would have broken most people. Yet, each time, he picked himself up, learned from the experience, and kept moving forward.

This kind of resilience is crucial in life. **Setbacks are inevitable**, but how you respond to them determines your future. Lincoln's life teaches us that success isn't about never failing—it's about getting back up after each fall and pressing on with renewed determination.

In your own life, you will undoubtedly face challenges, whether they come in the form of a failed project, a personal loss, or a setback in your career. The key is not to let these obstacles derail you. Instead, view them as opportunities to **learn and grow**. Just as Lincoln used his early failures to build a stronger foundation for his later success, you can use setbacks as stepping stones to greater achievements.

For practical application, when you encounter failure, take a moment to reflect on what went wrong and what you can learn from the experience. Don't dwell on the failure itself—focus on the lessons it provides. Lincoln's resilience wasn't just about persistence; it was about **adaptation**. He learned from his mistakes, adjusted his approach, and kept moving forward with clarity and purpose.

The next time you face a challenge, remind yourself of Lincoln's journey. No matter how many times he fell, he always got back up, and that's what made him great. **Resilience is the key to turning setbacks into successes.**

2. Lead with Integrity—Stay True to Your Values, Even in Difficult Times

Lincoln is often remembered as a leader of **uncompromising integrity**. He was known as "Honest Abe" for a reason—his commitment to truth, justice, and doing what was right, even when it was difficult, earned him the respect of both allies and enemies. Throughout his presidency, Lincoln faced enormous pressure to compromise on his principles, particularly when it came to slavery.

But he remained steadfast in his belief that the **Union must be preserved** and that slavery was morally wrong. His integrity was the foundation of his leadership, and it allowed him to make tough decisions with clarity and confidence.

This lesson is incredibly relevant in today's world, where compromise and moral ambiguity are often seen as necessary for success. But Lincoln's life shows us that true leadership comes from **staying true to your values**, even when the stakes are high. It's easy to take shortcuts or compromise on principles when things get tough, but real leaders stand firm in their convictions.

In your own life, whether you're leading a team, making a difficult decision, or facing personal challenges, remember that **integrity is the foundation of trust and respect**. When you act with honesty and stay true to your values, you inspire confidence in those around you. People are more likely to follow you, trust you, and support you when they know you won't waver in your commitment to doing what's right.

For practical application, take the time to identify your core values. What principles guide your decisions and actions? When you're faced with a tough choice, use these values as your compass. Ask yourself: **Is this decision aligned with my values, or am I compromising for short-term gain?** Lincoln's leadership was built on his unwavering commitment to his principles, and that's what made him an effective and respected leader. By leading with integrity, you'll build a foundation of trust that will carry you through the toughest challenges.

3. Unite Through Leadership—Bring People Together for a Common Purpose

Perhaps Lincoln's greatest achievement was his ability to **unite a divided nation**. At a time when the country was torn apart by civil war, Lincoln's leadership brought together people from vastly different backgrounds and beliefs for a common purpose: preserving the Union. He understood that leadership wasn't just about making decisions—it was about **bringing people together**, building consensus, and creating a shared vision for the future.

In your own life, whether you're leading a team at work, managing a project, or working with others in your personal life, Lincoln's ability to unite people offers a powerful lesson. **Leadership is not about forcing your will on others—it's about creating alignment**. It's about understanding the needs, concerns, and motivations of the people around you and finding common ground to move forward together.

Lincoln was able to unite the North by focusing on the greater good, not on individual differences. He communicated a clear, compelling vision that resonated with people from all walks of life. This ability to inspire and unite was key to his success as a leader.

For practical application, start by understanding the people you're working with. What are their concerns? What motivates them? How can you **align their goals with the larger mission**? Leadership isn't just about issuing orders—it's about **building relationships** and creating a sense of shared purpose. The more you understand the people around you, the more effectively you can lead them.

When faced with conflict or division, take a step back and ask yourself: **How can I bring people together?** How can I create a sense of unity, even in the face of disagreement? Lincoln's ability to unite a divided nation shows us that true leadership is about **inspiring collaboration** and finding common ground, even in the most challenging circumstances.

Nelson Mandela

Some leaders rise through power and control, while others ascend through vision and the sheer strength of their moral convictions. **Nelson Mandela** belongs firmly in the latter category. Few individuals in history have embodied the ideals of **forgiveness, resilience, and unity** as Mandela did. As the man who led South Africa through its most difficult and turbulent times—overcoming decades of apartheid, systemic racism, and his own 27 years in prison—Mandela became a symbol of hope, justice, and reconciliation not just for South Africa, but for the world. His story teaches us that true power doesn't come from domination; it comes from the ability to **forgive, unite, and lead with compassion**.

Mandela's greatness wasn't just in his ability to rally a nation or dismantle one of the most oppressive regimes in modern history. His true strength lay in his **unshakable belief in justice**, even when facing unimaginable adversity, and his capacity to put the well-being of others above his own suffering. He emerged from nearly three decades of imprisonment not filled with anger or a desire for revenge, but with an unwavering commitment to **peace and reconciliation**. His life is a powerful example of how **forgiveness is a form of strength**, and how true leadership comes from lifting others up.

In this chapter, we will delve into Nelson Mandela's extraordinary journey, the principles that guided him, and the valuable lessons that his life offers for anyone seeking to make an impact, overcome personal struggles, or lead with integrity and compassion.

Autobiography

Nelson Rolihlahla Mandela was born on July 18, 1918, in the small village of Mvezo in the Eastern Cape of South Africa. Born into the

Thembu royal family, Mandela's early life was shaped by his exposure to traditional African leadership, and the influence of his guardians, particularly Chief Jongintaba Dalindyebo, under whose care he was raised after his father's death. Mandela was given the opportunity to receive a formal education, which would prove critical to his later role as a leader and revolutionary.

Mandela attended the prestigious University of Fort Hare, the first university in South Africa for black Africans. However, his activism began early, as he became involved in student protests against the policies of the university, leading to his expulsion. This was a formative moment for Mandela, as it marked the beginning of his lifelong commitment to fighting against oppression. In 1941, Mandela moved to Johannesburg, where he worked in various jobs while studying law at the University of Witwatersrand. It was here that Mandela became deeply involved in the **African National Congress (ANC)**, a political organization committed to ending racial segregation and apartheid in South Africa.

As apartheid—the legal system of racial segregation—became increasingly oppressive in the 1940s and 1950s, Mandela's activism took a more radical turn. He co-founded the **ANC Youth League**, pushing for more direct action against the apartheid regime. By the 1960s, Mandela had become a prominent figure in the struggle, advocating for both peaceful protest and, when necessary, armed resistance. His involvement in the ANC's armed wing, **Umkhonto we Sizwe** ("Spear of the Nation"), led to his arrest in 1962, and in 1964, Mandela was sentenced to life imprisonment for sabotage against the apartheid government.

Mandela would spend the next **27 years in prison**, primarily on **Robben Island**, enduring harsh conditions, forced labor, and separation from his family. But even in prison, Mandela remained a symbol of the anti-apartheid movement. His reputation as a leader grew, and his unyielding spirit inspired not only those in South Africa but also people around the world.

In 1990, under mounting international pressure and a growing movement within South Africa, Mandela was released from prison. Rather than seek revenge for the years of injustice, Mandela advocated for **peace, forgiveness, and reconciliation.** He worked closely with President **F.W. de Klerk** to dismantle apartheid and transition South Africa toward democratic rule. In 1994, Mandela was elected as South Africa's first black president, leading the country through its first multiracial elections.

As president, Mandela focused on **nation-building**, working to heal the deep racial divisions that had long plagued the country. He established the **Truth and Reconciliation Commission** (TRC), which allowed victims of apartheid to speak about their experiences, while also granting amnesty to those who admitted to committing political crimes during the apartheid era. Mandela's presidency was marked by his emphasis on **forgiveness, unity, and equality.** He stepped down after one term in 1999, having set a powerful example of leadership rooted in humility and service.

Mandela passed away on December 5, 2013, but his legacy as a leader of unmatched moral authority endures. His life offers profound lessons in how to lead through adversity, how to overcome bitterness and hatred, and how to use power for the greater good of humanity.

Lessons and Applications

Nelson Mandela's life provides timeless lessons in **forgiveness, resilience, and compassionate leadership.** His journey from activist to prisoner to president offers profound insights into how to overcome personal and societal struggles, lead with empathy, and unite people around a common purpose. Let's explore three actionable and deeply practical lessons from Mandela's life, along with how you can apply these lessons to your own journey.

1. Embrace Forgiveness as a Form of Strength—Let Go of Bitterness to Lead with Clarity

One of the most powerful aspects of Nelson Mandela's leadership was his ability to **forgive those who had wronged him**. After spending 27 years in prison, separated from his family and subjected to brutal treatment, Mandela emerged not filled with hatred, but with a deep commitment to **forgiveness and reconciliation**. He knew that holding onto anger would only perpetuate the cycle of violence and division that had torn South Africa apart. Instead, he chose to let go of bitterness and work toward building a united, peaceful nation.

Forgiveness is often seen as a weakness or a way of letting someone off the hook. But Mandela's life demonstrates that forgiveness is, in fact, a form of strength. It takes courage to let go of resentment and anger, especially when the pain is deep. But by doing so, you free yourself from being defined by that pain and can focus on creating a positive future. Mandela understood that **forgiveness is a powerful tool for personal and societal healing**.

In your own life, there will be moments when you are wronged—whether by friends, colleagues, or circumstances beyond your control. It's easy to hold onto that anger and let it fuel your actions, but doing so often leads to destructive outcomes. If you want to lead with clarity and purpose, you need to **embrace forgiveness**. This doesn't mean ignoring injustice or forgetting wrongs—it means choosing not to be consumed by them.

For practical application, start by identifying a situation in your life where you've been holding onto resentment. Ask yourself: **How is this anger affecting my ability to move forward? What would it look like to forgive, even if it's difficult?** Forgiveness doesn't mean excusing the behavior—it means freeing yourself from its hold on you. Mandela's example shows us that by embracing forgiveness, you can lead with a clear mind and a compassionate heart, empowering yourself to create positive change.

2. Stay Unyielding in Your Purpose—Persistence Through Adversity

If there's one word that captures Nelson Mandela's spirit, it's **resilience**. He spent 27 years in prison, but during that time, he never wavered in his commitment to his cause. Mandela remained unshaken in his belief that South Africa could overcome apartheid and become a free, democratic nation. His unyielding resolve, even in the face of overwhelming adversity, is one of the most inspiring aspects of his life.

Mandela's story teaches us that **true greatness comes from persistence**, not from avoiding hardship. We all face challenges—whether they're personal struggles, setbacks in our careers, or obstacles in our pursuit of goals. But it's our ability to keep going, to stay true to our purpose, that determines our success. Mandela endured decades of imprisonment, but he never lost sight of his vision for a united South Africa. When he finally emerged from prison, he picked up where he left off, leading with the same determination that had sustained him during his incarceration.

In your own life, there will be moments when the challenges seem insurmountable. You may feel like giving up or abandoning your goals in the face of adversity. But Mandela's life teaches us that **the only way to fail is to stop trying**. Even when progress is slow or obstacles seem endless, staying committed to your purpose is what will ultimately lead to success.

For practical application, take a moment to reflect on a goal or challenge you've been working toward but feel stuck on. Ask yourself: **Am I allowing setbacks to deter me, or am I staying** persistent in the face of adversity? Mandela's life shows us that resilience isn't about never facing hardship—it's about pushing through, no matter how long it takes. Recommit to your purpose, and remind yourself that every challenge is an opportunity to grow stronger in your resolve.

3. Lead with Compassion and Humility—Empower Others Rather Than Seeking Power for Yourself

One of the most striking aspects of Nelson Mandela's leadership was his **humility and compassion**. After decades of fighting for justice, Mandela could have easily used his newfound power as president to seek revenge or dominate his political opponents. Instead, he chose to lead with **empathy and inclusivity**. He understood that true leadership isn't about wielding power for its own sake—it's about **empowering others and creating unity**.

Mandela's decision to form a government of national unity, including his former adversaries, demonstrated his commitment to healing rather than dividing. He prioritized the well-being of the nation over personal ambition, leading by example and showing that **compassion is a crucial component of strong leadership**.

In your own life, whether you're in a leadership position or not, you have the opportunity to lead with compassion. Leadership isn't about titles or positions—it's about how you treat others and the impact you make on the people around you. When you approach leadership with humility and a desire to uplift those around you, you create an environment where everyone can thrive.

For practical application, think about the people you interact with on a daily basis—whether they're colleagues, friends, or family members. Ask yourself: **Am I leading with empathy? How can I empower others rather than seeking control?** True leadership comes from lifting others up, not from dominating them. Mandela's life reminds us that by leading with compassion and humility, you can inspire lasting change and create a positive impact on the world around you.

Winston Churchill

In the darkest days of World War II, when Britain stood alone against the seemingly unstoppable force of Nazi Germany, one man's voice rang out with unwavering conviction, rallying a nation and giving hope to a world on the brink of despair. That man was **Winston Churchill**. Churchill wasn't just a wartime leader—he was the embodiment of **resolve, courage, and unshakable determination** in the face of overwhelming odds. His leadership was instrumental in the Allied victory, but his impact went beyond military strategy. Churchill's life and career offer profound lessons on **how to stand firm in the face of adversity, how to inspire others with your vision, and how to never, ever give up.**

Churchill's greatness wasn't just about his military success—it was about his ability to lead with **vision, confidence, and strength of character.** He faced countless failures, political defeats, and moments of deep personal doubt, but his resilience and ability to bounce back defined his legacy. His words during the war, from **"We shall fight on the beaches"** to **"Never, never, never give up,"** are more than just speeches—they are rallying cries for anyone striving to overcome their own battles, whether personal or professional.

In this chapter, we'll dive into Winston Churchill's extraordinary life, examining the qualities that made him a great leader and strategist. Most importantly, we'll break down how you can apply the lessons from his life to your own journey—whether you're leading others, facing difficult challenges, or striving to build resilience and mental toughness.

Autobiography

Winston Leonard Spencer Churchill was born on November 30, 1874, at Blenheim Palace, the ancestral home of the Duke of

Marlborough, one of Britain's most prominent aristocratic families. His father, **Lord Randolph Churchill**, was a prominent Conservative politician, and his mother, **Jennie Jerome**, was an American socialite. Despite his privileged upbringing, Churchill struggled academically in his early years, often rebelling against the rigid school systems. His difficult childhood and strained relationship with his parents left an indelible mark on him, driving his deep need for achievement and recognition throughout his life.

After a troubled academic career, Churchill found his calling in the military. He enrolled at the **Royal Military Academy Sandhurst**, where he excelled. His early military career took him to Cuba, India, Sudan, and South Africa, where he gained firsthand experience of warfare and a reputation for bravery. During the **Boer War** in South Africa, Churchill was captured by enemy forces but made a daring escape, which turned him into a national hero.

Churchill's early success as a soldier gave him the platform to launch a political career. In 1900, at the age of 25, he was elected to Parliament as a member of the Conservative Party. Over the next few decades, Churchill's political career was marked by numerous successes and setbacks. He served in various government roles, including **First Lord of the Admiralty**, where he played a key role in naval strategy during **World War I**. However, he also faced significant failures, most notably the disastrous **Gallipoli campaign**, which led to his temporary fall from political favor.

Churchill's career was filled with ups and downs, but it was in the 1930s that he faced some of his darkest moments. Out of power and politically marginalized, Churchill was considered a relic of a bygone era. However, he remained a fierce critic of **Nazi Germany** and **Adolf Hitler**, warning Britain about the dangers of appeasement when most politicians sought to avoid conflict. This period, often referred to as Churchill's **"wilderness years,"** was a time of deep personal and political isolation, but it also showed his unyielding resolve.

When World War II broke out in 1939, Churchill's warnings were finally heeded. In 1940, after the resignation of **Neville Chamberlain**, Churchill became Prime Minister at a time when Britain faced its greatest existential threat. The Nazi war machine had overrun much of Europe, and Britain stood alone against Hitler's forces. But Churchill, with his powerful oratory and strategic vision, became the nation's rallying figure. His speeches inspired not only the British people but the world, turning the tide of public sentiment and galvanizing Allied resistance.

Churchill's leadership during the war was marked by **bold decisions**, such as standing firm during the **Blitz**, resisting Nazi offers for negotiation, and forging critical alliances with the United States and the Soviet Union. He was known for his hands-on approach, frequently visiting bombed-out neighborhoods in London to show solidarity with the people and maintain morale. His strategic partnership with U.S. President **Franklin D. Roosevelt** and Soviet Premier **Joseph Stalin** was key to the ultimate defeat of Nazi Germany in 1945.

After the war, Churchill's political career faced further challenges. Despite his role as the hero of World War II, he was voted out of office in 1945 but returned as Prime Minister in 1951. In his later years, Churchill continued to be a dominant figure in global politics, championing causes such as European unity and standing against the spread of communism during the Cold War. He retired from public life in 1955 and was knighted by Queen Elizabeth II in 1953. Churchill passed away in 1965 at the age of 90, leaving behind a legacy as one of the greatest wartime leaders in history.

Lessons and Applications

Winston Churchill's life is filled with powerful lessons on **resolve, leadership, and resilience**. Whether you're facing personal challenges, leading a team through difficult times, or striving to achieve your goals, the qualities that made Churchill great can offer valuable insights. Let's explore three actionable lessons from Churchill's life and how you can apply them to your own journey.

1. Never Give Up—Resilience in the Face of Failure and Adversity

One of Churchill's most famous quotes is, "**Never, never, never give up.**" This wasn't just a catchphrase—it was the core of his character. Churchill's life was filled with setbacks and failures, from his early struggles in school to his political defeats and military disasters like Gallipoli. But through it all, Churchill never allowed failure to define him. He understood that resilience—the ability to **keep going in the face of adversity**—was the key to long-term success.

During World War II, Churchill's resilience became a beacon of hope for Britain. In the early years of the war, the outlook was bleak—France had fallen, the Soviet Union was under siege, and the United States had not yet entered the conflict. Britain stood alone, facing daily bombings by the Luftwaffe in what became known as the **Blitz**. Yet Churchill refused to entertain the idea of defeat. He rallied the British people with his unbreakable spirit, delivering speeches that echoed through the ages: "We shall fight on the beaches, we shall fight on the landing grounds... we shall never surrender."

In your own life, resilience is key to overcoming obstacles. There will be moments when the odds seem stacked against you, when failure feels inevitable, or when you're tempted to give up. But Churchill's life teaches us that **resilience is about pushing forward** when things seem most hopeless. Success isn't about avoiding failure—it's about **how you respond to failure**.

For practical application, start by embracing a mindset of resilience. When you face a setback, remind yourself that **failure is temporary**. Just as Churchill rebounded from his political and military defeats to lead Britain to victory, you can overcome your own challenges by refusing to give up. Setbacks are inevitable, but they don't have to be permanent. With resilience, you can turn failure into a stepping stone for future success.

2. Lead with Vision—Inspire Others with Bold Ideas and Strategic Thinking

Churchill was a visionary leader, known for his ability to **inspire others with bold ideas** and long-term thinking. While many of his contemporaries were content with short-term solutions, Churchill always looked beyond the immediate crisis to the larger strategic picture. His early warnings about Nazi Germany in the 1930s, when most politicians preferred appeasement, showed his ability to see the big picture and anticipate future challenges.

Churchill's vision wasn't just about military strategy—it was about **inspiring others with a sense of purpose and direction**. He knew that in times of crisis, people needed a leader who could articulate a clear, compelling vision of the future. His speeches during World War II weren't just motivational—they were strategic tools that gave the British people hope and helped them understand the importance of their sacrifices.

In your own life, whether you're leading a team or pursuing personal goals, **having a clear vision** is essential. People are more likely to follow you if they understand where you're going and why it matters. Just like Churchill used his vision to unite the British people during the war, you can use your vision to inspire and motivate those around you.

For practical application, take time to **clarify your vision**. What are you working toward? Why is it important? How can you communicate this vision to others in a way that inspires them to join you on the journey? Leadership isn't just about making decisions—it's about **painting a picture of the future** and rallying people around a common goal. By leading with vision, you'll not only inspire others but also keep yourself focused on the bigger picture, even when challenges arise.

3. Stay Calm Under Pressure—Composure and Confidence in Crisis

One of Churchill's greatest strengths was his ability to **stay calm under pressure**. During some of the most critical moments of World War II, when the future of Britain was in jeopardy, Churchill maintained a sense of composure and confidence that reassured both his fellow leaders and the general public. His calm, decisive leadership during the Battle of Britain and the Blitz helped maintain national morale and ensured that Britain remained resilient in the face of relentless attacks.

Churchill understood that **panic and fear are contagious**, especially in times of crisis. As a leader, he knew that his composure would set the tone for the rest of the country. He often visited bombed-out neighborhoods in London during the Blitz, speaking with citizens and showing them that their leader was unshaken by the destruction around them. This calm presence helped the British people endure the hardships of war with confidence.

In your own life, whether you're facing a personal crisis, a difficult decision, or a stressful situation at work, Churchill's example teaches us the importance of **staying calm under pressure**. When you remain composed, you're able to think more clearly, make better decisions, and inspire confidence in those around you. Panic and anxiety only cloud your judgment and lead to poor choices, while calmness allows you to assess the situation and respond effectively.

For practical application, practice maintaining your composure in stressful situations. When faced with a challenge, take a deep breath and remind yourself that **you control how you respond to the pressure**. Focus on what you can control, rather than the chaos around you. By staying calm and confident, you'll not only improve your decision-making but also inspire others to do the same.

Mahatma Gandhi

In a world often ruled by power struggles, aggression, and brute force, one man emerged to challenge the status quo, proving that real change can be achieved through **nonviolence** and **inner strength**. **Mahatma Gandhi**, known as the "Father of the Indian Nation," led one of the most remarkable revolutions in history—not with armies or weapons, but with **truth, love, and unwavering belief in justice**. His leadership in India's struggle for independence from British rule transformed not only his country but the global conversation on how to confront oppression and injustice.

Gandhi's greatness wasn't just about freeing India from colonial rule; it was about his philosophy of **Satyagraha**, or "truth force," which insisted that moral power could triumph over physical power. He showed the world that **nonviolence** is not a passive act of submission but an active and powerful force for social and political change. His teachings, rooted in ancient Indian wisdom, became a blueprint for civil rights movements across the world, inspiring leaders like **Martin Luther King Jr.** and **Nelson Mandela**.

In this chapter, we will explore the extraordinary life of Mahatma Gandhi and the timeless lessons he left behind—lessons on how to lead with moral courage, remain true to your values in the face of adversity, and harness the power of nonviolence to create lasting change.

Autobiography

Mohandas Karamchand Gandhi, later known as Mahatma Gandhi, was born on October 2, 1869, in Porbandar, a small coastal town in western India. Gandhi was raised in a deeply religious Hindu family, and his early years were influenced by the teachings of **Ahimsa** (nonviolence) and **Vaishnavism**, a spiritual tradition that emphasizes compassion and respect for all living beings. Despite his humble beginnings, Gandhi's journey would take him far beyond the small confines of his birthplace and into the annals of history as one of the greatest leaders of all time.

Gandhi's early life was marked by a struggle to find his place in the world. As a young man, he traveled to London to study law, where he was exposed to Western philosophy and literature. Although he was initially eager to fit into British society, Gandhi's experiences of racial discrimination abroad, particularly in **South Africa**, would shape his life's mission. It was in South Africa, while working as a lawyer, that Gandhi first encountered the harsh realities of institutionalized racism. He faced personal indignities, such as being thrown off a train for refusing to move to a third-class compartment despite holding a first-class ticket—an incident that became a turning point in his life.

In South Africa, Gandhi began to develop and refine his philosophy of **Satyagraha**, a form of nonviolent resistance against oppression. He organized protests against discriminatory laws, particularly those affecting Indian immigrants, and led boycotts of British goods. Through these early efforts, Gandhi discovered the power of **civil disobedience**—the idea that refusing to comply with unjust laws was a powerful form of resistance. His time in South Africa was a crucible for the ideas and principles that would later define his leadership in India's independence movement.

Returning to India in 1915, Gandhi found a country suffering under the weight of British colonialism. The British Empire controlled India's economy, resources, and political institutions, while exploiting its people. Gandhi quickly became a prominent figure in the struggle for Indian independence, but unlike other political leaders of the time, he advocated for a path of **nonviolent resistance**. He called on Indians to boycott British goods, engage in peaceful protests, and refuse to cooperate with British authorities.

One of Gandhi's most famous acts of resistance came in 1930, when he launched the **Salt March**, a 240-mile walk to the Arabian Sea to protest the British monopoly on salt production. This act of civil disobedience drew global attention and galvanized the Indian people, leading to widespread nonviolent protests across the country. Throughout the struggle, Gandhi was repeatedly arrested, yet he remained committed to his principles of nonviolence and truth.

Beyond politics, Gandhi also sought to reform Indian society. He championed the causes of the **untouchables** (the lowest caste in India), women's rights, and the promotion of rural self-sufficiency. He believed in living simply and practiced what he preached, adopting a minimalist lifestyle, spinning his own clothes, and advocating for economic independence from British industrial products.

Despite enduring imprisonment, ridicule, and internal opposition from both British authorities and within India itself, Gandhi's vision for a free India was ultimately realized. On August 15, 1947, India gained its independence from Britain, largely through nonviolent means. However, the victory was bittersweet, as Gandhi's efforts to prevent the partition of India into India and Pakistan failed, leading to one of the most violent periods in the region's history. Even in his later years, Gandhi continued to work tirelessly for unity and peace between Hindus and Muslims.

On January 30, 1948, Gandhi was assassinated by a Hindu nationalist who opposed his efforts to reconcile with Muslims. His death sent shockwaves around the world, but his legacy of nonviolence, peace, and the pursuit of truth has endured for generations.

Lessons and Applications

Mahatma Gandhi's life provides powerful lessons in **moral courage, nonviolence, and staying true to one's values**, even when the path is difficult. His ability to create massive change through peaceful means offers timeless principles that can be applied to your own life—whether you're navigating personal challenges, leading others, or striving to make a positive impact in the world. Let's explore three actionable and deeply practical lessons from Gandhi's life and how you can apply them to your journey.

1. Embrace Nonviolent Resistance—The Power of Peaceful Action

One of Gandhi's most profound contributions to the world was his unwavering belief in **nonviolent resistance**. He showed that true strength doesn't come from force or aggression but from the ability to confront injustice with peace and dignity. Gandhi's philosophy of **Ahimsa** (nonviolence) was at the core of everything he did. He believed that violence only perpetuates more violence, whereas nonviolent resistance could awaken the conscience of the oppressor and lead to lasting change.

The **Salt March** is a perfect example of Gandhi's nonviolent approach. Instead of engaging in violent rebellion, Gandhi led a peaceful protest against the British salt tax, demonstrating that ordinary people could stand up to oppressive systems without resorting to violence. His civil disobedience campaigns weren't about overthrowing the British through bloodshed—they were about exposing the injustice of the system and forcing the British to confront the moral implications of their rule.

In your own life, you can apply Gandhi's principle of nonviolence by embracing **peaceful action in the face of conflict**. Whether you're dealing with a difficult person, facing opposition at work, or encountering injustice in your community, remember that aggression rarely leads to productive outcomes. Instead, **focus on peaceful solutions** that align with your values.

For practical application, the next time you're faced with a conflict, take a step back before reacting. Ask yourself: **How can I respond to this situation with peace and dignity rather than anger or hostility?** By choosing nonviolence, you maintain control over your emotions and your actions, allowing you to resolve conflict in a way that fosters understanding and positive change.

Nonviolent resistance doesn't mean being passive—it means standing firm in your principles without resorting to aggression. In personal relationships, this could mean engaging in calm, constructive dialogue instead of heated arguments. In the workplace, it could mean advocating for change through respectful negotiation rather than confrontation. By applying nonviolent resistance in your own life, you embody Gandhi's belief that true strength lies in peace.

2. Stay True to Your Values—Moral Courage in the Face of Opposition

Throughout his life, Gandhi faced tremendous opposition—from the British government, from factions within India, and even from those close to him. Yet, he never wavered in his commitment to his values of **truth**, **nonviolence**, and **justice**. He understood that in times of crisis, it's easy to compromise your values for short-term gains, but doing so often leads to long-term consequences. Gandhi's **moral courage** was one of his greatest assets—he remained steadfast in his beliefs, even when it would have been easier to give in to pressure.

Gandhi's adherence to **Satyagraha**, or "truth force," was rooted in his conviction that **truth and justice will ultimately prevail**, even when the odds seem overwhelming. He believed that by staying true to your values, you strengthen not only yourself but also the integrity of your cause. His ability to maintain moral clarity in the face of adversity inspired millions of people to join his movement, knowing that he would never ask them to do something that went against their shared values.

In your own life, you will undoubtedly face moments when your values are tested—whether in your personal relationships, career, or broader societal challenges. It's easy to compromise when the pressure mounts, but Gandhi's life teaches us that **staying true to your values is the foundation of real strength and success.**

For practical application, begin by clearly identifying your core values. What do you stand for? What principles guide your decisions and actions? When you face a difficult choice, ask yourself: **Does this align with my values, or am I compromising for the sake of convenience or approval?** By staying grounded in your values, you build inner strength and integrity, allowing you to navigate challenges with clarity and purpose.

In times of crisis or when facing opposition, remember Gandhi's example. **Moral courage is about standing firm in your convictions**, even when others try to persuade you to take an easier path. Whether it's standing up for fairness in the workplace, maintaining honesty in your personal relationships, or advocating for justice in your community, staying true to your values will guide you through the most difficult challenges.

3. Lead by Example—Inspire Others Through Humility and Service

Gandhi wasn't just a political leader—he was a living example of the principles he preached. He didn't ask others to make sacrifices that he wasn't willing to make himself. He led by example, living a simple life, practicing self-sufficiency, and embracing humility. His leadership wasn't about power or status—it was about **service to others**. By aligning his personal life with his public actions, Gandhi inspired millions of people to follow his path.

One of the most striking aspects of Gandhi's leadership was his emphasis on **self-discipline and personal responsibility**. He believed that if you wanted to change the world, you first had to change yourself. Whether it was spinning his own clothes as part of the Swadeshi movement or fasting to protest violence, Gandhi's personal actions were a reflection of his larger goals. This kind of leadership—leading by example—had a profound impact on those around him.

In your own life, you can apply Gandhi's approach by **living the values and principles you wish to see in the world**. Whether you're leading a team at work, influencing your family, or contributing to your community, people are far more likely to follow you if they see you **living your beliefs**. Leadership isn't just about what you say—it's about what you do.

For practical application, consider how your actions align with your values. Are you living in a way that reflects your beliefs, or are there areas where you could do more to lead by example? Whether it's practicing humility, showing kindness to others, or demonstrating discipline in your daily life, small actions can have a big impact. Just as Gandhi inspired an entire nation through his example, you can inspire those around you by staying true to your values and leading with integrity.

Catherine the Great

In an era dominated by male rulers, a woman from a relatively obscure German principality rose to become one of the most powerful and influential leaders in European history. **Catherine the Great**, Empress of Russia, was a ruler who redefined what it meant to lead, govern, and influence an empire. Her reign spanned over 30 years, and during that time, she expanded Russia's borders, modernized its institutions, and championed the arts and education. Catherine's brilliance wasn't just in her ability to govern—she was a master of **adaptability, political savvy, and strategic influence**. Her success came not from brute force, but from her **visionary leadership, intellectual rigor, and ability to navigate the complex dynamics of power**.

Catherine didn't come to power through conventional means, nor was she born into Russian royalty. Yet, her story is one of resilience, ambition, and a relentless drive to achieve greatness despite the odds. Her reign transformed Russia into a global powerhouse and her legacy endures to this day. The lessons we can learn from her life go far beyond politics—they touch on how to adapt to changing circumstances, how to wield influence strategically, and how to maintain a clear, long-term vision even when facing opposition.

This chapter will explore Catherine the Great's remarkable life, examining the qualities that made her a transformative leader. We will also break down how you can apply her timeless lessons to your own life—whether you're navigating career challenges, striving for personal growth, or leading others through times of uncertainty.

Autobiography

Born as **Sophie Friederike Auguste von Anhalt-Zerbst** on May 2, 1729, in Stettin, Prussia (now Szczecin, Poland), Catherine the Great did not initially seem destined for greatness. She was the daughter of minor German nobility, raised in a world of small courts and provincial expectations. However, from a young age, she exhibited a **sharp intellect** and a desire for more than what her circumstances seemed to offer. She was well-educated, showing a passion for philosophy, history, and literature—interests that would later play a significant role in her approach to ruling.

At 16, Sophie was selected as a potential bride for **Grand Duke Peter of Russia**, the heir to the Russian throne. She traveled to Russia, converted to the Orthodox faith, and took the name **Catherine**. In 1745, she married Peter, a union that was far from happy. Peter, who would later become **Peter III of Russia**, was considered weak, immature, and more interested in his hobbies than in ruling. Catherine, on the other hand, was ambitious and quickly immersed herself in Russian culture, learning the language and aligning herself with powerful factions at court.

In 1762, following the death of Empress Elizabeth, Peter ascended to the throne as Emperor Peter III. However, his reign was short-lived. His unpopular policies and erratic behavior alienated key members of the Russian military and nobility. Sensing an opportunity, Catherine orchestrated a **coup d'état** with the support of the military and key political figures. Within six months of Peter's reign, Catherine had him deposed and took the throne as **Empress of Russia**.

Her ascent to power wasn't easy, but Catherine proved to be a shrewd and capable ruler. Under her leadership, Russia underwent significant expansion and modernization. Catherine's reign, often referred to as the **Golden Age of Russia**, was marked by territorial conquests, including the annexation of Crimea and the expansion into Siberia and Alaska. She also sought to modernize Russia's institutions, bringing Western ideas and reforms to the Russian court, economy, and education system.

Catherine was deeply influenced by the **Enlightenment**, corresponding with philosophers like **Voltaire** and **Diderot**, and she attempted to implement many of the principles of reason, education, and governance that were central to Enlightenment thought. She founded schools, encouraged the development of arts and sciences, and worked to reform Russian law and administration. Yet, Catherine was not naive; she understood that certain reforms, like abolishing serfdom, could destabilize the empire, and she carefully balanced her desire for progress with the realities of Russian society.

Catherine's personal life was as complex as her political career. She maintained several influential relationships with military leaders, advisors, and intellectuals, often leveraging these connections to strengthen her rule. Despite her reliance on key individuals, Catherine remained firmly in control, ensuring that her authority was never undermined by those closest to her.

Her reign lasted until her death in 1796, leaving behind a legacy as one of the most effective and influential rulers in Russian history. Catherine the Great's success wasn't just in the expansion of Russia's borders, but in her ability to **navigate power dynamics, strategically influence her court and nation, and adapt to the ever-changing political landscape.**

Lessons and Applications

Catherine the Great's life offers powerful lessons on **visionary leadership, adaptability, and strategic influence.** Whether you're navigating career challenges, managing complex relationships, or striving to make your mark in the world, Catherine's ability to succeed in a male-dominated and hostile environment can serve as a guide for achieving your own ambitions. Let's explore three actionable lessons from her life and how you can apply them to your journey.

1. Adaptability is Key—Learn to Thrive in New Environments

One of the most defining traits of Catherine the Great was her ability to **adapt to new environments**. Born in Germany and raised in a minor noble family, Catherine was not destined to become the ruler of Russia. Yet, she understood early on that survival—and success—depended on her ability to **embrace her new circumstances** and learn quickly. When she arrived in Russia as a teenager, she immediately immersed herself in the culture, learning the language and adopting Russian customs. This allowed her to earn the respect of the Russian nobility and connect with the people she would eventually lead.

When Peter III proved to be a disastrous ruler, Catherine adapted once again—this time by aligning herself with key military and political leaders to secure her position as empress. She wasn't rigid or confined by her original status; instead, she used every new challenge as an opportunity to grow and strengthen her influence.

In your own life, adaptability is crucial. Whether you're starting a new job, moving to a new city, or navigating a personal challenge, the ability to **embrace change and adjust to new environments** will set you apart. Like Catherine, you must be willing to learn, to evolve, and to take risks in unfamiliar territory.

For practical application, whenever you find yourself in a new or challenging situation, take a proactive approach. **Learn everything you can about your new environment**—whether it's a workplace, a social circle, or a new city. Ask questions, observe those who are successful, and adopt the habits or strategies that will help you thrive. Instead of resisting change, embrace it as an opportunity to grow. Catherine's success came from her ability to see new environments not as threats, but as arenas for her to expand her power and influence.

2. Master the Art of Strategic Influence—Leverage Relationships to Achieve Your Goals

Catherine the Great understood that power doesn't come from acting alone—it comes from knowing how to **influence the right people** at the right time. Throughout her reign, Catherine formed strategic alliances with military leaders, advisors, and intellectuals, many of whom helped her solidify her control over the Russian Empire. She didn't rely solely on her title as empress to exert authority; she used her relationships to **amplify her power** and create a loyal base of support.

Catherine's ability to navigate complex political dynamics allowed her to implement reforms, expand Russia's borders, and maintain her hold on power for over three decades. She didn't just lead by decree—she understood the importance of **building alliances and cultivating loyalty.**

In your own life, whether you're working in business, leading a team, or pursuing personal goals, understanding how to build and leverage relationships is key to success. Strategic influence isn't about manipulation—it's about **building mutual trust and aligning your goals with the interests of others.** By learning how to connect with the right people and create win-win situations, you can accomplish far more than you could on your own.

For practical application, start by identifying the key people in your life or career who can help you achieve your goals. These could be mentors, colleagues, or even friends who have valuable connections or knowledge. Take the time to **invest in these relationships**—offer help, listen to their needs, and look for ways to create value for them. Just as Catherine cultivated relationships with influential figures in the Russian court, you can build a network of allies who will support you on your path to success.

3. Maintain a Clear Vision—Balance Long-Term Goals with Realistic Short-Term Action

Catherine the Great was a visionary leader, but what made her truly successful was her ability to balance her **long-term vision** for Russia with **pragmatic short-term actions**. She admired the Enlightenment and sought to modernize Russia by bringing in Western ideas, reforming the education system, and encouraging the arts and sciences. However, Catherine also understood that certain reforms, like abolishing serfdom, could destabilize the empire and create backlash from the nobility. She knew when to **pursue her goals aggressively** and when to hold back to ensure the stability of her reign.

Her ability to see the big picture while carefully managing the day-to-day realities of ruling allowed Catherine to implement lasting change without alienating key factions in her empire. She remained committed to her vision of a **stronger, more enlightened Russia**, but she did so with patience and strategy, ensuring that each step forward was sustainable.

In your own life, having a clear vision for your future is essential, but it's equally important to balance that vision with **realistic, achievable short-term goals**. Too often, people become discouraged when their long-term dreams don't materialize quickly enough. Catherine's life teaches us that **progress is incremental** and that success comes from carefully managing the present while keeping your eyes on the future.

For practical application, take time to clarify your long-term vision. What do you want to achieve in the next five, ten, or twenty years? Once you have that vision in mind, break it down into **smaller, actionable steps** that you can focus on in the short term.

By balancing your ambitious goals with practical daily actions, you can steadily work toward achieving your vision without becoming overwhelmed or discouraged. Like Catherine, you must be both a visionary and a pragmatist.

Philosophers and Thinkers

Socrates

In the pantheon of great thinkers, **Socrates** stands as a towering figure whose influence extends far beyond the boundaries of ancient Athens. Known as the "father of Western philosophy," Socrates did not leave behind written works. Instead, his legacy is carried on through the writings of his students, most notably **Plato**. His life and teachings continue to resonate because of his commitment to a simple yet profound idea: **the unexamined life is not worth living**.

Socrates was a man who lived for one purpose—to challenge the accepted truths of his day and to seek a deeper understanding of life, ethics, and the nature of knowledge itself. Through his relentless questioning, he forced others to confront their own ignorance and pushed them toward **self-knowledge and intellectual humility**. He taught that wisdom comes not from having the right answers, but from **asking the right questions**. His philosophical method, now known as the **Socratic Method**, remains a powerful tool for self-improvement, intellectual growth, and understanding the world around us.

Socrates lived during a time of great turmoil in Athens, yet he never swayed from his belief that **truth and virtue** were worth pursuing, even at great personal cost. In the end, his dedication to questioning and truth-seeking led to his trial and execution, but his ideas have survived the millennia, influencing philosophers, leaders, and thinkers ever since.

In this chapter, we will explore the life of Socrates, examining the principles that defined his philosophy and how you can apply the lessons of **self-inquiry, intellectual humility, and the relentless pursuit of truth** to your own life.

Autobiography

Socrates was born around 470 BCE in Athens, Greece, into a modest family. His father, Sophroniscus, was a stonemason, and his mother, Phaenarete, was a midwife. Although little is known about his early life, Socrates received an education typical of Athenian boys, which included lessons in rhetoric, music, gymnastics, and philosophy. Despite his humble beginnings, Socrates would go on to challenge the intellectual elite of Athens and leave an indelible mark on Western thought.

Unlike many philosophers of his time, Socrates did not establish a formal school, nor did he write down his ideas. Instead, he spent his days in the **agora**, the public square of Athens, engaging in conversations with anyone who would listen. His mission was to question people about their beliefs—whether they were politicians, craftsmen, or ordinary citizens—and to expose the contradictions in their thinking. He believed that by showing people their ignorance, he could help them move closer to wisdom.

At the core of Socrates' philosophy was his belief that **true wisdom lies in recognizing one's ignorance**. He famously declared, "I know that I know nothing," a statement that reflects both his intellectual humility and his commitment to lifelong learning. Unlike other thinkers who claimed to possess knowledge, Socrates maintained that questioning everything—even one's own beliefs—was the only path to true understanding.

Socrates developed a unique method of inquiry, now known as the **Socratic Method**, which involved asking a series of probing questions to help someone examine their own beliefs and challenge assumptions. This method wasn't about giving answers; it was about guiding people toward deeper reflection and self-awareness. Socrates believed that by engaging in this process, individuals could discover the truth for themselves, rather than relying on the opinions of others.

Though his questioning style gained him a following among younger Athenians, it also made him unpopular with many of the city's leaders. His unrelenting critiques of traditional beliefs and the Athenian government led to accusations that he was corrupting the youth and disrespecting the gods. In 399 BCE, Socrates was put on trial for impiety and corrupting the youth of Athens. Despite having the opportunity to escape or plead for leniency, Socrates remained steadfast in his principles. He defended his actions, arguing that he had done nothing but encourage people to think critically and live virtuous lives.

Ultimately, Socrates was found guilty and sentenced to death by consuming **hemlock**, a poisonous plant. His death marked the end of his life, but his ideas lived on, preserved by his students like **Plato** and **Xenophon**, who recorded his teachings and dialogues. Socrates' willingness to die for his beliefs cemented his status as a martyr for truth and intellectual freedom, making him a symbol of the power of questioning authority and the pursuit of wisdom.

Lessons and Applications

Socrates' life provides powerful lessons in **self-examination, critical thinking, and the relentless pursuit of truth.** His dedication to asking questions, seeking knowledge, and encouraging others to reflect on their own lives offers timeless wisdom that can be applied to anyone striving for personal growth and intellectual development. Let's break down three actionable and practical lessons from Socrates' life and explore how you can incorporate them into your own journey.

1. Embrace Intellectual Humility—The First Step Toward Wisdom Is Recognizing What You Don't Know

One of the most famous statements attributed to Socrates is, "I know that I know nothing." This wasn't an admission of defeat but a demonstration of his **intellectual humility**. Socrates understood that the first step toward gaining knowledge was recognizing one's own ignorance. Too often, people assume they know more than they actually do, and this false confidence prevents them from learning and growing.

Socrates' commitment to questioning his own beliefs—and encouraging others to do the same—stemmed from his belief that **true wisdom** is found not in having all the answers but in being willing to admit that you don't know everything. This humility allows you to remain open to new ideas, perspectives, and knowledge.

In your own life, embracing intellectual humility can be transformative. Instead of feeling the need to have all the answers, recognize that **there is always more to learn**. This mindset opens you up to growth, allows you to learn from others, and fosters a deeper understanding of the world around you.

For practical application, start by asking yourself: **What are the areas in my life where I assume I already know the answers?** Challenge yourself to question your own assumptions and seek out new perspectives. Whether in your career, relationships, or personal beliefs, adopting Socrates' mindset of "knowing nothing" can lead to greater self-awareness and intellectual growth. The more you embrace the idea that there is always more to learn, the more you'll be able to develop your own wisdom.

Intellectual humility also allows you to engage with others more openly. Instead of arguing from a place of certainty, approach conversations with curiosity. Ask questions, listen, and be willing to change your mind. Socrates' dialogues were driven by his curiosity and openness to new ideas—qualities that are essential for anyone seeking to become more thoughtful and self-aware.

2. Question Everything—Critical Thinking as a Tool for Personal Growth

At the heart of Socrates' philosophy was the practice of **questioning everything**. He didn't take ideas at face value, and he didn't accept the status quo without scrutiny. Instead, Socrates believed that by asking the right questions, individuals could uncover deeper truths and **challenge the assumptions that shaped their lives**. This process of constant inquiry is known as the **Socratic Method**, and it's a tool that can be used to sharpen your thinking, clarify your beliefs, and uncover hidden biases.

Socrates understood that **critical thinking** is essential for personal growth. By questioning our own beliefs and the world around us, we can strip away illusions and get closer to the truth. This requires intellectual courage—it's not always easy to confront the possibility that we've been wrong or that our deeply held beliefs might be flawed. But the reward is a deeper understanding of ourselves and the world.

In your own life, adopting Socrates' approach to questioning can lead to profound personal growth. Instead of accepting things as they are, take the time to **ask questions** and challenge the assumptions that underlie your decisions, beliefs, and actions. Why do you believe what you believe? What evidence do you have to support your views? Are there alternative perspectives you haven't considered?

For practical application, try integrating the **Socratic Method** into your daily life. When faced with a problem, instead of jumping to conclusions or accepting the first solution that comes to mind, ask yourself a series of questions: **Why is this the best solution? What assumptions am I making? What are the possible alternatives?** This method of inquiry helps you think more critically and ensures that you make decisions based on sound reasoning rather than habit or bias.

This practice can also be applied to your interactions with others. Instead of arguing or debating, ask questions that challenge people to think more deeply about their own positions. This can lead to more productive and insightful conversations, just as it did in Socrates' dialogues.

3. Pursue Self-Knowledge—The Unexamined Life Is Not Worth Living

Perhaps Socrates' most famous maxim is, "The unexamined life is not worth living." For Socrates, the ultimate goal of philosophy was **self-knowledge**—understanding oneself at the deepest level. He believed that without this self-awareness, life lacked meaning and direction. Self-knowledge wasn't just an abstract concept for Socrates—it was the foundation of ethical living and personal fulfillment.

Socrates spent his life encouraging others to examine their own beliefs, values, and motivations. He knew that **true fulfillment** comes not from external success but from understanding oneself. Self-knowledge allows you to live in alignment with your values, make better decisions, and find meaning in your actions.

In your own life, the pursuit of **self-knowledge** is critical for personal growth and fulfillment. Understanding who you are—your strengths, weaknesses, motivations, and values—enables you to live a more authentic and meaningful life. Socrates' teachings remind us that self-examination is an ongoing process. It's not something that you achieve once and then forget; it's a lifelong journey.

For practical application, begin by setting aside time for **self-reflection**. This could take the form of journaling, meditation, or simply taking a walk and contemplating your thoughts. Ask yourself questions like: **What are my core values? Am I living in**

alignment with those values? What motivates my decisions? What fears or desires influence my actions? The more you engage in self-reflection, the more self-awareness you'll cultivate.

The pursuit of self-knowledge also involves being open to feedback from others. Socrates valued dialogue and discussion because it provided an opportunity for self-improvement. In your life, seek out honest feedback from people you trust. Be willing to listen to their perspectives and consider how their insights can help you grow.

Confucius

In a world often marked by conflict and disorder, there are figures whose teachings transcend the chaos, offering wisdom for living with integrity, discipline, and purpose. One such figure is **Confucius**, the ancient Chinese philosopher whose ideas on **ethical leadership, virtue, and self-discipline** have shaped civilizations for over two millennia. Confucius didn't just offer abstract concepts—his teachings were grounded in the belief that **personal transformation leads to social harmony**. His life was a testament to the idea that greatness isn't just about power or wealth, but about cultivating a strong moral character, leading by example, and contributing to the greater good.

Confucius's teachings have influenced entire cultures, and his philosophy, known as **Confucianism**, continues to guide individuals on how to live a virtuous and balanced life. His wisdom is timeless because it focuses on **practical actions**: how to improve oneself, how to treat others with respect, and how to lead with integrity. In a world where many are searching for purpose and direction, Confucius's message is clear: **the path to success and fulfillment lies in cultivating virtue and discipline in everyday life.**

In this chapter, we'll delve into the life of Confucius, exploring the core principles of his philosophy and, most importantly, how you can apply his lessons to your own life. Whether you're seeking personal growth, leadership wisdom, or ethical guidance, Confucius's teachings offer valuable insights for anyone looking to live a life of purpose and integrity.

Autobiography

Confucius was born in 551 BCE in the small state of **Lu**, in what is now modern-day Shandong, China. His given name was **Kong**

Qiu, and he was born into a family of modest means. His father, a military officer, died when Confucius was just a young boy, leaving his mother to raise him in relative poverty. Despite these hardships, Confucius was determined to receive an education, showing an early interest in learning and moral philosophy. His thirst for knowledge led him to study the classical texts of Chinese culture, and over time, he became known for his wisdom and insight.

By the time he was in his twenties, Confucius had developed a reputation as a skilled teacher. His ability to think deeply about ethics, government, and personal conduct made him a sought-after scholar, and he soon began attracting disciples who were eager to learn from him. Though Confucius spent much of his early career in education, he was also deeply involved in the political life of his time. He believed that **good governance** was crucial to creating a just society, and he sought positions of influence to enact reforms that aligned with his ethical vision.

However, despite his ambitions, Confucius's time in government was marked by frustration. He served briefly as a government official in the state of Lu, but his efforts to institute moral and political reforms were often met with resistance. Disillusioned by the corruption and moral decay he saw in the ruling elite, Confucius left office and began traveling from state to state, seeking a ruler who would embrace his philosophy of ethical leadership and governance. Though he never found a government willing to fully adopt his ideas, his teachings continued to resonate with his disciples and future generations.

Confucius spent the latter part of his life teaching and refining his ideas, which were eventually compiled by his followers in the text known as the **Analects**. This collection of sayings and conversations captures the core of Confucian philosophy, focusing on themes such as **virtue, filial piety, respect for tradition**, and **the importance of moral leadership**. Confucius believed that by cultivating personal virtue and adhering to ethical principles, individuals could not only improve themselves but also contribute to the betterment of society as a whole.

Confucius passed away in 479 BCE, but his ideas endured. Over time, his teachings became the foundation of Chinese social, political, and educational thought, shaping the values of countless generations. His influence extends beyond China, impacting cultures across East Asia and even the West, where his ideas about ethics and leadership continue to be studied and applied.

Lessons and Applications

Confucius's life offers timeless lessons in **ethical living, leadership through example, and the cultivation of virtue.** Whether you're leading a team, working toward personal growth, or striving to live with greater integrity, his teachings provide practical insights that can be applied in any context. Let's break down three actionable and deeply practical lessons from Confucius's philosophy, and explore how you can incorporate them into your own life.

1. Cultivate Discipline—The Foundation of Personal and Professional Success

One of the core principles of Confucian philosophy is the importance of **self-discipline.** Confucius believed that personal discipline was the foundation upon which all other virtues are built. Without discipline, it is impossible to cultivate virtue, achieve success, or live in accordance with ethical principles. Confucius himself was known for his rigorous personal discipline, maintaining a strict adherence to his values and principles in both his personal and public life.

For Confucius, discipline wasn't just about following rules—it was about consistently striving to improve oneself, day after day. He taught that true discipline comes from within, from a desire to better oneself and live a life of virtue. This internal discipline translates into all areas of life, from how we manage our time and resources to how we treat others and fulfill our responsibilities.

In your own life, cultivating discipline is crucial for achieving your goals and living in alignment with your values. Whether you're working toward a personal fitness goal, developing a new skill, or advancing in your career, discipline is the key to success. It's easy to get distracted or to give in to short-term temptations, but Confucius reminds us that **lasting success comes from consistent effort and self-control.**

For practical application, start by identifying an area of your life where you could benefit from greater discipline. This could be in your work habits, your fitness routine, or even your relationships. Once you've identified the area, set small, manageable goals that will help you build discipline over time. Confucius taught that great accomplishments come from small, consistent efforts, so focus on **progress rather than perfection.**

Additionally, practice self-reflection to hold yourself accountable. At the end of each day, ask yourself: **Did I live in accordance with my values today? Did I maintain discipline in the areas that matter most?** By regularly assessing your progress, you can make adjustments and continue to grow in your discipline, just as Confucius encouraged.

2. Lead by Example—The Most Effective Form of Leadership

Confucius placed a strong emphasis on the idea of **leading by example**. He believed that leaders should inspire others not through commands or coercion, but through their own behavior and character. In his view, the best leaders are those who **live in accordance with the values they wish to see in others.** This principle of leadership is known as **moral leadership**, and it's as relevant today as it was in ancient China.

Confucius taught that a leader's personal conduct sets the tone for those they lead. If a leader is virtuous, disciplined, and ethical, their followers will naturally be inclined to emulate those qualities. Conversely, if a leader is corrupt or self-serving, it will be impossible to inspire loyalty, respect, or positive change. Confucius's idea of leadership goes beyond formal authority—it's about **influencing others through integrity, consistency, and moral conviction**.

In your own life, whether you're leading a team at work, raising a family, or simply trying to make a positive impact in your community, Confucius's lesson on leading by example is invaluable. People are far more likely to follow someone who practices what they preach, and genuine leadership comes from **living the values you advocate**.

For practical application, take a close look at the values you want to inspire in others. Are you living those values yourself? If you want others to work hard, be honest, or show respect, are you demonstrating those qualities in your own actions? Leading by example isn't just about doing the right thing when people are watching—it's about **consistently living in alignment with your principles**, regardless of the circumstances.

To put this into practice, focus on embodying the qualities you wish to see in others. If you're in a leadership role, show up with integrity, be transparent in your decision-making, and treat others with respect. If you're working toward personal growth, let your actions reflect your commitment to improvement. By leading with your actions, you'll inspire those around you to follow suit, just as Confucius taught.

3. Value Relationships and Social Harmony—Success Is Built on Strong Connections

At the heart of Confucius's teachings is the importance of **relationships and social harmony**. He believed that society functions best when people fulfill their roles and responsibilities to one another, creating a harmonious and orderly environment. Confucius placed great emphasis on the concept of **filial piety** (respect for one's parents and elders) and believed that strong family relationships were the foundation of a stable society. However, his ideas about relationships extended beyond the family—he believed that all human interactions should be governed by mutual respect, empathy, and ethical behavior.

For Confucius, success wasn't just about individual achievement; it was about contributing to the well-being of others and fostering harmonious relationships. He taught that in order to be truly successful, one must cultivate **strong, ethical relationships** in both personal and professional life. This means treating others with kindness, being reliable, and fulfilling your obligations to those around you.

In your own life, the quality of your relationships will have a direct impact on your success and fulfillment. Whether in business, friendships, or family life, strong relationships built on trust, respect, and mutual support are the foundation for long-term success. Confucius reminds us that **no one succeeds in isolation**, and that our interactions with others are central to our personal and professional growth.

For practical application, take the time to invest in your relationships. Whether it's spending more time with family, supporting your colleagues, or nurturing your friendships, make an effort to build strong connections based on respect and integrity. Confucius taught that small, consistent actions—like showing gratitude, offering help, or listening attentively—can strengthen relationships over time and contribute to a more harmonious and fulfilling life.

Additionally, practice **empathy and understanding** in your interactions with others. Confucius believed that relationships thrive when people seek to understand each other's perspectives and act with compassion. When faced with conflict or challenges in your relationships, ask yourself: **How can I approach this situation with empathy and integrity?** By valuing relationships and prioritizing social harmony, you'll not only improve your personal connections but also create a more positive and successful environment around you.

Friedrich Nietzsche

There are few thinkers in history who provoke as much thought, challenge, and even controversy as **Friedrich Nietzsche**. A philosopher who rejected traditional morality and dared to question everything, Nietzsche wasn't interested in easy answers or comforting beliefs. His work was centered on the idea that **life's greatest challenge is to overcome oneself**—to rise above mediocrity, victimhood, and societal norms, and to create a life defined by personal meaning, strength, and authenticity. His famous declaration, "**God is dead**," was not a simple denial of religion but a call for individuals to face the **freedom and responsibility** that come with creating their own values in a world where the old certainties no longer held sway.

Nietzsche's philosophy is one of **power, self-overcoming, and the relentless pursuit of individual greatness.** He advocated for the creation of the **Übermensch**—the "overman" or "superman"—who would rise above the limitations of conventional morality and societal expectations to live a life of higher purpose and meaning. In his view, **hardship and suffering** weren't things to be avoided but were essential crucibles in which strength, wisdom, and individuality are forged.

In this chapter, we'll explore Nietzsche's life and philosophy, drawing out lessons on how to confront life's challenges, master oneself, and create a personal path to greatness. Whether you're struggling with adversity, feeling trapped by societal expectations, or simply seeking a deeper sense of meaning, Nietzsche's bold ideas offer a path toward greater **freedom, strength, and self-mastery.**

Autobiography

Friedrich Nietzsche was born on October 15, 1844, in Röcken, a small village in Prussia (modern-day Germany). His father was a Lutheran minister who died when Nietzsche was just five years old, leaving him to be raised primarily by his mother and sister. Nietzsche's early years were marked by intellectual curiosity and academic achievement. He showed promise as a student, excelling in classical studies, philosophy, and languages. By the age of 24, Nietzsche was appointed professor of classical philology at the University of Basel, making him one of the youngest ever to hold such a position.

Despite his academic success, Nietzsche's life was fraught with personal difficulties. He suffered from **chronic illness**, particularly debilitating migraines and vision problems, which would plague him throughout his life. These health issues forced him to retire from his professorship at the age of 34, leaving him with limited income and few prospects. However, it was during this time of personal hardship that Nietzsche produced some of his most profound philosophical works.

Nietzsche's philosophy was shaped by his experiences of isolation, illness, and struggle. In his writings, he rejected the Christian values of his upbringing, criticizing what he saw as the **weakness** and **passivity** inherent in traditional morality. He argued that individuals should not seek comfort in religion or society's expectations but should instead **forge their own path** by embracing the challenges of life and developing their own values. This radical individualism is captured in his concept of the **will to power**—the idea that life's fundamental drive is the pursuit of power, not necessarily political or social dominance, but power over oneself and one's circumstances.

In books like **Thus Spoke Zarathustra, Beyond Good and Evil,** and **The Genealogy of Morals,** Nietzsche explored the themes of self-overcoming, nihilism, and the creation of new values. His declaration that "God is dead" was not a nihilistic rejection of meaning but a challenge to humanity to create its own meaning in a world where traditional religious and moral frameworks no longer held sway. For Nietzsche, the highest goal was to become the **Übermensch**—a being who transcends conventional morality, embraces hardship, and creates life-affirming values from a place of personal strength and creativity.

Nietzsche's later years were marked by increasing isolation and mental illness. In 1889, at the age of 44, Nietzsche suffered a mental collapse, from which he never fully recovered. He spent the last 11 years of his life in a state of mental and physical decline, cared for by his mother and sister. Despite this tragic end, Nietzsche's philosophical legacy only grew after his death in 1900, and his ideas continue to influence thinkers, artists, and leaders across the world.

Lessons and Applications

Friedrich Nietzsche's life and philosophy offer profound lessons on **overcoming adversity, mastering oneself, and living a life of deep personal meaning**. His emphasis on the importance of struggle, self-overcoming, and the creation of one's own values provides practical insights for anyone seeking to live a more powerful and purposeful life. Let's break down three actionable lessons from Nietzsche's philosophy and explore how you can apply them to your own journey.

1. Embrace Struggle as a Path to Strength—"That Which Does Not Kill Us Makes Us Stronger"

One of Nietzsche's most famous quotes, "That which does not kill us makes us stronger," encapsulates a core principle of his philosophy: **struggle is not something to be avoided, but embraced.** Nietzsche believed that adversity, suffering, and hardship are essential parts of the human experience and that it is through these challenges that we develop strength, resilience, and wisdom. For Nietzsche, life's difficulties are not obstacles to happiness but opportunities for growth and transformation.

In your own life, you will inevitably face challenges—whether it's personal loss, career setbacks, or emotional struggles. Nietzsche's philosophy encourages you to **reframe these hardships** as opportunities for growth. Instead of avoiding discomfort or seeking escape, face your struggles head-on and use them as catalysts for becoming stronger, more resilient, and more self-aware.

For practical application, the next time you encounter a challenge, ask yourself: **How can I grow from this experience? What strengths or skills can I develop by facing this adversity?** Rather than succumbing to frustration or despair, embrace the struggle as part of your journey toward self-mastery. Nietzsche teaches us that **strength is forged in the fire of adversity**, and by embracing the discomfort of life's challenges, you can cultivate the mental and emotional toughness necessary to overcome any obstacle.

This principle also applies to daily life. Small challenges, like maintaining discipline in your work or facing difficult conversations, are opportunities to build resilience. Nietzsche reminds us that true strength isn't just about overcoming massive life events—it's about **developing the daily discipline to face discomfort** and grow from it.

2. Become Who You Are—Forge Your Own Path and Create Your Own Values

One of Nietzsche's most powerful ideas is his challenge to individuals to **become who they truly are**. In a world where societal expectations, cultural norms, and religious doctrines often dictate how people should live, Nietzsche believed that true freedom comes from the **creation of one's own values**. He rejected the idea that morality should be imposed by external forces, arguing instead that each person must **define their own path**, create their own meaning, and live in accordance with their own inner truth.

Nietzsche's concept of the **Übermensch**—the individual who transcends conventional morality and creates their own values—serves as a model for this kind of radical self-determination. The Übermensch doesn't conform to society's expectations but instead **redefines success and fulfillment** on their own terms. Nietzsche believed that the greatest individuals are those who have the courage to **reject the comfort of conformity** and embrace the freedom—and responsibility—of self-creation.

In your own life, it's easy to fall into the trap of living according to the expectations of others—whether it's family, friends, or society at large. Nietzsche's challenge is to **take control of your own life**, define what is meaningful to you, and pursue that path with courage and conviction. This means rejecting the need for external validation and instead focusing on what truly matters to you.

For practical application, start by asking yourself: **What values or beliefs have I inherited from others that don't truly resonate with me? What do I believe is the highest purpose of my life?** Take time to reflect on what you want out of life, independent of societal norms or expectations. Nietzsche encourages you to **live authentically**, even if it means going against the grain. The more you align your actions with your true values, the more fulfilling and meaningful your life will become.

By taking ownership of your own values and defining your path, you can achieve a sense of freedom and empowerment that few people experience. Nietzsche teaches us that **self-mastery** begins with the courage to reject conformity and create a life that reflects our deepest truths.

3. Harness the Will to Power—Develop the Inner Strength to Master Yourself and Your Circumstances

At the core of Nietzsche's philosophy is the concept of the **will to power**. This is not simply a desire for dominance over others, but a deeper drive to **master oneself, overcome obstacles, and shape the world according to one's own vision**. Nietzsche believed that the will to power is the fundamental force behind all human action and that those who learn to harness this power within themselves can achieve greatness.

The will to power is about **inner strength and self-mastery**. It's the ability to push through adversity, to remain disciplined in the pursuit of your goals, and to continually strive to improve yourself. For Nietzsche, true power doesn't come from controlling others—it comes from the ability to **control yourself** and shape your life according to your highest values and aspirations.

In your own life, the will to power manifests in your ability to **take control of your thoughts, emotions, and actions**. It's about developing the inner strength to persevere in the face of difficulty, to maintain focus on your goals, and to consistently push yourself toward self-improvement. Nietzsche's philosophy encourages you to see every challenge as an opportunity to exercise your will to power and grow stronger as a result.

For practical application, begin by identifying areas of your life where you feel out of control—whether it's in your habits, emotions, or external circumstances. Ask yourself: **How can I develop the inner strength to master this area of my life? What actions can I take to exert more control over my thoughts and behavior?** The will to power is about taking responsibility for your own life and recognizing that **you have the ability to shape your destiny** through discipline, perseverance, and self-mastery.

By cultivating the will to power, you'll develop the inner strength necessary to achieve your goals and overcome any obstacle.

Nietzsche teaches us that **true power comes from within**, and by mastering yourself, you can create a life of purpose, meaning, and strength.

Marcus Aurelius

Few figures in history exemplify the balance of power and humility like **Marcus Aurelius**, the Roman Emperor whose writings on **self-discipline, integrity, and Stoicism** continue to inspire leaders, philosophers, and thinkers today. In a world often consumed by greed, ambition, and personal gain, Marcus Aurelius stood apart as a ruler who sought not just to govern an empire, but to govern himself. His personal reflections, compiled in the now famous text known as **Meditations**, reveal a man who, despite the immense responsibility of leading the Roman Empire, never lost sight of his commitment to virtue, wisdom, and the betterment of his soul.

Marcus Aurelius lived by the principles of **Stoicism**, a philosophy that teaches the importance of inner calm, rational thinking, and accepting the things we cannot control. In a time of war, political strife, and personal loss, he demonstrated that true power doesn't come from dominance over others, but from **mastery of oneself**. His teachings, though written nearly two thousand years ago, remain as relevant as ever, especially for anyone seeking to lead, grow, and thrive in the face of adversity.

This chapter will explore the life of Marcus Aurelius, linking his greatness to practical insights that we can apply to our own lives. Through his wisdom and philosophy, we can learn to face challenges with resilience, to lead with integrity, and to cultivate a calm and disciplined mind in a chaotic world.

Autobiography

Marcus Aurelius Antoninus Augustus was born on April 26, 121 AD, in Rome. He came from a prominent Roman family, and early in his life, he caught the attention of Emperor Hadrian, who saw great potential in the young Marcus. At the age of 17, he was adopted by **Antoninus Pius**, Hadrian's successor, and groomed to eventually take on the role of emperor himself. Under the guidance of Antoninus Pius, Marcus received an education that would shape both his mind and character, studying **philosophy, law, and rhetoric**.

Though Marcus was destined for power, he was always more interested in **wisdom and virtue** than in wealth or status. He was deeply influenced by the Stoic philosophy of the time, especially the teachings of **Epictetus**, which emphasized the importance of rational thinking, self-control, and inner peace. Throughout his life, Marcus strove to live according to these Stoic principles, seeing his role as emperor not as an opportunity for personal gain, but as a duty to serve the greater good.

In 161 AD, after the death of Antoninus Pius, Marcus Aurelius ascended to the throne, ruling alongside his adoptive brother, **Lucius Verus**, until Lucius's death in 169 AD. Marcus's reign was marked by external conflicts, particularly with the **Germanic tribes** on Rome's northern borders and the **Parthians** in the east. These wars consumed much of his time and energy, yet Marcus continued to reflect deeply on his role as both a leader and a human being, often writing down his thoughts in the quiet moments between battles. These reflections would later become his **Meditations**, one of the most famous works of Stoic philosophy.

Marcus Aurelius was not only a philosopher-king but also a man who endured significant personal hardship. He faced the loss of several of his children, constant military pressures, and political challenges within the empire. Yet, through all of this, he maintained a sense of duty, self-control, and humility, striving to govern Rome with fairness and justice.

Despite the demands of ruling the Roman Empire, Marcus never lost sight of his commitment to self-improvement. His writings reveal a man constantly struggling to live up to his own high standards, reflecting on the nature of virtue, the fleetingness of life, and the importance of doing good for its own sake. He passed away in 180 AD, leaving behind a legacy not only as one of Rome's most respected emperors but also as a philosopher whose teachings have endured through the ages.

Lessons and Applications

Marcus Aurelius's life offers timeless lessons in **self-discipline, Stoic resilience, and leading with integrity.** His reflections in **Meditations** provide a road map for navigating life's challenges with wisdom and inner strength. Let's break down three actionable and practical lessons from his philosophy and explore how you can apply them to your own life.

1. Focus on What You Can Control—Master Your Mind, Not the World

One of the central teachings of Stoicism, and something Marcus Aurelius returned to again and again, is the idea that we should only focus on the things we can control and let go of the things we cannot. In his **Meditations**, he wrote, "You have power over your mind—not outside events. Realize this, and you will find strength." For Marcus, the key to inner peace and strength was to master his own thoughts, emotions, and reactions, rather than trying to control the external world.

Life is full of uncertainties—whether it's a difficult boss, financial struggles, or even global events beyond our control. Marcus teaches us that we shouldn't waste energy worrying about things that are out of our hands. Instead, we should **focus on what we can control**: our thoughts, our actions, and how we respond to the challenges we face. This mindset allows us to maintain calm and clarity even in chaotic situations.

For practical application, start by identifying areas of your life where you are focusing too much on things you can't control. Are you stressing over how others perceive you? Worrying about future events that may never happen? Once you've identified these areas, make a conscious effort to shift your focus inward. Ask yourself: **What can I control in this situation? How can I respond with integrity and wisdom, regardless of the outcome?** By focusing on your own thoughts and actions, you'll free yourself from unnecessary anxiety and develop a sense of inner strength that can withstand life's challenges.

In moments of stress or frustration, remember that you have the power to choose your response. Marcus Aurelius faced the weight of an empire, yet he understood that the real battle was within his own mind. You too can apply this lesson by cultivating mental discipline, letting go of what you can't control, and focusing on what truly matters—your own actions and character.

2. Cultivate Inner Discipline—Master Yourself Through Daily Habits

For Marcus Aurelius, **self-discipline** wasn't just a philosophical idea—it was a daily practice. In **Meditations**, he reflected on the importance of doing the hard work of self-improvement, even when it was uncomfortable or inconvenient. He wrote, "At dawn, when you have trouble getting out of bed, tell yourself: I have to go to work—as a human being. What do I have to complain of, if I'm going to do what I was born for—the things I was brought into the world to do?"

Marcus understood that **discipline** is the foundation of a virtuous life. Whether it was rising early to tend to his duties as emperor or maintaining his composure in the face of adversity, Marcus believed that self-discipline was the key to living with integrity and purpose. He didn't see discipline as a burden, but as the path to becoming the best version of himself.

In your own life, cultivating inner discipline is essential for achieving your goals, maintaining your values, and navigating life's challenges. Whether you're striving for personal fitness, career success, or simply becoming a better person, discipline is the key to making consistent progress. It's not about grand gestures or occasional bursts of effort—it's about the small, daily actions that build character over time.

For practical application, begin by identifying one area of your life where you could benefit from greater discipline. This could be your morning routine, your work habits, or even how you manage your time. Set small, manageable goals, and commit to them every day. Just as Marcus Aurelius reminded himself that his work was part of his purpose, remind yourself that discipline is the path to becoming who you want to be.

Discipline isn't about perfection—it's about consistency. Even on days when motivation is low or obstacles seem overwhelming, stay committed to your goals. Marcus Aurelius faced the immense responsibility of ruling an empire, yet he always returned to his principles of self-discipline and self-control. You can apply this lesson by developing daily habits that align with your long-term goals, knowing that each small action brings you closer to becoming your best self.

3. Lead with Integrity—Let Your Actions Reflect Your Values

Perhaps one of the most powerful lessons from Marcus Aurelius's life is the importance of **leading with integrity**. As emperor of Rome, Marcus had immense power, yet he always strove to use that power wisely and ethically. He believed that true leadership was not about dominance or control, but about setting an example for others to follow. In **Meditations**, he wrote, "Waste no more time arguing about what a good man should be. Be one."

Marcus understood that **integrity** is not about what you say, but about how you live. He believed that leaders should embody the values they wish to see in the world and that actions speak louder than words. His reign was marked by his commitment to justice, fairness, and compassion, even in times of war and crisis. He sought to be a ruler who served the greater good, rather than one who sought personal glory or power.

In your own life, whether you're leading a team, managing relationships, or striving to make a positive impact in your community, **integrity is the foundation of true leadership**. It's about living in alignment with your values, even when it's difficult or inconvenient. Marcus Aurelius teaches us that integrity isn't about perfection—it's about consistently striving to do what is right, regardless of the circumstances.

For practical application, take a close look at your actions and ask yourself: **Do my actions align with the values I claim to hold? Am I leading by example in my personal and professional life?** True leadership comes from within, and by living with integrity, you inspire trust, respect, and admiration from those around you.

Marcus Aurelius ruled one of the greatest empires in history, yet his greatest legacy is his commitment to living a life of virtue. You too can apply this lesson by focusing less on what you say and more on what you do. Let your actions reflect your values, and lead by example in every area of your life. Whether you're a parent, a manager, or simply someone striving to be better, integrity is the key to true leadership and personal fulfillment.

Sun Tsu

When you think of warfare and strategy, few names are as universally recognized as **Sun Tzu**. His timeless work, **The Art of War**, has transcended its military origins and become a masterclass on **strategy, leadership, and understanding the nature of conflict**. While Sun Tzu was a military general in ancient China, the wisdom he left behind applies far beyond the battlefield. Whether you're leading a business, managing a team, or navigating personal challenges, the principles he outlined over 2,500 years ago offer **pragmatic and actionable lessons** for anyone striving to achieve success and overcome obstacles.

Sun Tzu's philosophy revolves around the idea that the **greatest victories are won without fighting**, and that understanding yourself, your opponent, and the environment is the key to triumph. He advocated for careful planning, the importance of adaptability, and the value of understanding timing. His teachings are not just about physical combat but about mastering **strategic thinking**, turning challenges into opportunities, and avoiding unnecessary conflict. In this chapter, we will dive deep into Sun Tzu's life and legacy, pulling out actionable lessons that can help you succeed in whatever arena you find yourself in.

Autobiography

Sun Tzu, also known as **Sunzi**, is believed to have been born around 544 BCE in the ancient Chinese state of Qi during the late **Spring and Autumn period** (771-476 BCE). This era in Chinese history was marked by constant warfare between rival states, where military prowess and strategic thinking were highly valued. Sun Tzu grew up in a time where the balance of power could shift at a moment's notice, and survival often depended on military skill and cunning.

Details about Sun Tzu's life are sparse, as much of what we know comes from legend and historical texts. He is said to have served as a general under **King Helü** of the state of Wu, where he became renowned for his ability to win battles with minimal bloodshed. His reputation as a military strategist grew, and he was recognized for his emphasis on **strategic flexibility, deception, and the importance of moral and psychological factors** in warfare. Sun Tzu understood that brute force was not always the most effective means of achieving victory. Instead, he valued intelligence, foresight, and careful planning.

It was during this time that Sun Tzu is believed to have composed **The Art of War**, a collection of military strategies and philosophies that would later become one of the most influential works on strategy ever written. The Art of War covers everything from tactics and troop deployment to understanding the psychology of your opponent. It emphasizes the importance of knowing when to engage in conflict and, more importantly, when to avoid it. His central premise is that the **supreme art of war is to subdue the enemy without fighting**.

Sun Tzu's insights into warfare were far ahead of their time, and his work has influenced countless leaders, not just in the realm of military strategy, but also in politics, business, sports, and personal development. Though the exact circumstances of his death are unclear, Sun Tzu's ideas have endured for centuries and remain as relevant today as they were during ancient times.

Lessons and Applications

Sun Tzu's life and teachings offer profound lessons on **strategic thinking, adaptability, and winning through wisdom rather than force**. His approach to conflict, whether on the battlefield or in daily life, emphasizes the power of **preparation, understanding, and flexibility**. Let's explore three key lessons from Sun Tzu's philosophy and how you can apply them to your own life, whether you're facing personal challenges, professional competition, or seeking to achieve long-term goals.

1. Know Yourself and Your Opponent—Master the Power of Self-Awareness and Observation

One of Sun Tzu's most famous maxims is, "**If you know the enemy and know yourself, you need not fear the result of a hundred battles. If you know yourself but not the enemy, for every victory gained you will also suffer a defeat. If you know neither the enemy nor yourself, you will succumb in every battle.**" This statement speaks to the importance of **self-awareness and understanding your competition or challenge**. Sun Tzu believed that true power comes from knowing both your own strengths and weaknesses as well as those of your opponent.

In today's world, "knowing your enemy" doesn't necessarily refer to a literal adversary—it could be a business competitor, a challenging project, or even a personal obstacle you're trying to overcome. By gaining a deep understanding of the situation, including both your position and the nature of the challenge, you can craft a more effective strategy. **Self-awareness** is key to this process. Understanding your own abilities, limitations, and tendencies allows you to make smarter decisions, avoid pitfalls, and leverage your strengths.

For practical application, start by **assessing your own strengths and weaknesses**. Whether it's in your career, personal relationships, or any area where you're striving to succeed, ask yourself: **What do I excel at? Where do I need to improve? How do I typically react to pressure or competition?** By gaining clarity on who you are and how you operate, you'll be in a better position to strategize effectively.

Next, study the **environment and the "opponent"** you're facing. If it's a competitor, understand their strengths, weaknesses, and patterns. If it's a personal challenge, break it down and analyze what it will take to overcome it. Sun Tzu emphasized the importance of **intelligence gathering**—knowing the terrain, the climate, and the disposition of both your forces and your opponent's. In a business context, this could mean market research; in a personal context, it could mean understanding the dynamics of a relationship or situation.

By combining **self-awareness** with a thorough understanding of the challenge, you can approach any situation from a position of strength, just as Sun Tzu advocated.

2. Adaptability is Key—Be Flexible in Strategy and Responsive to Change

One of Sun Tzu's core teachings is the value of **adaptability**. He wrote, **"In war, the way is to avoid what is strong and strike at what is weak."** Sun Tzu understood that rigid plans often lead to failure because they do not account for the ever-changing nature of life and conflict. Instead, he believed that the best strategy is one that is flexible, allowing you to respond to new information and shifting circumstances.

In life, unexpected challenges are inevitable. Whether it's a sudden change in the marketplace, a personal setback, or a shift in your priorities, the ability to **adapt** is crucial to success. Sun Tzu emphasized that a great leader or strategist knows when to stick to the plan and when to pivot. **Rigidity** often leads to missed opportunities or prolonged struggles, while **adaptability** allows you to capitalize on new developments and maintain the upper hand.

For practical application, adopt a mindset of **strategic flexibility** in your daily life. When pursuing a goal or facing a challenge, create a plan, but remain open to adjusting it as needed. Instead of becoming fixated on one way of achieving success, constantly **evaluate new information and opportunities**. Ask yourself: **Is my current approach still the best one? What new factors should I consider? How can I adjust my strategy to take advantage of the situation?**

One of the ways to stay adaptable is to embrace **continuous learning**. Sun Tzu advocated for constant observation and the use of intelligence to adapt quickly. In your life, this means keeping your mind open to new ideas, seeking feedback, and learning from both your successes and your failures. By doing so, you'll be able to change direction when necessary and stay ahead of the competition or challenges you face.

Remember, success doesn't always go to the person with the most resources or the strongest initial position—it goes to the person who can adapt quickly and intelligently in the face of new challenges. This lesson is one of Sun Tzu's greatest insights and remains just as relevant today as it was on the battlefields of ancient China.

3. Win Without Fighting—The Best Victory Is Achieved Through Strategy, Not Force

Perhaps the most profound lesson from Sun Tzu's **Art of War** is the idea that the **greatest victory is one that is achieved without fighting**. Sun Tzu wrote, "**The supreme art of war is to subdue the enemy without fighting.**" This principle is not only about avoiding conflict whenever possible but also about using strategy, diplomacy, and wisdom to achieve your goals without unnecessary confrontation or destruction.

In today's world, this lesson can be applied to everything from business negotiations to interpersonal relationships. **Conflict is often costly**—whether it's the energy and time spent in a workplace argument or the resources expended in a business rivalry. Sun Tzu teaches us that true mastery lies in **winning through intelligence, strategy, and finesse**, not brute force.

For practical application, strive to **resolve conflicts or challenges through strategy rather than confrontation**. This could mean negotiating a better deal in a business transaction, finding a creative solution to a personal disagreement, or outmaneuvering a competitor through strategic thinking rather than direct confrontation. Ask yourself: **How can I achieve my goals without unnecessary conflict? What strategies can I use to influence the outcome in my favor without escalating tensions?**

This lesson also applies to personal challenges. Instead of confronting obstacles with sheer willpower alone, think about how you can **outthink the problem**. Maybe you need to find a new angle or a different approach. Often, the smartest way forward isn't through head-on confrontation, but by working around the obstacle, using patience and strategy.

By learning to win without fighting, you conserve your energy, resources, and focus, allowing you to achieve your goals more efficiently and effectively. This ability to **outsmart and outmaneuver** rather than overpower your opponent is one of Sun Tzu's most powerful teachings, and it's a principle that can lead to lasting success in all areas of life.

Immanuel Kant

Among the greatest minds in Western philosophy, **Immanuel Kant** stands as a titan whose work reshaped the way we think about ethics, rationality, and human existence. Kant's philosophy was not just about abstract theories; it was about how we, as individuals, can lead meaningful, moral lives grounded in reason and self-discipline. Kant's famous principle, the **categorical imperative**, is one of the most profound ethical contributions in human history. It essentially says: **act only according to that maxim whereby you can, at the same time, will that it should become a universal law.** This guiding principle challenges us to act in ways that we would want everyone else to act, making moral behavior not just a choice, but a **duty** rooted in rational thought.

Kant's philosophy is deeply practical, urging us to think critically about our actions and to rise above selfish inclinations in favor of what is rationally and morally right. His ideas center on the power of the human mind to **understand the world and to make moral decisions** based on reason, rather than emotion or personal desire. For anyone seeking to live a life of discipline, ethical integrity, and intellectual clarity, Kant's philosophy provides a clear path forward.

In this chapter, we will explore Immanuel Kant's life, linking his greatness to practical insights that can help us all live with more purpose, self-discipline, and moral clarity. Whether you're navigating personal or professional challenges, Kant's teachings provide valuable lessons on **how to think deeply, act morally, and discipline yourself to pursue what is right, not just what is easy.**

Autobiography

Immanuel Kant was born on April 22, 1724, in **Königsberg, Prussia** (modern-day Kaliningrad, Russia), into a modest family. His father was a harness maker, and his mother, though uneducated, was deeply religious and instilled in Kant a strong sense of morality and devotion. Kant's early life was marked by discipline, religious instruction, and a strong work ethic—traits that would later come to define both his personal life and his philosophy.

As a young man, Kant showed exceptional academic talent and was sent to the **University of Königsberg**, where he studied philosophy, mathematics, and the natural sciences. He was heavily influenced by the works of philosophers such as **Descartes, Leibniz**, and **Newton**, but his own thinking quickly began to diverge from the established traditions. After completing his studies, Kant spent several years working as a private tutor before returning to academia to earn his doctorate and eventually becoming a professor at the University of Königsberg.

Kant was known for his **rigid discipline and routine**. He reportedly lived such a punctual and ordered life that the citizens of Königsberg would set their clocks by his daily walks. But this intense structure in his personal life allowed Kant to produce some of the most profound philosophical works in history. His **Critique of Pure Reason** (1781) is one of the most influential books in Western philosophy, addressing the relationship between **human experience and knowledge**, and exploring how we perceive and understand the world around us.

Kant's later works, such as the **Critique of Practical Reason** and the **Groundwork of the Metaphysics of Morals**, delved into **moral philosophy**, where he developed the concept of the **categorical imperative**. In Kant's view, moral decisions should be guided by rational principles that are universally applicable to all people. He believed that **moral duty** was not dependent on individual desires or outcomes but was an objective fact that we are obligated to follow, simply because we are rational beings capable of understanding what is right and just.

Kant lived his entire life in Königsberg, never traveling far from his birthplace, but his ideas reached across the globe, influencing generations of thinkers, leaders, and everyday individuals. His philosophy continues to shape modern ethics, political theory, and epistemology. Kant passed away in 1804, leaving behind a legacy as one of the most disciplined and rational thinkers in history.

Lessons and Applications

Immanuel Kant's life and work offer timeless lessons on **moral clarity, the power of reason, and the importance of self-discipline.** His philosophy challenges us to think beyond personal desires and to align our actions with universal principles of right and wrong. Let's break down three actionable and deeply practical lessons from Kant's philosophy and explore how you can incorporate them into your own life.

1. Act Out of Duty, Not Desire—Embrace the Power of Moral Responsibility

At the core of Kant's ethical philosophy is the idea that we should act according to **moral duty**, rather than out of personal desire or self-interest. For Kant, morality is not a matter of convenience or preference; it's about adhering to **rational principles that we would want to apply universally.** His famous **categorical imperative** challenges us to ask ourselves: **Would I want everyone to act this way? Would this behavior be acceptable if it became a universal law?** If the answer is no, then we have a moral duty not to engage in that action.

Kant's philosophy teaches us that **doing what is right** is often difficult because it requires us to put aside our personal inclinations in favor of what is just and rational. This sense of moral responsibility can be applied to everyday decisions, from how we treat others to how we conduct ourselves in our careers.

For practical application, start by reflecting on your daily actions and decisions. Ask yourself: **Am I acting out of a sense of duty, or am I acting out of convenience or personal gain?** When faced with a moral choice, try to detach yourself from your immediate desires and think critically about the broader implications of your actions. Would you want your behavior to set a precedent for others? If the answer is no, then you have a moral duty to act differently.

Kant's idea of **moral duty** may seem strict, but it offers a path to living with integrity and consistency. By acting out of duty rather than desire, you align yourself with values that transcend personal interests, and you contribute to a more just and fair world. This mindset not only helps you make better decisions but also earns you the respect and trust of others, as people can see that you act out of principle rather than self-interest.

2. Discipline Your Mind—Rational Thinking Leads to Clarity and Strength

Kant's philosophy is rooted in **rationality**—the idea that we must use our reason to understand the world and make decisions that are logically sound. He believed that the ability to think critically and objectively is what separates humans from other animals and that this capacity for reason gives us the power to understand moral truths and guide our lives accordingly.

In a world full of distractions, temptations, and emotional influences, Kant's emphasis on **disciplining the mind** is more relevant than ever. He teaches us that **rational thinking** is the key to clarity and strength in decision-making. When we allow our emotions, biases, or impulses to drive our decisions, we often act irrationally, leading to mistakes and regrets. But when we discipline ourselves to think critically, to weigh evidence, and to consider the logical consequences of our actions, we gain clarity and control over our lives.

For practical application, start by cultivating **self-discipline in your thinking**. When faced with a decision, big or small, resist the urge to act impulsively or emotionally. Instead, take a step back and ask yourself: **What is the rational choice here? What are the long-term consequences of this decision?** By practicing rational thinking, you can avoid the pitfalls of emotional decision-making and make choices that are more likely to lead to success and fulfillment.

You can also apply this lesson to your daily habits. Just as Kant maintained a disciplined routine to structure his life, you can create mental habits that promote clarity and focus. Set aside time each day for **reflection and critical thinking**, whether through journaling, meditation, or simply taking a walk to clear your mind. By developing the habit of disciplined thought, you'll become more effective in all areas of your life, from personal relationships to professional goals.

3. Live by Universal Principles—Create a Life of Consistency and Integrity

Kant believed that morality should be based on **universal principles**, meaning that the rules we live by should apply to everyone, everywhere, at all times. This idea forms the basis of his **categorical imperative**, which asks us to act only in ways that we would want to become universal laws. In other words, our actions should not just be good for us—they should be good for society as a whole.

Living by **universal principles** brings consistency and integrity to your life. When you base your actions on solid, universal values—such as honesty, fairness, and respect—you create a foundation for trust, both with yourself and with others. People will know what to expect from you, and you will be able to navigate life with a clear sense of purpose and direction.

For practical application, start by identifying the **core principles** that you believe should govern your life. These might include values such as honesty, responsibility, or kindness. Once you've identified these principles, use them as a guide for all of your actions and decisions. Ask yourself: **Does this decision align with my core values? Am I acting in a way that I would want others to act?**

By holding yourself to these universal standards, you create a sense of **integrity** that will guide you through life's challenges. Even when faced with difficult choices or external pressures, you can rely on your core principles to make decisions that are consistent and morally sound. This consistency builds inner strength and earns the respect and admiration of those around you.

John Locke

In the pantheon of great thinkers who have shaped modern political thought and human understanding, **John Locke** holds a central place. Often called the "Father of Liberalism," Locke's ideas have profoundly influenced everything from the development of modern democracy to our understanding of individual rights and the nature of knowledge. His writings on **natural rights, government by consent**, and **the pursuit of knowledge** continue to inspire individuals who seek to create a better world, where freedom and reason guide human progress. For Locke, the mind was a blank slate at birth, and through experience, we build knowledge, learn, and grow—an idea that would become foundational in the study of human psychology and education.

Locke's philosophy wasn't just about abstract ideas; it was about **how individuals can lead meaningful, autonomous lives**. He advocated for personal freedom and responsibility, believing that the best society is one where people are empowered to pursue their own happiness, within the framework of a just and fair legal system. His ideas on governance—especially the notion that governments should derive their power from the consent of the governed—laid the groundwork for the American Revolution, and his influence is evident in the Declaration of Independence and other foundational documents of modern democratic states.

In this chapter, we will dive deep into the life and philosophy of John Locke, exploring how his ideas can help us become more knowledgeable, more free, and more engaged in building a just society. By following Locke's lessons, we can cultivate our minds, take control of our destiny, and contribute to the world in meaningful ways.

Autobiography

John Locke was born on August 29, 1632, in the small village of Wrington, Somerset, England, to a relatively modest family. His father was a lawyer and served as a captain in the English Civil War, fighting for the Parliamentary forces. Locke grew up in an environment where **political ideas and debates were part of everyday life**, which would later influence his thinking about government and individual rights.

At the age of 14, Locke entered the **Westminster School in London**, where he developed a deep interest in philosophy, science, and medicine. From there, he went on to **Christ Church, Oxford**, where he completed his studies. However, Locke found the classical curriculum at Oxford stifling and unconnected to the real world. He became more interested in the new scientific ideas of the time, inspired by the work of **René Descartes** and his contemporary **Robert Boyle**.

Locke eventually became a **physician** and entered into public service as an advisor and diplomat. His work brought him into contact with some of the leading political figures of the day, including **Anthony Ashley Cooper, the Earl of Shaftesbury**, a key figure in the development of England's constitutional government. Locke became Shaftesbury's personal physician and confidant, and through this relationship, he gained firsthand experience in the workings of political power and government. During this time, Locke began to develop his ideas on **civil government, natural rights, and the role of reason** in human affairs.

Locke's most famous work, **Two Treatises of Government** (1689), was written in defense of the **Glorious Revolution**, which saw the overthrow of King James II in favor of a constitutional monarchy under William and Mary. In this work, Locke argued that governments must be based on **the consent of the governed** and that individuals have inherent **natural rights** to **life, liberty, and**

property—rights that no government could take away. His political philosophy would go on to influence the **American Revolution** and the drafting of the U.S. Constitution.

Equally important was Locke's **An Essay Concerning Human Understanding** (1690), in which he explored the nature of human knowledge and the development of ideas. In this work, Locke introduced the concept of the **tabula rasa**, or blank slate, suggesting that humans are not born with innate knowledge but instead gain understanding through experience. This was a radical departure from previous philosophical ideas and laid the groundwork for modern theories of **empiricism and education**.

Locke spent the final years of his life in relative peace, continuing to write and refine his ideas while living in Essex, England. He passed away on October 28, 1704, but his ideas continue to resonate, forming the bedrock of modern liberal thought, democratic governance, and the understanding of human knowledge.

Lessons and Applications

John Locke's life and philosophy offer powerful lessons on **knowledge, personal freedom, and the creation of a just society**. His ideas challenge us to think deeply about how we understand the world, how we exercise our freedoms, and how we can contribute to a society where individual rights are respected and protected. Let's explore three actionable and practical lessons from Locke's philosophy and how you can apply them to your own life.

1. Knowledge is Power—Embrace Lifelong Learning and the Power of Empiricism

At the core of Locke's philosophy is the belief that **knowledge comes from experience**. In his **Essay Concerning Human Understanding**, Locke famously argued that the mind is like a blank slate at birth and that all knowledge is gained through experience and reflection. This idea, known as **empiricism**, suggests that we are not born with innate ideas, but rather, we build our understanding of the world through our interactions with it.

For Locke, the pursuit of knowledge was a lifelong endeavor. He believed that by constantly seeking out new experiences, learning from them, and reflecting on our understanding, we could grow as individuals and contribute meaningfully to society. This idea is as relevant today as it was in Locke's time. In a world that is constantly changing, the ability to **adapt, learn, and grow** is crucial for success.

For practical application, adopt a mindset of **lifelong learning**. Whether through formal education, reading, or simply being curious about the world around you, commit to continually expanding your knowledge. Ask yourself: **What am I learning today? How can I apply my experiences to gain a deeper understanding of the world?** Approach every situation—whether in your career, relationships, or personal development—as an opportunity to learn and grow.

Locke's emphasis on **empiricism** also reminds us of the importance of critical thinking. Don't take things at face value. Test your beliefs and ideas against reality. Engage in conversations with others to broaden your perspective, and be willing to change your mind when new evidence presents itself. By grounding your understanding in experience and reflection, you'll develop a stronger, more adaptable mind capable of navigating life's challenges.

2. Defend Your Natural Rights—Protect Your Freedom and Take Responsibility for Your Life

One of Locke's most enduring contributions to political philosophy is his concept of **natural rights**—the idea that every individual has the inherent right to **life, liberty, and property**, which no government can infringe upon. These rights are not granted by any authority but are intrinsic to human existence. For Locke, the role of government is not to control its citizens, but to **protect their rights** and ensure that they are free to pursue their own happiness.

This idea is foundational to the modern concept of **personal freedom** and the belief that individuals should be able to live their lives as they see fit, as long as they do not harm others. But Locke also emphasized that with this freedom comes responsibility. It is up to each person to **take control of their own life**, make informed decisions, and contribute to the well-being of society.

For practical application, reflect on how you exercise your **freedom** in daily life. Are you taking full responsibility for your actions and decisions, or are you allowing others to dictate your choices? Locke's philosophy encourages you to **assert control over your own life**—whether that means pursuing a career you're passionate about, standing up for your beliefs, or simply making decisions that align with your values.

Additionally, Locke's idea of **natural rights** reminds us of the importance of defending not just our own freedoms, but the freedoms of others. In a just society, we must respect the rights of all individuals and work to protect those rights from being infringed upon. This can mean advocating for social justice, speaking out against oppression, or simply treating others with the respect and dignity they deserve.

3. Consent is Key—Govern Your Own Life and Make Thoughtful, Informed Choices

A central principle of Locke's political philosophy is the idea that **governments derive their authority from the consent of the governed**. In other words, people should only be subject to laws and leaders that they have freely agreed to. This idea of **consent** goes beyond political theory—it's a powerful lesson in personal autonomy and decision-making.

In Locke's view, true freedom comes from making **informed, thoughtful choices** based on rational understanding. Just as individuals in a society must consent to their government, you must also **take charge of your own life** by actively participating in the decisions that affect you. This means not simply going along with the crowd or accepting things as they are, but taking the time to **understand your options** and making choices that align with your values and goals.

For practical application, start by **questioning the decisions** you make every day. Are you making these choices consciously, or are you letting others influence your path? Locke's philosophy challenges you to be proactive in your life—whether that's in your career, relationships, or personal development. Take ownership of your decisions, and ensure that they are **based on reason, not external pressures**.

This principle can also apply to how you manage relationships and work with others. Seek **mutual consent** in all your interactions. Whether you're negotiating a contract, managing a team, or building a relationship, aim to create agreements that both parties freely consent to. Locke's vision of a society governed by consent reminds us that healthy, productive relationships are built on **communication, understanding, and respect** for each person's autonomy.

Revolutionaries and Reformers

Martin Luther King Jr.

Few figures in modern history have had as profound an impact on the fight for justice, equality, and human dignity as **Dr. Martin Luther King Jr.** His life was a testament to the power of **courageous leadership**, **nonviolent resistance**, and a relentless commitment to truth and justice. King didn't just speak about the ideals of freedom—he embodied them, facing down hatred, violence, and oppression with grace, resilience, and unwavering moral conviction. His leadership in the **Civil Rights Movement** transformed not only the United States but also the global understanding of what it means to fight for human rights and equality.

King's philosophy of **nonviolent resistance**, inspired by **Mahatma Gandhi**, showed the world that great change could be achieved without violence or hatred. Instead, King emphasized the need for love, understanding, and **moral courage** in the face of injustice. His words and actions have inspired generations of leaders, activists, and everyday individuals who seek to build a better, more equitable world. He demonstrated that **real power comes from standing up for what is right**, even when the path is difficult.

In this chapter, we will explore the life of Martin Luther King Jr., drawing practical lessons from his leadership and his enduring commitment to nonviolence and justice. His example offers powerful guidance on how we can each become stronger, more principled, and more courageous in the face of our own challenges, no matter how daunting they may seem.

Autobiography

Martin Luther King Jr. was born on January 15, 1929, in **Atlanta, Georgia**, into a family deeply rooted in the church and the pursuit of equality for African Americans. His father, **Martin Luther King**

Sr., was a prominent Baptist preacher, and his mother, **Alberta Williams King**, was a schoolteacher. Growing up in the segregated South, King experienced firsthand the injustices of racism, but he was also exposed to the strength and resilience of the Black church, which played a central role in shaping his moral and spiritual outlook.

King was a gifted student, excelling academically throughout his early education. He went on to attend **Morehouse College** in Atlanta, where he earned his undergraduate degree. From there, King pursued a seminary education at **Crozer Theological Seminary** in Pennsylvania, where he was introduced to the teachings of **Mahatma Gandhi** and the philosophy of **nonviolent resistance**. This idea would come to shape King's approach to the struggle for civil rights.

After earning his Ph.D. in theology from **Boston University**, King became pastor of **Dexter Avenue Baptist Church** in Montgomery, Alabama. It was here, in 1955, that King's leadership would come to national prominence, following the **Montgomery Bus Boycott** sparked by the arrest of **Rosa Parks**, who refused to give up her seat to a white passenger. King, then only 26 years old, was chosen to lead the boycott, which lasted over a year and became a turning point in the American Civil Rights Movement. His leadership during this period solidified his reputation as a courageous and visionary leader, committed to achieving justice through peaceful means.

In the years that followed, King became the face of the Civil Rights Movement, leading marches, organizing protests, and delivering powerful speeches that called for an end to segregation and racial discrimination. His most famous address, the **"I Have a Dream" speech**, delivered during the **March on Washington** in 1963, captured the hearts and minds of millions, articulating a vision of a future where people would be judged not by the color of their skin but by the content of their character.

King's commitment to nonviolence, even in the face of brutal opposition, set him apart as a leader of unparalleled moral strength. He faced arrests, bombings, threats, and physical attacks, yet he never wavered in his belief that **love and nonviolence** were the most powerful tools for achieving true justice. His efforts culminated in the passing of the **Civil Rights Act of 1964** and the **Voting Rights Act of 1965**, landmark pieces of legislation that dismantled legal segregation and secured voting rights for African Americans.

Despite these victories, King's work was far from over. He expanded his focus to include issues of poverty and economic injustice, launching the **Poor People's Campaign** in 1968. Tragically, King's life was cut short when he was assassinated on April 4, 1968, in Memphis, Tennessee, where he had been supporting striking sanitation workers. Though his life was taken, his legacy endures, serving as a beacon of hope and a model for what true leadership and moral courage look like.

Lessons and Applications

Martin Luther King Jr.'s life offers profound lessons in **courage, nonviolence, and leading by example**. His philosophy and leadership provide actionable insights for anyone seeking to stand up for what is right, face adversity with strength, and lead with integrity. Let's explore three deeply practical lessons from King's life and how you can apply them to your own journey.

1. Stand Firm in the Face of Adversity—True Courage is Doing What's Right, Even When It's Hard

One of the most remarkable aspects of King's leadership was his **unshakable courage**. He faced threats to his life, imprisonment, and constant harassment, yet he remained committed to his cause. King understood that standing up for what's right is never easy, and that **true courage** is about remaining firm in your convictions, even when the path ahead is filled with danger, doubt, or fear. He once said, "**The ultimate measure of a man is not where he stands in moments of comfort and convenience, but where he stands at times of challenge and controversy.**"

King's courage wasn't just about confronting external challenges—it was about the **internal strength** required to lead others in a fight for justice. He refused to back down, even when the cost was high. He believed that real change could only come through persistent effort, even in the face of overwhelming odds.

In your own life, you will face moments where standing up for what you believe in will be difficult. Whether it's confronting injustice in your workplace, making a tough decision in your personal life, or taking a risk to pursue a higher goal, **courage will be required**. King's example teaches us that true strength is found in the ability to **persist through fear** and uncertainty.

For practical application, start by identifying an area in your life where you've been avoiding confrontation or a difficult decision. Ask yourself: **Am I avoiding this because it's hard, or because it's not right? What would Martin Luther King Jr. do in this situation?** Take one step toward facing this challenge head-on. Whether it's having a difficult conversation, standing up for someone else, or simply acting on your principles, remember that **courage is a muscle**—the more you use it, the stronger it becomes.

Courage isn't just about facing external battles—it's about overcoming your own self-doubt and fear. By standing firm in your values and convictions, you build the inner strength to handle whatever life throws at you. **Courage, like King's, is the foundation of lasting success.**

2. Embrace Nonviolence—Lead with Love, Not Force

At the heart of Martin Luther King Jr.'s philosophy was the principle of **nonviolence**. Inspired by the teachings of **Gandhi**, King believed that violence only begets more violence, and that **love and understanding** are the most powerful forces for achieving lasting change. He taught that true power comes not from physical force, but from the ability to transform hearts and minds through peaceful means.

In a world often driven by aggression, competition, and conflict, King's commitment to **nonviolent resistance** is more relevant than ever. He understood that achieving justice through violence only deepens divisions and leads to greater suffering. Instead, he advocated for the **transformative power of love and compassion**, even toward one's enemies.

For practical application, begin by reflecting on how you respond to conflict in your own life. Do you react with anger, aggression, or defensiveness? King's philosophy teaches us to **pause, reflect, and respond with calm and empathy**. The next time you find yourself in a disagreement, whether at work or in your personal life, practice King's approach of **nonviolence in thought, word, and action**. Ask yourself: **How can I respond with understanding rather than anger? How can I lead this conversation toward resolution, not division?**

King's approach wasn't passive—it was deeply active and strategic. Nonviolence doesn't mean avoiding confrontation or being weak. It means confronting challenges with strength, clarity, and a commitment to **building bridges** rather than burning them. In your own leadership, adopt this principle by prioritizing dialogue, seeking common ground, and leading with compassion, even when it's difficult.

This philosophy can be applied in everyday situations, from managing difficult conversations at work to navigating personal relationships. By practicing **nonviolence and leading with love,** you not only create better outcomes but also cultivate a deeper sense of inner peace and purpose. King's legacy reminds us that **the strongest leaders are those who lift others up, not tear them down.**

3. Lead by Example—Be the Change You Want to See

Perhaps one of the most powerful lessons from Martin Luther King Jr.'s life is the idea that **real leaders lead by example.** King didn't just speak about justice—he **lived** it. He marched alongside his followers, faced arrest and imprisonment, and endured personal threats and attacks, all while maintaining his commitment to nonviolence and love. He once said, **"A genuine leader is not a searcher for consensus but a molder of consensus."** King understood that **true leadership is about inspiring others through your actions, not just your words.**

In your own life, this lesson is incredibly valuable. Whether you're leading a team at work, raising a family, or simply trying to improve yourself, the most effective way to inspire others is to **embody the change you want to see.** Talk is cheap—but when people see you acting with integrity, courage, and conviction, they are far more likely to follow your lead.

For practical application, think about an area of your life where you want to see improvement or change. It could be within your organization, your community, or even within yourself. Ask yourself: **Am I living the values I want to see in others? How can I set a better example through my actions?** Commit to **leading by example** in one area of your life—whether that's through showing more discipline at work, being more present with your family, or standing up for a cause you believe in.

King's leadership wasn't about perfection—it was about **consistency** and **authenticity.** He didn't wait for others to act—he took the first step, knowing that by setting the right example, others would follow. In your own leadership, practice this by focusing less on what others are doing and more on **how you can lead with integrity**. By aligning your actions with your values, you create a ripple effect that can inspire real change, just as King did.

Malcolm X

Few figures in American history embody the journey of personal transformation and the relentless pursuit of freedom like **Malcolm X**. His life was a radical evolution—from a troubled youth involved in crime, to a leader of the **Nation of Islam**, to an advocate for global human rights and Black empowerment. Malcolm X was unapologetically bold in his demand for justice, truth, and equality, challenging not only white America's systemic racism but also the complacency and compromise he saw in other civil rights leaders of his time. For Malcolm, the journey wasn't just about racial equality—it was about **self-determination, personal evolution, and the freedom to shape one's own destiny**.

What set Malcolm apart was his ability to adapt and grow. He didn't shy away from controversial or hard truths, and his willingness to embrace change—both personally and ideologically—gave him a unique power. His speeches and ideas weren't just about fighting for civil rights; they were about **empowerment**, about taking control of one's life and refusing to let others define you. Malcolm X's message was simple: **liberate your mind, empower yourself, and stand unflinchingly for what you believe is right.**

In this chapter, we will explore Malcolm X's life in depth and uncover the lessons his journey offers to all of us. From the power of personal transformation to the importance of standing boldly for your beliefs, Malcolm's example is a roadmap for anyone seeking to break free from societal constraints and become their most authentic and powerful self.

Autobiography

Malcolm X, born **Malcolm Little** on May 19, 1925, in **Omaha, Nebraska**, grew up in a world defined by racial violence, poverty, and systemic injustice. His father, Earl Little, was a Baptist minister and a supporter of **Marcus Garvey's Universal Negro Improvement Association (UNIA)**, which advocated for Black pride and independence. This activism made the family a target for white supremacists, and their home was burned to the ground when Malcolm was just four years old. His father's murder, when Malcolm was six, was officially ruled an accident, but many believed it to be the work of the **Black Legion**, a white supremacist group. This early trauma would leave a deep mark on Malcolm's view of the world.

Malcolm's mother, Louise Little, struggled to support her eight children after Earl's death. She was eventually institutionalized due to mental health issues, and the children were placed in foster care. From there, Malcolm's life spiraled. As a teenager, he fell into a life of crime, moving to **Harlem, New York**, where he engaged in drug dealing, gambling, and robbery. By 1946, he was arrested and sentenced to ten years in prison for burglary.

It was during his time in prison that Malcolm's transformation began. Through the guidance of his siblings, he was introduced to the teachings of **Elijah Muhammad** and the **Nation of Islam (NOI)**. The NOI preached a message of Black empowerment, self-sufficiency, and the rejection of white society's oppression. Malcolm immersed himself in books, studying everything from history to philosophy to religion, and developed a new sense of purpose. Upon his release in 1952, Malcolm changed his surname from "Little" to "X," symbolizing the rejection of his "slave name" and the unknown African heritage taken from him through slavery.

Malcolm quickly rose to prominence within the Nation of Islam, becoming its most dynamic and visible spokesperson. His fiery oratory, combined with his sharp intellect and fearless critique of America's racial inequalities, drew national attention. Malcolm's speeches, which condemned white America for its brutal history of racism and demanded justice **"by any means necessary,"** resonated with many Black Americans, especially those who felt disillusioned by the nonviolent approaches of other civil rights leaders like **Martin Luther King Jr.**

However, Malcolm's journey didn't stop there. After a pilgrimage to **Mecca** in 1964, Malcolm experienced a profound shift in his worldview. He embraced **Sunni Islam**, renouncing the racial exclusivity of the Nation of Islam and adopting a more inclusive vision of global human rights. He believed that racism wasn't just an American problem, but a human problem, and that the struggle for freedom extended beyond race to include the fight for justice everywhere. He founded the **Organization of Afro-American Unity (OAAU)**, which sought to unite people of African descent around the world.

Malcolm X was assassinated on February 21, 1965, at the age of 39. Though his life was cut short, his legacy continues to inspire generations of people seeking freedom, justice, and personal empowerment. His autobiography, co-written with **Alex Haley**, remains one of the most powerful and influential books in American history.

Lessons and Applications

Malcolm X's life offers powerful lessons on **personal transformation, self-determination, and the courage to speak truth to power.** His ability to reinvent himself, to stand boldly for what he believed in, and to fight for justice in the face of immense opposition provides valuable insights for anyone striving to break free from limitations and achieve greatness. Let's explore three actionable lessons from Malcolm X's life and how you can apply them to your own journey.

1. Embrace Personal Transformation—It's Never Too Late to Redefine Yourself

Malcolm X's life is a testament to the power of **personal transformation**. Born into a world of systemic racism and violence, and later falling into a life of crime, Malcolm could have easily been another statistic. But his time in prison became a turning point, where he completely redefined himself through education, faith, and self-reflection. Malcolm's transformation didn't stop there—after embracing the Nation of Islam, he again redefined himself after his pilgrimage to Mecca, evolving his philosophy and broadening his vision to include global human rights.

The lesson here is clear: **it's never too late to redefine who you are**. No matter where you start in life, or how difficult your past has been, you always have the power to change and evolve. Malcolm's journey shows that growth is a continual process, and the ability to embrace change is one of the most powerful tools for personal empowerment.

For practical application, start by reflecting on where you are in your life right now. Are there areas where you feel stuck or limited by your past? What aspects of yourself do you want to redefine? Remember, transformation requires **both introspection and action**. Just as Malcolm immersed himself in education and spiritual reflection, you too can begin your transformation by seeking knowledge, new experiences, and challenging your current beliefs. Ask yourself: **What steps can I take today to become the person I truly want to be?**

Don't be afraid to **break free from past identities** that no longer serve you. Whether it's shedding old habits, embracing new beliefs, or pursuing a different path in life, Malcolm's example teaches us that transformation is not only possible, but necessary for growth. Be willing to evolve, to rethink who you are, and to embrace the endless possibilities for your future.

2. Stand Unapologetically for What You Believe—Courage is the Foundation of True Power

Malcolm X was known for his fearless and unapologetic stance on **speaking truth to power**. He didn't mince words when it came to confronting racism, inequality, and systemic oppression. He was often criticized for his boldness, but it was precisely this courage that made his message so powerful. Malcolm understood that to create real change, you must be willing to stand boldly for what you believe in, even if it makes others uncomfortable.

Courage is the foundation of true power. It takes courage to speak out against injustice, to challenge the status quo, and to advocate for what you know is right. Many people shy away from these moments because they fear backlash, rejection, or failure. Malcolm's life teaches us that **being bold in your convictions** is not only necessary for progress but is also a key ingredient in personal success.

For practical application, reflect on the areas in your life where you've hesitated to speak up or take action. Are there situations where you've allowed fear to hold you back from standing for what you believe in? The next time you face a challenging situation, channel the courage of Malcolm X by standing firm in your convictions. Whether it's at work, in your relationships, or within your community, don't be afraid to speak your truth, even if it goes against the grain.

Courage doesn't always mean taking radical or confrontational steps—it can also mean having the inner strength to **stay true to your values**, even when it's hard. The more you practice speaking up and acting on your beliefs, the more confident and empowered you'll become. Just as Malcolm X refused to apologize for fighting for justice, you too can find strength in being unapologetically yourself.

3. Empower Yourself Through Knowledge—Education

is the Key to Freedom

One of the most remarkable aspects of Malcolm X's journey was his commitment to **self-education**. During his time in prison, Malcolm read voraciously, devouring books on history, philosophy, religion, and politics. He understood that **knowledge is the key to empowerment**, and that education gives you the tools to understand the world, challenge false narratives, and advocate for yourself and others. As he famously said, "**Education is the passport to the future, for tomorrow belongs to those who prepare for it today.**"

Malcolm's emphasis on education wasn't just about academic knowledge—it was about understanding your history, your rights, and the systems of power that shape society. He knew that the more informed and educated you are, the more control you have over your own destiny.

For practical application, make **self-education** a priority in your life. In today's world, access to knowledge is easier than ever, whether through books, online courses, podcasts, or documentaries. Identify areas where you want to grow—whether it's in your career, personal development, or understanding social and political issues—and commit to learning something new every day. Ask yourself: **How can I use knowledge to empower myself and create the future I want?**

Education isn't just about gaining information; it's about **developing critical thinking**, questioning assumptions, and using what you learn to improve your life and the lives of others. Just as Malcolm X used education to transform himself and his community, you too can harness the power of knowledge to create lasting change. Empower yourself through learning, and you'll find that the possibilities for growth and success are limitless.

Joan of Arc

In the annals of history, **Joan of Arc** stands as a symbol of unwavering conviction and courage in the face of insurmountable odds. A teenage peasant girl from a small village in France, Joan's belief in her divine mission led her to change the course of her country's history during one of its darkest times. She wasn't a soldier trained in warfare or a noble with wealth and influence—she was a young woman with nothing but her faith and determination, yet she inspired an army and turned the tide of a war that had ravaged France for decades.

Joan's rise to prominence during the **Hundred Years' War** between France and England is nothing short of extraordinary. At just 17 years old, she led French troops to a series of improbable victories, breaking the siege of Orléans and paving the way for the coronation of **Charles VII** as king. Joan's story is a testament to the power of **courage**, **vision**, and **the belief that one person can make a difference**, no matter their background or circumstances.

Her life is also a reminder of the sacrifices often required of those who dare to challenge the status quo and pursue a cause larger than themselves. Burned at the stake at the age of 19, Joan's legacy of strength and faith continues to inspire generations. In this chapter, we'll dive deep into Joan of Arc's life and uncover the powerful lessons we can apply to our own struggles, aspirations, and paths to success.

Autobiography

Jeanne d'Arc, commonly known as Joan of Arc, was born around January 6, 1412, in the village of **Domrémy** in northeastern France. She came from a humble peasant family, the daughter of Jacques d'Arc and Isabelle Romée. Joan's upbringing was typical for a rural peasant girl, and she grew up tending to animals and helping with the farm. Yet, despite her unremarkable beginnings, Joan always had a strong religious faith that would later drive her to undertake one of the most audacious missions in history.

At the time of Joan's youth, France was embroiled in the **Hundred Years' War** with England, a conflict that had left the country divided and devastated. The English, allied with the **Burgundians**, controlled vast portions of northern France, including Paris. The French monarchy was weak and discredited, with the rightful heir to the throne, **Charles VII**, struggling to secure his claim as king. Amid this political chaos, Joan began to experience what she described as **visions from God**, guiding her to support Charles VII and help drive the English from France.

In 1429, at the age of 17, Joan traveled to the court of Charles VII, claiming that she had been sent by God to lead his armies to victory. It's worth noting how remarkable this act was—Joan was a young, uneducated woman claiming a divine mandate in a time when women had little to no influence, especially in matters of war and politics. Charles, desperate for any advantage, eventually gave her a chance to prove herself. Clad in armor, Joan was placed at the head of the French army and tasked with relieving the besieged city of **Orléans**.

Joan's leadership and inspirational presence rallied the French troops, who achieved a stunning victory at Orléans. This victory marked a turning point in the war and led to a series of successful campaigns that ultimately resulted in Charles VII's coronation as king in **Reims Cathedral**, a symbolic moment that Joan had predicted. Her ability to motivate and inspire others was extraordinary, particularly given the skeptical and patriarchal society in which she operated.

However, Joan's meteoric rise was followed by a swift and tragic fall. In 1430, she was captured by the Burgundians and sold to the

English, who sought to discredit her and the French cause. She was put on trial for **heresy** and **witchcraft**, accused of cross-dressing (for wearing male military clothing) and claiming to hear divine voices. Despite her unwavering faith and defense of her actions, Joan was condemned and burned at the stake in **Rouen** on May 30, 1431. She was just 19 years old.

Though Joan's life was brief, her impact was immense. Nearly 25 years after her death, a second trial was held, and she was posthumously exonerated of all charges. In 1920, Joan of Arc was canonized as a saint by the **Roman Catholic Church**. Today, she stands as one of France's greatest heroes and a symbol of courage, faith, and the power of conviction.

Lessons and Applications

Joan of Arc's life offers profound lessons in **courage, conviction, and the power of believing in your mission**. Her journey from peasant girl to military leader and martyr provides valuable insights for anyone facing their own battles—whether personal, professional, or spiritual. Let's explore three key lessons from Joan's life and how you can apply them to your own.

1. Believe in Your Vision—Commit to Your Purpose, Even When Others Doubt You

One of the most remarkable aspects of Joan of Arc's life is her **unwavering belief** in her divine mission. Despite being a young woman with no formal training or political connections, Joan was utterly convinced that she had been chosen by God to lead France to victory. This belief fueled her courage and resilience in the face of enormous opposition. She faced skepticism not only from her enemies but also from those who should have been her allies. Yet, Joan never wavered in her conviction.

The lesson here is simple but powerful: **when you believe deeply in your purpose, others' doubts and opposition lose their power** over you. Joan's story shows that conviction is often the fuel needed to push through adversity. People may doubt you, ridicule your ambitions, or tell you that your goals are unrealistic. But if you have clarity about your vision and believe in its importance, that belief becomes a powerful force that propels you forward.

For practical application, reflect on your own vision or purpose. Ask yourself: **What do I believe in so strongly that I'm willing to pursue it, even if others doubt me?** Whether it's a personal goal, a professional ambition, or a cause you're passionate about, write down your vision and commit to it. **Ignore the naysayers**—the world is full of people who will tell you why something can't be done. Joan didn't let the skepticism of powerful men dissuade her, and neither should you.

Keep in mind that believing in your vision doesn't mean ignoring reality or acting recklessly. It means having the courage to stay committed to your goals, even when the path is hard. Like Joan, you will encounter obstacles and detractors, but your conviction will be the key to overcoming them.

2. Act with Courage—Bravery Isn't the Absence of Fear, It's Taking Action Despite It

Joan of Arc's life is defined by her extraordinary courage. She faced dangers that most people would flee from—leading troops into battle, defying the powerful institutions of her time, and standing firm in her beliefs even when it led to her death. Courage, in Joan's case, wasn't about being fearless. It was about taking action in the face of fear because she believed so strongly in the righteousness of her cause.

Too often, we wait for fear to go away before we take action. But Joan's story teaches us that **courage is not the absence of fear—it's** the decision to move forward in spite of it. Real bravery comes from recognizing your fear and pushing through it because you know what you're fighting for is worth the risk.

For practical application, identify an area of your life where you've been holding back because of fear. Maybe it's a career move you're afraid to make, a relationship you're scared to pursue, or a difficult conversation you've been avoiding. Ask yourself: **What would Joan of Arc do in this situation?** Chances are, she wouldn't let fear stop her from taking action. Start by taking one small step toward your goal, even if it scares you. Courage is like a muscle—the more you exercise it, the stronger it becomes.

Also, remember that acting with courage doesn't mean acting without preparation. Joan didn't march into battle without strategy or support. She built alliances, sought guidance, and made calculated decisions. Similarly, as you take courageous steps in your own life, prepare yourself as best as you can. **Plan, strategize, and then act**, knowing that even with the best preparation, there will still be moments where you'll need to push past fear.

3. Stay True to Your Principles—Stand Firm in Your Values, No Matter the Cost

Perhaps the most enduring lesson from Joan of Arc's life is her **unwavering commitment to her values**. Even when faced with death, Joan refused to deny her faith or betray her principles. Her trial was an opportunity to save herself by recanting her claims of divine guidance, but Joan chose to stay true to her beliefs, even knowing that it would lead to her execution.

In today's world, where compromises are often made for convenience or personal gain, Joan's example is a powerful reminder of the importance of **staying true to your principles**. Whether in your career, personal life, or relationships, there will be times when you're tempted to take the easy way out, to compromise on your values to avoid conflict or achieve a short-term benefit. Joan's life teaches us that **true strength lies in holding firm to your values, no matter the cost.**

For practical application, reflect on your own principles and values. What are the **non-negotiables** in your life? Are there areas where you've been compromising or bending your values to fit in or avoid discomfort? Joan's story challenges you to stand firm, even when it's difficult. Ask yourself: **What am I willing to sacrifice to stay true to what I believe in?** Whether it's in business, relationships, or personal decisions, commit to living in alignment with your values.

Staying true to your principles isn't just about grand gestures—it's about the **small, everyday decisions** that define who you are. Whether it's speaking up for someone who's being treated unfairly, refusing to participate in unethical behavior at work, or being honest even when it's inconvenient, **your integrity is your greatest asset.** Joan's life shows us that staying true to your values may be costly in the short term, but it's the foundation of true greatness.

Simón Bolívar

Simón Bolívar is one of history's most iconic freedom fighters, a man whose name is synonymous with **independence, revolution, and the relentless pursuit of liberty.** Often called **El Libertador,** Bolívar was a military and political leader who played a crucial role in liberating much of Latin America from Spanish colonial rule. His efforts led to the independence of countries like **Venezuela, Colombia, Ecuador, Peru, and Bolivia,** and his vision for a united and independent Latin America inspired generations of leaders, revolutionaries, and ordinary people.

Bolívar's greatness lay not just in his military prowess but in his **unshakable vision of freedom.** He believed that the people of Latin America deserved to govern themselves, free from the control of a distant empire. Throughout his life, Bolívar faced overwhelming odds, including political divisions, military defeats, and personal betrayals. Yet, his **determination** and **belief in the cause of independence** never wavered. Bolívar's ability to **lead by example,** fight through adversity, and remain steadfast in his vision of a free and united Latin America provides powerful lessons for anyone seeking to achieve greatness against the odds.

In this chapter, we'll explore the life of Simón Bolívar, drawing out practical lessons from his journey that you can apply to your own struggles and ambitions. Bolívar's example teaches us that **vision and determination,** combined with the courage to stand for what is right, can turn even the most improbable dreams into reality.

Autobiography

Simón Bolívar was born on July 24, 1783, in **Caracas, Venezuela,** into a wealthy aristocratic family of Spanish descent. His parents died when he was still a child, leaving him under the care of relatives and tutors who would shape his early education. Bolívar was sent to Europe in his youth, where he continued his studies and was exposed to the ideas of the **Enlightenment**—concepts like **liberty, equality, and self-governance** that would profoundly influence his thinking.

While in Paris, Bolívar witnessed firsthand the aftermath of the **French Revolution**, which cemented his belief in the principles of **popular sovereignty** and the right of people to overthrow unjust rulers. During this time, he also met **Alexander von Humboldt**, a German scientist and explorer who predicted that the Spanish colonies in the Americas would soon seek independence. These experiences ignited Bolívar's vision of a **free Latin America** and planted the seeds of the revolution he would one day lead.

Returning to Venezuela in 1807, Bolívar joined the growing movement for independence from Spanish rule. He quickly emerged as a key leader in the struggle, advocating for the complete liberation of Latin America from colonial oppression. His charisma, intelligence, and military skill made him a natural leader of the cause. Bolívar's early efforts met with both success and failure—at times he faced defeat, exile, and even near execution—but his **resilience** and **unwavering belief in the cause** kept him fighting.

Bolívar's most famous military campaigns include the daring **crossing of the Andes** in 1819, a feat that is often compared to Hannibal's crossing of the Alps. This risky and arduous march led to the surprise defeat of Spanish forces at the **Battle of Boyacá**, which secured the independence of modern-day Colombia. Bolívar continued his campaigns, eventually liberating **Venezuela, Ecuador, Peru**, and the region that would later be named **Bolivia** in his honor.

Despite his military successes, Bolívar struggled to achieve his political vision of a united Latin America, which he called **Gran Colombia**. His dream of a single, powerful nation that could stand on equal footing with the great powers of Europe and North America was ultimately thwarted by internal divisions, regional rivalries, and political infighting. In his final years, Bolívar grew disillusioned with the fragmentation of the independence movement, famously stating, "**I have plowed the sea.**"

Simón Bolívar died of tuberculosis on December 17, 1830, in Santa Marta, Colombia, at the age of 47. Although his vision of a united Latin America was never fully realized, Bolívar remains a towering figure in the history of the Americas, revered for his relentless dedication to the cause of freedom and independence. His life and legacy continue to inspire those who fight for justice, self-determination, and the right of all people to live free from oppression.

Lessons and Applications

Simón Bolívar's life offers profound lessons in **vision, resilience, and the pursuit of freedom**. His determination to fight for the independence of an entire continent, despite facing immense challenges, provides valuable insights for anyone seeking to achieve their own goals in the face of adversity. Let's explore three key lessons from Bolívar's life and how you can apply them to your own journey.

1. Cultivate a Grand Vision—Great Leaders Think Beyond Themselves

One of the most defining aspects of Bolívar's leadership was his **grand vision** for a free and united Latin America. He wasn't just fighting for the independence of Venezuela or Colombia—he dreamed of a **continental revolution** that would rid all of Latin America of colonial rule and create a united republic that could stand strong on the global stage. Bolívar's vision extended beyond the immediate political struggles of his time to a larger goal of transforming the entire region for the better.

The lesson here is that **great leaders think beyond their immediate circumstances.** Bolívar's ability to inspire others came from his passion for something larger than himself—a vision that transcended borders and individual ambition. When you cultivate a grand vision for your life, your career, or your community, you tap into a source of motivation and resilience that will sustain you through the toughest challenges.

For practical application, take some time to reflect on your own goals. Are you thinking big enough? Are you focusing only on short-term achievements, or are you working toward something larger that will have a lasting impact? Ask yourself: **What is my grand vision for the future? What am I trying to build or achieve that will make a difference beyond my immediate life?** When you have a grand vision, you not only inspire yourself but also those around you.

Keep in mind that having a grand vision doesn't mean ignoring the details or the steps needed to get there. Bolívar had to navigate complex political and military challenges on his path to independence, but his larger vision was always his guiding star. Similarly, while you work toward your goals, always keep your long-term vision in sight. It will help you make decisions with purpose and push through obstacles that might otherwise discourage you.

2. Resilience in the Face of Adversity—Persistence Is Key to Achieving Greatness

Bolívar's life is a testament to the power of **resilience.** Throughout his campaigns, he faced **military defeats, political betrayals, and personal setbacks.** There were moments when the cause of independence seemed hopeless, and yet, Bolívar never gave up. His ability to rebound from failure and continue fighting, even when the odds were stacked against him, was one of his greatest strengths as a leader.

Too often, people give up on their goals when they encounter failure or difficulty. Bolívar's life teaches us that **persistence is key to achieving greatness**. Setbacks are inevitable, but how you respond to them is what defines your path. Bolívar didn't see failure as the end—he saw it as a temporary obstacle that he could overcome with enough effort and determination.

For practical application, reflect on how you respond to setbacks in your own life. Do you let failure stop you, or do you use it as fuel to keep going? The next time you encounter a challenge, think of Bolívar's resilience. Ask yourself: **How can I turn this setback into an opportunity for growth? What lessons can I learn from this failure that will make me stronger?** By viewing adversity as part of the journey, rather than a barrier, you'll develop the mental toughness needed to keep moving forward.

One of the keys to resilience is **staying focused on your purpose**. Bolívar never lost sight of his ultimate goal, even when everything seemed to be falling apart. In your own life, keep your vision at the forefront of your mind, especially during difficult times. Remind yourself why you started in the first place, and let that purpose carry you through the rough patches. Persistence, coupled with a clear sense of purpose, is what separates those who achieve greatness from those who give up too soon.

3. Fight for Freedom—Stand for What You Believe in, Even When It's Unpopular

Bolívar's entire life was dedicated to the cause of **freedom**. He believed deeply in the right of people to govern themselves and to live free from the tyranny of colonial rule. Bolívar's fight for independence was not always popular, and he often faced opposition from both Spanish forces and rival factions within Latin America.

Yet, Bolívar never wavered in his belief that the struggle for freedom was worth any price.

The lesson here is that **true leadership requires the courage to stand for what you believe in, even when it's unpopular or difficult.** Bolívar didn't fight for convenience or personal gain—he fought for the principles of liberty and justice, even when doing so made him enemies or led to hardship. In today's world, where it's easy to follow the crowd or avoid confrontation, Bolívar's example challenges us to **stand firm in our beliefs** and to fight for the causes we care about.

For practical application, reflect on the principles or causes that matter most to you. Are there situations in your life where you've been hesitant to speak up or take action because it's unpopular or uncomfortable? The next time you find yourself in such a situation, ask yourself: **What would Bolívar do?** Use his example as inspiration to stand firm in your convictions, even when it's difficult.

Fighting for what you believe in doesn't always mean leading a revolution—it can mean standing up for fairness at work, advocating for someone who's been mistreated, or working toward positive change in your community. The key is to have the **moral courage** to take action, rather than staying silent or complacent. Bolívar's legacy reminds us that the fight for freedom—whether personal or political—is always worth pursuing.

Che Guevara

Few figures in modern history ignite the imagination and controversy as much as **Ernesto "Che" Guevara**. To some, he was a **freedom fighter**, an icon of rebellion, and a visionary who sought to liberate the oppressed from imperialism and inequality. To others, he was a ruthless revolutionary, willing to sacrifice anything and anyone in the name of his ideals. Whatever your perspective, there is no denying that Che Guevara was a man driven by a deep conviction and a relentless commitment to fighting for his vision of a better world. His image, immortalized on t-shirts, posters, and murals, has come to symbolize the spirit of revolution, courage, and resistance to oppression.

What makes Guevara so compelling is not just his role in the Cuban Revolution, but the **clarity of his ideals** and his **willingness to take action**. He wasn't content to talk about change—he lived it. Che left behind a life of privilege and comfort to pursue his belief in the right of all people to be free from oppression, inequality, and exploitation. His transformation from a young medical student into an international revolutionary leader demonstrates the power of **action** and **dedication** to a cause larger than oneself.

In this chapter, we will delve into Che Guevara's life, examining how his beliefs shaped his actions and what we can learn from his unwavering commitment to change. While Guevara's methods and legacy are often debated, there is much to draw from his **passion, determination, and resolve** for anyone seeking to make a difference in their own life or the world.

Autobiography

Ernesto "Che" Guevara was born on June 14, 1928, in **Rosario, Argentina**, to a middle-class family with progressive political views.

From a young age, Guevara was influenced by the leftist ideals of his family and their deep empathy for the working class. Despite suffering from chronic asthma, Che excelled academically and was known for his curiosity, intellectual rigor, and a fierce desire to understand the world beyond Argentina's borders.

In 1948, Che began studying **medicine** at the University of Buenos Aires, driven by a desire to help those who were suffering from disease and poverty. However, his perspective on the world was dramatically reshaped by a series of journeys through **Latin America**, most famously his motorcycle trip with friend **Alberto Granado** in 1951-1952. This journey, chronicled in his memoir **"The Motorcycle Diaries,"** exposed Guevara to the extreme poverty, inequality, and political oppression faced by the people of Latin America. He witnessed firsthand the exploitation of indigenous communities, the vast disparities in wealth, and the destructive influence of foreign corporations on local economies. These experiences sparked his transformation from a medical student into a committed revolutionary.

Guevara's growing conviction that the region's problems could not be solved through reform, but only through **armed revolution**, led him to immerse himself in Marxist literature and revolutionary thought. He became convinced that the only way to free the oppressed masses from exploitation was to overthrow capitalist governments and replace them with socialist systems that prioritized the needs of the people over corporate profits.

In 1954, Guevara traveled to **Guatemala**, where he witnessed the CIA-backed coup that overthrew the left-wing government of **Jacobo Árbenz**, solidifying his belief that the United States would go to any length to maintain control over Latin America's resources. It was during this time that Guevara met **Raúl Castro**, who introduced him to his brother **Fidel Castro**, the exiled leader of the Cuban revolutionary movement. Che joined the Castros and their

26th of July Movement, dedicated to overthrowing the U.S.-backed Cuban dictator **Fulgencio Batista**.

Guevara quickly rose through the ranks of the Cuban guerrillas, becoming one of Castro's most trusted commanders. His military strategy, leadership, and unyielding commitment to the cause were instrumental in the success of the **Cuban Revolution**, which culminated in Batista's overthrow in 1959. After the revolution, Guevara held several important positions in the Cuban government, including overseeing the nationalization of industries and serving as president of the **National Bank of Cuba**.

However, Che was not content to rest on the success of the Cuban Revolution. He believed that the fight for freedom and socialism needed to spread beyond Cuba's borders. In the mid-1960s, Guevara left Cuba to support revolutionary movements in Africa and Latin America, most notably in **Congo** and **Bolivia**. It was in Bolivia that Guevara's life came to a tragic end. In 1967, after leading a failed insurgency, he was captured by the Bolivian army, acting on CIA intelligence, and executed on October 9, 1967.

Despite his death, Che Guevara's legacy as a revolutionary icon has endured. His writings, speeches, and image continue to inspire those who seek justice and equality in the face of oppression. His story is one of **unrelenting commitment to ideals**, and while his methods and ideology may not align with everyone's beliefs, there are valuable lessons to be drawn from his life about passion, action, and dedication.

Lessons and Applications

Che Guevara's life offers profound lessons in **conviction, action, and relentless pursuit of one's ideals**. His transformation from medical student to revolutionary leader provides powerful insights for anyone striving to create change—whether in their own life or on a larger scale. Let's explore three key lessons from Guevara's life and how you can apply them to your own journey.

1. Transform Your Convictions Into Action—Don't Just Believe in Change, Fight for It

One of the defining characteristics of Che Guevara was his **unwavering commitment to action**. Guevara wasn't satisfied with merely holding strong beliefs about injustice or inequality—he dedicated his entire life to **fighting for the change** he wanted to see in the world. Whether leading guerrilla fighters in the Cuban jungle or advocating for socialism on the world stage, Che didn't just talk about revolution—he lived it.

The lesson here is clear: **beliefs alone are not enough.** It's easy to have opinions or convictions, but it's the action you take to support those beliefs that truly makes a difference. Che understood that change doesn't happen without a willingness to get your hands dirty and make sacrifices for the cause. He was willing to endure personal hardship, exile, and even face death for the ideals he held dear.

For practical application, reflect on your own beliefs and values. Ask yourself: **What do I believe in strongly enough that I'm willing to take action for it?** Whether it's standing up for social justice, working toward a personal goal, or making a difference in your community, it's time to move beyond words and take action. Identify one concrete step you can take today to move closer to making your convictions a reality.

Remember, action doesn't have to be grand or revolutionary to be meaningful. Che started small—joining a cause, organizing, and slowly building momentum. In your own life, begin by taking small, manageable steps. Each action, no matter how small, brings you closer to realizing your vision. Don't wait for the perfect moment or for someone else to lead the way—**take the initiative and start creating the change you want to see.**

2. Be Relentless—Great Achievements Require Sacrifice and Unyielding Commitment

Guevara's life exemplifies the idea that **great achievements require great sacrifices**. He gave up a comfortable life in Argentina to fight in the jungles of Cuba, knowing that success was far from guaranteed. Even after the Cuban Revolution, when he could have remained in a position of power, he chose to continue the struggle for revolution in other countries, often at great personal risk. Guevara's willingness to make sacrifices for what he believed in is a powerful reminder that **commitment to a cause** often demands personal hardship, long hours, and an unyielding resolve.

In your own life, you may not be fighting in a revolution, but any significant goal will require similar dedication and persistence. Whether you're building a business, improving your health, or mastering a skill, **the road to success is rarely easy**. There will be obstacles, failures, and moments when you're tempted to quit. Che's life reminds us that the key to success is **pushing through those moments** and remaining relentless in pursuit of your goals.

For practical application, consider the sacrifices you're willing to make for your goals. Are you prepared to work harder, endure discomfort, or face setbacks to achieve what you want? Ask yourself: **How badly do I want to succeed?** Che's story teaches us that true success comes from refusing to give up, no matter how difficult the path becomes. Setbacks are inevitable, but your **determination and resilience** are what will carry you through.

One way to stay relentless is to **focus on your long-term vision**. Che never lost sight of his ultimate goal—a world free from imperialism and oppression. Even in the face of overwhelming odds, he remained committed to his vision. In your own life, keep your goals at the forefront of your mind and use them as motivation to persevere when challenges arise. **Stay focused, stay relentless, and keep moving forward.**

3. Embrace Hard Work and Discipline—Commit to Continuous Learning and Improvement

Che Guevara was not just a revolutionary in spirit—he was a man of **discipline, hard work, and intellectual rigor**. He constantly studied military strategy, Marxist theory, and history to improve his leadership skills and deepen his understanding of the global struggle for justice. Guevara's dedication to **self-improvement** was a key factor in his ability to inspire others and achieve success in his campaigns. He knew that the ability to lead and to fight effectively came not just from passion but from knowledge, strategy, and preparation.

The lesson here is that **discipline and continuous learning** are essential to success in any field. Whether you're leading a movement, building a business, or working on personal growth, hard work and discipline will always be necessary. Guevara's commitment to studying, planning, and self-improvement is a reminder that you should never stop learning or striving to be better, no matter how skilled you think you are.

For practical application, adopt a mindset of **continuous improvement**. Ask yourself: **What areas of my life or work can I improve through study or practice?** Whether it's learning a new skill, deepening your understanding of a particular subject, or improving your physical fitness, there's always room for growth. Create a plan for consistent self-improvement, whether it's through daily study, practice, or reflection. **Discipline yourself to stick to that plan** and track your progress over time.

Just as Che studied strategy to improve his effectiveness as a revolutionary, you should invest in developing your own skills and knowledge to achieve your goals. Discipline and hard work aren't always glamorous, but they are the foundation of success. **Embrace the grind, commit to self-improvement, and over time, you will see the results of your efforts.**

Harriet Tubman

In the dark and dangerous world of slavery in 19th-century America, one woman stood as a beacon of hope and defiance: **Harriet Tubman**. Known as the **"Moses of her people,"** Tubman is one of the most inspiring figures in American history. She not only escaped the horrors of slavery herself but returned again and again to lead others to freedom, risking her life every time. Tubman's legacy is not just one of courage, but of **relentless persistence and leadership through action**. Her story is one of **selflessness, bravery, and determination** that serves as a powerful lesson for anyone facing their own battles, whether they are personal, professional, or societal.

Tubman's life teaches us that **true power comes from acting on your convictions**, no matter the obstacles. She fought against a system designed to crush her spirit, yet she refused to be a victim. Instead, she became a leader, showing others the path to freedom. Her story reminds us that real courage doesn't always come from grand speeches or titles, but from the quiet, relentless determination to do what's right, even when the odds are against you.

In this chapter, we will explore Harriet Tubman's extraordinary life, and draw out lessons that can help you cultivate the same resilience, courage, and leadership in your own journey. Whether you're facing challenges that seem insurmountable or striving to lead others through difficult circumstances, Tubman's life offers valuable insights into **how to act with courage, fight with persistence, and lead with integrity**.

Autobiography

Harriet Tubman was born **Araminta Ross** around 1822 on a plantation in **Dorchester County, Maryland**. Born into slavery, Tubman experienced the brutality and dehumanization that defined the lives of enslaved African Americans in the southern United States. Her early life was marked by extreme hardship. She was forced to work from a young age, subjected to beatings, and suffered a traumatic head injury at the age of 12 when an overseer struck her with a heavy metal weight. This injury caused lifelong seizures, severe headaches, and visions that she would later interpret as divine messages guiding her mission.

Despite these challenges, Tubman's **spirit was unbreakable**. In 1849, at the age of 27, she made the courageous decision to escape slavery. With nothing but the clothes on her back, Tubman fled to Pennsylvania, where she found freedom. But unlike many others who escaped the brutality of slavery, Tubman could not rest knowing that her family and others remained in chains. Instead of enjoying her newfound freedom, she made a daring decision: she would return to the South and lead others to freedom through the **Underground Railroad**.

The **Underground Railroad** was not a literal railway but a network of secret routes, safe houses, and abolitionists who helped enslaved people escape to free states or Canada. Tubman became one of its most famous "conductors," leading over 13 missions and helping more than 70 enslaved individuals escape to freedom, including members of her own family. She was fearless in the face of danger. Slave catchers hunted her with a bounty on her head, but she was never caught. Tubman carried a pistol, both for protection and to discourage those she helped from turning back out of fear. She famously told them, **"You'll be free or die."**

Her success as a conductor on the Underground Railroad earned her the nickname **"Moses"**, drawing a parallel to the biblical figure who led his people out of slavery. But Tubman's contributions to the fight for freedom didn't end with her work on the Underground Railroad. During the **American Civil War**, she served as a scout, nurse, and spy for the Union Army, using her knowledge of covert operations to lead raids that freed hundreds of enslaved people.

After the war, Tubman continued her advocacy, working tirelessly for the abolition of slavery and the rights of women. She lived the rest of her life in **Auburn, New York**, where she dedicated herself to helping the poor, elderly, and disenfranchised. Harriet Tubman died on March 10, 1913, at the age of 91, but her legacy as a **freedom fighter, leader, and advocate for justice** continues to inspire people around the world.

Lessons and Applications

Harriet Tubman's life is filled with lessons on **courage, persistence, and leading by example**. Her incredible journey from enslavement to freedom, and her relentless work to liberate others, offers profound insights for anyone seeking to overcome challenges and make a difference. Let's dive into three key lessons from Tubman's life and explore how you can apply them to your own journey.

1. Courage in the Face of Fear—Act Boldly, Even When the Stakes Are High

One of the most remarkable qualities of Harriet Tubman was her **unshakable courage**. It's hard to imagine the fear she must have faced each time she returned to the South to lead others to freedom. She was risking her life every single time, knowing that if she were caught, the punishment would be severe, likely ending in her death. Yet, Tubman didn't let fear stop her. She acted boldly because she believed so deeply in her mission to free others from slavery.

The key lesson here is that **true courage isn't the absence of fear**, but the ability to act in spite of it. Tubman's bravery wasn't about being fearless—it was about refusing to let fear control her actions. She understood that **the stakes were high**, but she was willing to face those risks because the cause of freedom was worth it.

For practical application, think about areas in your life where fear has been holding you back. Maybe it's fear of failure, fear of rejection, or fear of stepping outside of your comfort zone. Ask yourself: **What would Harriet Tubman do in this situation?** The next time you face a decision or challenge that feels overwhelming, remember Tubman's courage and take bold action, even if you feel afraid. Start by identifying a small step you can take toward your goal, and commit to moving forward, no matter the obstacles.

You don't have to wait for fear to disappear before you act. Courage is about acknowledging the fear and moving forward anyway. Whether it's standing up for what's right, taking a risk in your career, or pursuing a personal goal, **bold action in the face of fear** is the hallmark of true courage.

2. Persistence in the Pursuit of Freedom—Never Give Up, No Matter the Obstacles

Harriet Tubman's story is one of **relentless persistence**. She didn't just escape slavery and rest on her laurels—she went back into dangerous territory again and again to lead others to freedom. Each mission she undertook was filled with peril, but Tubman's determination never wavered. She was committed to her cause, and no matter how difficult or dangerous the journey, she pressed on.

The lesson here is about the power of **persistence**. Whatever your goal—whether it's personal freedom, career success, or making a positive impact in the world—there will always be obstacles. The key to success isn't avoiding those obstacles, but learning how to overcome them. Tubman's life reminds us that **the road to freedom or success is never easy**, but persistence will see you through.

For practical application, reflect on the challenges you're facing right now. Are there moments when you've considered giving up because the path seems too hard or the obstacles too great? Take a page from Tubman's playbook and commit to persistence. Ask yourself: **How can I push through this challenge? What steps can I take to keep moving forward?** The next time you encounter a setback, remember that persistence is the key to achieving anything worthwhile.

One way to stay persistent is to **focus on your purpose**. Tubman's purpose—freeing others from slavery—was so clear and powerful that it fueled her persistence, even when the odds were against her. In your own life, get clear on why you're pursuing your goals. When you have a strong sense of purpose, it becomes easier to keep going, even when things get tough. **Stay the course, and don't let setbacks derail your progress.**

3. Lead by Example—True Leadership is About Action, Not Titles

Harriet Tubman didn't hold any official titles or positions of power. She wasn't a general, a politician, or a wealthy influencer. Yet, she was one of the most effective and respected leaders of her time. How? By leading through her **actions**, not her words. Tubman didn't wait for permission or recognition—she saw what needed to be done, and she did it. Her leadership came from the fact that she was willing to act when others might hesitate. She led by example, inspiring others to follow her because of her bravery and integrity.

The lesson here is that **leadership isn't about titles—it's about action**. You don't need to wait for someone to grant you authority or give you permission to lead. You can start leading today by taking action toward your goals and doing what's right. Tubman showed that true leaders don't just talk about change—they make it happen through their actions.

For practical application, think about how you can lead by example in your own life. Ask yourself: **What actions can I take that**

will inspire others to follow or support me? Whether it's in your career, your community, or your personal life, leadership comes from **doing**, not just talking. Be the person who takes the first step, who pushes through obstacles, and who acts with integrity, and you'll find that others naturally look to you for guidance.

Leadership also means being **willing to take risks** for what you believe in. Tubman risked everything to lead others to freedom. In your own life, leadership may require stepping out of your comfort zone, making difficult decisions, or standing up for what's right, even when it's unpopular. Don't wait for the perfect moment or for others to lead the way—**be the one who acts**, and you'll inspire others to follow.

Florence Nightingale

Florence Nightingale is best known as the **founder of modern nursing**, but her legacy reaches far beyond the medical field. Nightingale's story is one of purpose-driven action, tireless dedication, and a belief in the power of **systematic improvement**. At a time when women's roles were severely restricted, and nursing was seen as a lowly, almost disreputable profession, Nightingale not only elevated the field but also revolutionized the way we understand **healthcare, sanitation, and data-driven change**. She didn't just care for the sick—she transformed the entire system, improving care and saving countless lives in the process.

In the face of overwhelming adversity, from societal resistance to the harsh conditions of the **Crimean War**, Nightingale showed an unyielding commitment to her mission. Her meticulous approach to improving sanitary conditions in hospitals, her use of statistics to make informed decisions, and her pioneering leadership in healthcare have made her a timeless role model in **leadership, dedication, and compassion**. Nightingale teaches us that when you find your purpose and commit yourself fully to it, you can not only achieve greatness but also leave an indelible mark on the world.

In this chapter, we will explore the life of Florence Nightingale and draw out the lessons her journey offers to anyone striving to make an impact, improve themselves, and become a force for positive change. **Dedication, compassion, and the relentless pursuit of improvement** are the cornerstones of Nightingale's legacy, and we will see how these qualities can be applied to your own path toward greatness.

Autobiography

Florence Nightingale was born on May 12, 1820, into a wealthy British family in **Florence, Italy**, the city after which she was named. Raised in a privileged environment, she received an excellent education, studying a wide range of subjects, including languages, mathematics, and history—an unusual opportunity for women of her time. However, despite the expectations of high society that she would marry well and lead a quiet domestic life, Nightingale had other plans.

At an early age, Nightingale felt a calling, which she described as a **divine vocation** to help the sick and suffering. In her 20s, she shocked her family by declaring her intention to become a nurse—a profession that, at the time, was looked down upon by the upper class. Nursing was considered a job for the poor and uneducated, not for someone of her social standing. But Nightingale's passion for helping others and her **unyielding sense of purpose** led her to pursue her goal against all odds.

In 1853, the **Crimean War** broke out, and news of the appalling conditions in British military hospitals reached the public. Soldiers were dying not just from battle wounds, but from **infectious diseases** spread by unsanitary conditions. Nightingale volunteered her services and was soon asked by the **British government** to lead a team of nurses to **Scutari**, a military hospital in the Crimea. What she encountered there was horrifying: filth, overcrowding, poor ventilation, and a lack of basic medical supplies. Thousands of soldiers were dying unnecessarily.

Nightingale immediately set to work, implementing strict sanitary practices, organizing the hospital staff, and ensuring that soldiers received better food, clean water, and proper care. Her reforms had a dramatic impact, reducing the hospital's mortality rate from 42% to just 2%. She became known as the **"Lady with the**

Lamp," a name inspired by her habit of making rounds late at night to check on her patients.

But Nightingale didn't stop there. She understood that lasting change required more than short-term fixes. After the war, she dedicated herself to improving public health, hospital design, and sanitation in Britain and beyond. She established the first scientifically based nursing school at **St. Thomas' Hospital** in London, where she set standards for nursing education that continue to influence the profession today. Her work also extended into public health reform, and she used **statistics and data analysis** to advocate for better healthcare policies—one of the first people in history to apply statistical methods to public health.

Nightingale's contributions to healthcare, sanitation, and data-driven decision-making earned her international recognition. She spent the rest of her life working tirelessly to improve healthcare systems, writing books, and training nurses. She passed away on August 13, 1910, at the age of 90, having left an enduring legacy as one of the world's most influential women.

Lessons and Applications

Florence Nightingale's life offers timeless lessons in **purpose-driven action, compassion, and relentless dedication to improvement**. Her journey from privileged young woman to the world's most famous nurse provides a powerful example of how finding and committing to your purpose can lead to profound change, both in your life and the world around you. Let's explore three key lessons from Nightingale's life and how you can apply them to your own journey.

1. Find and Follow Your Purpose—Let Your Passion Drive You, Even When Others Doubt You

Florence Nightingale's life was defined by her sense of **purpose**. From a young age, she felt a calling to help those in need, and she pursued that calling with relentless determination, even when society, her family, and the expectations placed upon her suggested that she should live a very different life. Nightingale refused to conform to the norms of her time, choosing instead to dedicate herself to a cause that she knew was her true mission. This unwavering commitment to her purpose not only shaped her career but also transformed the field of nursing and public health.

The key lesson here is that **purpose is a powerful motivator**. When you have a clear sense of purpose, it gives you the strength to overcome obstacles and push forward, even when others doubt you or when the path ahead seems difficult. Nightingale's life teaches us that your purpose is what fuels you during hard times, guiding you through adversity and keeping you focused on the bigger picture.

For practical application, reflect on your own sense of purpose. Ask yourself: **What is my true calling? What am I passionate about that can drive me to make a difference in my life or the lives of others?** Take time to identify the cause, mission, or goal that resonates most deeply with you, and make a plan to pursue it. Remember, finding your purpose may not happen overnight—it requires reflection, experimentation, and sometimes going against the grain, just as Nightingale did.

Once you have a clear sense of purpose, use it as your guiding star. When challenges arise or when others doubt your path, return to your purpose as a source of strength and motivation. **Let your passion for your mission push you forward**, even when the road ahead is tough or unclear.

2. Lead Through Compassion—True Leadership is

Rooted in Empathy and Caring for Others

At the heart of Florence Nightingale's work was her **compassion for others**. She didn't just see herself as a healthcare professional; she saw herself as a caregiver, someone who was responsible for the well-being of others. Her deep empathy for the suffering soldiers in Crimea drove her to improve the conditions they faced. She didn't just provide medical treatment—she created an environment where they could recover with dignity and care. Nightingale's leadership was grounded in her understanding that **true success is not just about achieving goals, but about uplifting and caring for others in the process.**

The lesson here is that **compassion is a powerful form of leadership**. Whether you're leading a team, a business, or simply navigating your personal relationships, empathy and understanding for others will always make you a more effective leader. Nightingale's success wasn't just about her medical knowledge or organizational skills—it was her genuine concern for others that inspired those around her and allowed her to make such a lasting impact.

For practical application, reflect on how you can incorporate **compassion into your leadership style**. Ask yourself: **How can I better understand and care for the people I lead or interact with?** Whether in your career, personal life, or community, leading with empathy can transform the way you approach challenges and the way others respond to you. Make an effort to listen, to understand the needs of those around you, and to act in ways that support their well-being.

Compassionate leadership doesn't mean being soft or compromising your standards—it means recognizing the humanity in others and creating an environment where people feel valued, respected, and supported. Just as Nightingale's compassionate care helped soldiers recover in war-torn hospitals, your empathy can create a more productive, positive, and meaningful environment in whatever you do.

3. Relentlessly Pursue Improvement—Never Settle for "Good Enough," Always Strive for Better

Florence Nightingale was never content with the status quo. She understood that **improvement is a continuous process**, and she applied this mindset throughout her life, whether it was improving sanitation in military hospitals, reforming public health systems, or advancing nursing education. Nightingale's approach was rooted in her belief that there was always a better way to do things and that by using data, research, and observation, she could continually improve healthcare outcomes. She was meticulous, detail-oriented, and driven by a commitment to **constant progress**.

The lesson here is that **greatness is achieved through relentless dedication to improvement**. Nightingale didn't stop once she had improved conditions in Crimea—she continued to push for better healthcare, better systems, and better education long after the war was over. Her life teaches us that success isn't a one-time achievement; it's the result of a continuous effort to refine, improve, and evolve in everything you do.

For practical application, adopt a mindset of **continuous improvement** in your own life. Ask yourself: **What areas of my life or work can I improve, even if they're already functioning well?** Whether it's your career, your fitness, your relationships, or your personal growth, there is always room to grow and develop. Start by identifying one area where you can make a small improvement, and commit to making incremental changes over time.

Don't settle for "good enough." Just as Nightingale applied data and analysis to improve healthcare systems, you can use feedback, self-reflection, and ongoing learning to enhance your performance and results. Remember, **improvement is a process**, not a destination. The more you embrace this mindset, the more you will continue to grow, achieve, and make a meaningful impact in whatever you pursue.

Artists and Creators

Vincent van Gogh

Few artists in history are as widely recognized and revered as **Vincent van Gogh**, a man whose vibrant, emotionally charged paintings forever altered the world of art. His unique style, characterized by bold colors, dynamic brushstrokes, and deeply personal themes, has made him one of the most influential figures in modern art. But beyond his artistic genius, van Gogh's life story is one of **passion, perseverance**, and a relentless quest to express the truth of his inner world. Despite a life filled with **struggle, rejection, and personal demons**, van Gogh remained true to his vision, producing more than 2,000 works of art in a short, turbulent career that continues to inspire millions.

Van Gogh's greatness doesn't come from wealth or status—he sold only one painting during his lifetime and spent most of his days in poverty. What makes van Gogh extraordinary is his **uncompromising dedication** to his art and the way he channeled his emotional pain into **creative expression**. His work speaks to the universal human experience, touching on themes of loneliness, beauty, suffering, and hope. Van Gogh teaches us that even in the face of adversity, we can create something meaningful by staying committed to our passion and remaining authentic to who we are.

In this chapter, we'll explore the life of Vincent van Gogh, diving into the struggles and triumphs that shaped his artistic legacy. More importantly, we'll draw out the lessons his life offers for anyone pursuing a dream or seeking to find purpose in their work. Van Gogh's journey is a reminder that **greatness doesn't come from external validation**, but from the passion you pour into your craft and the courage to be your most authentic self.

Autobiography

Vincent Willem van Gogh was born on March 30, 1853, in **Groot-Zundert, Netherlands**, to a religious family. His father was a Protestant minister, and his upbringing was steeped in spirituality, a theme that would later influence his artistic work. Van Gogh was the eldest of six children, and from a young age, he showed an interest in drawing. However, his path to becoming an artist was far from straightforward.

As a young man, van Gogh struggled to find his place in the world. He worked in various occupations, including as an art dealer, a teacher, and a missionary in a mining community in Belgium. It wasn't until his late twenties that van Gogh decided to pursue art seriously. His early works were somber and dark, reflecting his difficult experiences and the influence of his early mentors. **"The Potato Eaters"** (1885) is one of the most famous paintings from this period, showcasing the lives of poor working-class families.

Van Gogh's artistic career truly began to blossom when he moved to **Paris in 1886**. There, he was exposed to the work of **Impressionist and Post-Impressionist artists**, including Claude Monet, Paul Gauguin, and Georges Seurat. These influences transformed van Gogh's style, leading him to embrace the vibrant colors and expressive techniques that would define his later work. His time in Paris also deepened his relationship with his younger brother, **Theo**, who supported him both financially and emotionally throughout his life.

In 1888, van Gogh moved to **Arles in the south of France**, seeking inspiration in the bright, natural landscapes of Provence. It was here that he produced some of his most iconic works, including **"Sunflowers"**, **"The Starry Night"**, and **"Irises."** However, his time in Arles was also marked by increasing mental instability. Van Gogh famously cut off part of his own ear after a heated argument with fellow artist Paul Gauguin, an event that signaled the worsening of his mental health struggles.

Despite his inner turmoil, van Gogh continued to paint prolifically. His paintings from this period are imbued with intense emotion, reflecting both the beauty and the pain he experienced. His distinctive use of color, bold brushstrokes, and swirling forms gave his work a sense of vitality and movement that was unlike anything else at the time.

In May 1889, van Gogh voluntarily entered the **Saint-Paul-de-Mausole asylum** in Saint-Rémy-de-Provence, where he continued to paint while receiving treatment. Some of his most famous works, including **"The Starry Night,"** were created during this period. His time in the asylum provided temporary relief from his mental health issues, but van Gogh's struggles with depression and anxiety persisted.

On July 27, 1890, at the age of 37, van Gogh tragically shot himself in the chest, succumbing to his injuries two days later. His death marked the end of a life filled with personal battles, but it also signaled the beginning of his posthumous recognition as one of the greatest artists in history. Today, van Gogh's work is celebrated for its emotional depth, its innovative style, and its ability to connect with viewers on a profound level.

Lessons and Applications

Vincent van Gogh's life offers powerful lessons in **passion, perseverance, and authenticity**. His relentless pursuit of his artistic vision, even in the face of rejection and personal hardship, provides valuable insights for anyone striving to create something meaningful or navigate the challenges of self-expression. Let's explore three key lessons from van Gogh's life and how you can apply them to your own journey.

1. Follow Your Passion Relentlessly—Even When the World Doesn't Understand You

Vincent van Gogh's life was defined by his **unwavering dedication to his art**. He didn't paint for fame, money, or recognition—in fact, he received little of these during his lifetime. Van Gogh painted because he was driven by a deep, almost spiritual need to express himself through his work. Even when his paintings were criticized or ignored, he continued to pursue his artistic vision with unrelenting passion. His work wasn't shaped by the trends or opinions of others—it was shaped by his own experiences, emotions, and view of the world.

The lesson here is that **passion is the fuel for greatness**. Van Gogh didn't let external validation dictate his path, and neither should you. Whatever your passion—whether it's art, music, writing, business, or any other pursuit—the key to success is staying true to what drives you, even when the world doesn't immediately understand or appreciate it. Van Gogh's life teaches us that the most important thing is to **follow your passion relentlessly**, regardless of external recognition.

For practical application, reflect on your own passions and ask yourself: **Am I pursuing what truly drives me, or am I holding back because of fear or doubt?** If there's something you're passionate about but haven't fully committed to, take a page from van Gogh's book and go all in. Start by dedicating more time, energy, and focus to the things that light you up, even if they don't bring immediate rewards. Remember, van Gogh painted over 2,000 works in his lifetime, most of which were unappreciated until after his death. **The process matters more than the outcome**, and staying true to your passion will eventually lead to greatness.

2. Persevere Through Hardship—Greatness Comes From Resilience, Not Ease

Van Gogh's life was filled with struggle—financial hardship, mental health challenges, and constant rejection. Yet, through it all, he remained fiercely dedicated to his craft. His ability to keep going, despite personal suffering and a lack of recognition, is one of the most inspiring aspects of his life. Van Gogh's perseverance shows that **greatness is not born from ease, but from resilience in the face of adversity.**

The key lesson here is that **persistence is essential to success**. Whether you're trying to build a career, achieve a personal goal, or create something meaningful, the path will be filled with obstacles. Van Gogh's life teaches us that the people who succeed are not those who never face hardship, but those who keep going, even when it seems impossible. His story is a reminder that **the most important work often comes out of the most difficult times.**

For practical application, reflect on the challenges you're currently facing. Are there moments when you've considered giving up because the path seems too hard? The next time you encounter a setback, think of van Gogh's persistence. Ask yourself: **How can I push through this challenge and use it as fuel for my work?** Just as van Gogh channeled his struggles into his art, you can use your own hardships as a source of strength and inspiration. The road to greatness is rarely smooth, but your ability to persevere will make all the difference.

One way to build resilience is to **embrace the process**, rather than focusing solely on the end goal. Van Gogh painted because he loved the act of creating, not because he was chasing fame or success. In your own pursuits, try to find joy and meaning in the process itself, rather than worrying about immediate outcomes. **Greatness is a long game**, and persistence is the key to staying on that path.

3. Be True to Yourself—Authenticity is Your Greatest Strength

Van Gogh's work is celebrated not just for its technical brilliance, but for its **authenticity**. His paintings are deeply personal, reflecting his emotions, struggles, and unique perspective on the world. Van Gogh didn't try to fit into the mold of what was popular or acceptable at the time—he created art that was true to him, regardless of how it was received. His authenticity is what makes his work so powerful and enduring.

The lesson here is that **authenticity is your greatest strength**. In a world that often pressures us to conform or fit into predefined boxes, van Gogh's life reminds us that true greatness comes from embracing who you are and expressing yourself without compromise. Whether in your career, relationships, or creative pursuits, being true to yourself is what will set you apart and make your work meaningful.

For practical application, reflect on how you can bring more authenticity into your life. Ask yourself: **Am I staying true to who I am, or am I trying to meet the expectations of others?** The next time you're faced with a decision—whether it's in your work or personal life—ask yourself: **What would the most authentic version of me do?** Van Gogh's legacy teaches us that when you embrace your true self, your work and life become more fulfilling, and your impact becomes more profound.

Being authentic doesn't mean disregarding the opinions of others—it means **staying true to your values, passions, and vision**, even when it's challenging. Just as van Gogh poured his heart and soul into his art, you can pour your authenticity into everything you do. **The world doesn't need more people who conform—it needs more people who are brave enough to be themselves.**

William Shakespeare

When we think of **William Shakespeare**, we think of greatness. Revered as one of the greatest writers in history, Shakespeare's work has transcended time, language, and culture, influencing everything from storytelling to human psychology. He created characters and plots that are as alive today as they were in the late 16th and early 17th centuries. From **Hamlet** and **Macbeth** to **Romeo and Juliet** and **Othello**, his creations delve deep into the core of human experience—love, power, ambition, betrayal, and the search for meaning.

Shakespeare's genius doesn't just lie in his ability to entertain—it lies in his unparalleled insight into the human condition. His plays are timeless because they reflect universal truths about who we are, what drives us, and what we fear. But Shakespeare's greatness wasn't just about innate talent. His journey was marked by a **relentless work ethic**, **adaptability**, and a unique ability to capture the complexities of life. He wasn't born a literary master; he developed into one through perseverance, continuous improvement, and an understanding of his audience's needs.

For anyone striving for greatness, whether in creative fields or any other endeavor, Shakespeare provides a roadmap of what it means to be **uncompromising in your creative vision** while constantly refining your craft. This chapter will explore the life and lessons of William Shakespeare, showing us that the key to greatness lies in creativity, adaptability, and the courage to express ourselves in ways that resonate deeply with others.

Autobiography

William Shakespeare was born on **April 23, 1564**, in **Stratford-upon-Avon, England**. His father, **John Shakespeare**, was a successful glove maker and a prominent figure in the town, while his mother, **Mary Arden**, came from a well-to-do family. Shakespeare's early life was relatively comfortable, but little is known about his childhood beyond his education at the local grammar school, where he would have studied Latin, literature, and the classics—an education that would later serve as a foundation for his literary achievements.

In 1582, at the age of 18, Shakespeare married **Anne Hathaway**, who was eight years his senior. The couple had three children, but Shakespeare's early adult life remained largely undocumented. It wasn't until the late 1580s that Shakespeare surfaced in **London**, where he began his career as an actor and playwright.

By the early 1590s, Shakespeare had become a well-known figure in the London theater scene, producing plays for the **Lord Chamberlain's Men**, a popular acting troupe. His early works, such as **Titus Andronicus** and **The Taming of the Shrew**, showcased his talent for storytelling, blending tragic and comic elements to captivate audiences. Shakespeare's reputation continued to grow with his **history plays**, such as **Henry IV** and **Richard III**, which offered powerful insights into politics, power, and leadership.

As Shakespeare matured as a writer, his plays became more complex and profound, culminating in some of his greatest works, including **Hamlet**, **Othello**, **King Lear**, and **Macbeth**. These tragedies explore the darker sides of human nature—ambition, madness, betrayal, and the tragic consequences of flawed decisions. What sets Shakespeare apart, however, is his ability to weave deep philosophical themes into compelling stories that continue to resonate with audiences worldwide.

Throughout his career, Shakespeare didn't just write for aristocrats or intellectuals; he wrote for everyone, from the elite to the common people who crowded the theaters of London. His understanding of human nature and his ability to adapt his work to the tastes of diverse audiences is one reason why his plays remain so powerful today.

Shakespeare retired to Stratford-upon-Avon in 1613, having written 38 plays, 154 sonnets, and several other poems. He passed away on **April 23, 1616**, leaving behind a body of work that would influence literature, theater, and culture for centuries to come. Although Shakespeare lived in a world vastly different from our own, his genius transcended time, and his life offers powerful lessons about creativity, self-expression, and the pursuit of excellence.

Lessons and Applications

William Shakespeare's life offers valuable insights into **creativity, adaptability, and mastering one's craft**. His ability to navigate both artistic and practical challenges provides a blueprint for anyone striving to leave a lasting impact on their chosen field. Let's explore three key lessons from Shakespeare's life and how you can apply them to your own journey.

1. Master Your Craft—Dedication to Improvement is the Path to Excellence

William Shakespeare's success was not just the result of innate genius—it was the product of **relentless dedication to his craft**. He was not born with a quill in his hand or an immediate mastery of the English language. He developed his skills over time, constantly refining his ability to write plays that entertained, moved, and challenged his audiences. From the historical accuracy of his history plays to the poetic complexity of his tragedies, Shakespeare's greatness came from an obsession with **perfecting his art**.

One of Shakespeare's greatest strengths was his **adaptability**—he studied the works of other writers, observed what audiences responded to, and continued to evolve his style. His early plays, while successful, were simpler and less refined than his later works, demonstrating his growth as a playwright over the course of his career.

The key lesson here is that **mastery is a process**, not a destination. Shakespeare didn't settle for mediocrity or rely on his early successes. Instead, he pushed himself to improve, honing his skills through constant writing, rewriting, and performing. Whatever your field, whether it's creative, technical, or managerial, the pursuit of excellence requires a commitment to **continuous improvement** and a willingness to learn from both success and failure.

For practical application, reflect on your own approach to your work. Ask yourself: **Am I dedicated to truly mastering my craft, or am I coasting on early successes?** Make a commitment to improve, no matter where you are in your career. This could involve setting aside time each day to practice, seeking feedback from mentors, or studying the work of those who have mastered the field before you. **The road to excellence is a long one**, but the dedication to improvement is what separates the great from the good.

2. Embrace Creativity—Use Your Unique Voice to Stand Out

Shakespeare's enduring success comes not just from his skill as a writer, but from his **ability to express himself uniquely**. His characters, from the brooding Hamlet to the ambitious Lady Macbeth, resonate because they reflect human experiences in ways that no one had articulated before. He wasn't afraid to push boundaries, experiment with language, and tackle complex emotional themes. Shakespeare's unique voice, filled with poetic imagery, wit, and insight into the human psyche, is what sets him apart from other writers of his time.

The lesson here is that **creativity is your greatest asset**. It's easy to fall into the trap of imitating others or trying to follow trends, but true success comes from tapping into what makes you unique and using that to stand out in your field. Shakespeare wasn't trying to be the next someone else—he was focused on developing his own style, his own voice, and telling the stories only he could tell.

For practical application, think about how you can embrace your own creativity and express yourself authentically. Ask yourself: **What makes my work unique? How can I use my personal experiences, perspective, and voice to create something that stands out?** Whether you're writing, designing, building a business, or leading a team, your creativity is what will set you apart from the rest.

One way to cultivate creativity is to **experiment**. Shakespeare wasn't afraid to blend genres, use new words, or tackle difficult subjects. In your own work, try new approaches, even if they feel risky or unconventional. **Creativity requires courage**, and the willingness to step outside your comfort zone can lead to breakthrough ideas that elevate your work to new levels.

3. Adapt to Your Audience—Greatness Comes From Understanding and Connecting With Others

While Shakespeare was an artistic genius, he was also a shrewd businessman. He didn't write plays in isolation—he wrote for an audience, and he knew how to **connect with people from all walks of life**. His plays were performed in the **Globe Theatre**, where both the wealthy elite and the common folk gathered to be entertained. Shakespeare understood that in order to be successful, he needed to write in a way that spoke to **universal themes** while also tailoring his work to the tastes of his diverse audience.

The key lesson here is that **greatness comes from understanding and connecting with others**. Whether you're leading a team, selling a product, or creating art, it's essential to understand the needs, desires, and expectations of your audience. Shakespeare was able to balance artistic integrity with audience appeal because he understood the human condition and crafted his stories in ways that resonated with people from all backgrounds.

For practical application, think about how you can **better connect with your audience**—whether that audience is clients, customers, colleagues, or fans. Ask yourself: **What do they value? What problems are they facing, and how can my work provide a solution or meet their needs?** By tailoring your approach to meet the needs of your audience, you can create stronger connections and increase the impact of your work.

At the same time, remember that **connection doesn't mean compromise**. Shakespeare didn't water down his work to please everyone; he simply understood how to package his creativity in a way that resonated with his audience. In your own work, seek to understand your audience without losing your unique voice or vision. **The key to success is balancing authenticity with audience engagement**, just as Shakespeare did.

Ludwig van Beethoven

Ludwig van Beethoven is synonymous with **musical genius**, but his life story is about far more than just composing extraordinary symphonies. Beethoven is the embodiment of **resilience, unwavering determination**, and the refusal to let circumstances dictate one's fate. From a young age, Beethoven faced adversity—personal loss, a tumultuous family life, and, most famously, the gradual loss of his hearing. Yet, despite the unimaginable challenges, he created some of the most iconic and influential works of music the world has ever known.

Beethoven's life teaches us that **greatness comes not from perfection**, but from the ability to rise above our limitations and channel our struggles into something meaningful. He didn't just create music; he revolutionized it, pushing the boundaries of what was possible and leaving a legacy that has inspired generations of musicians, artists, and creators. His symphonies, sonatas, and concertos continue to move audiences because they are not just masterful compositions—they are reflections of the human spirit's power to overcome.

In this chapter, we will explore the life of Ludwig van Beethoven, a man who defied the odds and achieved greatness through sheer force of will, innovation, and an unrelenting commitment to his art. More importantly, we'll draw out lessons from his journey that can be applied to anyone striving to reach their own potential. Beethoven teaches us that **adversity is not an obstacle—it is an opportunity to transcend limitations** and create something extraordinary.

Autobiography

Ludwig van Beethoven was born on December 17, 1770, in **Bonn, Germany**, into a family with a strong musical tradition. His father, **Johann van Beethoven**, was a singer and musician, but he was also an alcoholic who pushed young Ludwig relentlessly, often harshly, to become a musical prodigy in the vein of **Mozart**. By the time Beethoven was a teenager, it was clear that he had immense talent. At just 13, he was already employed as an assistant organist at the court of Bonn and had begun composing his first works.

In 1792, Beethoven moved to **Vienna**, the cultural heart of European music, where he studied with renowned composer **Joseph Haydn**. It was in Vienna that Beethoven truly flourished as a composer and performer. His early works, including his **Piano Sonatas** and **Symphonies Nos. 1 and 2**, earned him recognition as a rising star in the classical music world. He quickly gained a reputation not only for his musical brilliance but for his fiery personality and uncompromising nature. Beethoven wasn't afraid to break rules or challenge traditional forms, a quality that would come to define his work.

However, in his late twenties, Beethoven began to experience a devastating setback: he was losing his hearing. For a composer, this was an unthinkable tragedy. By the time he was in his early thirties, his hearing loss had become severe, and eventually, he became almost completely deaf. The anguish this caused Beethoven is well documented in his **Heiligenstadt Testament**, a letter he wrote in 1802 in which he confessed his despair and thoughts of suicide due to his deafness. And yet, despite this unimaginable obstacle, Beethoven chose to persevere.

Rather than retreat from his art, Beethoven's deafness seemed to ignite an even deeper passion for composing. In the years following his personal crisis, he produced some of his most groundbreaking and celebrated works, including his **Third Symphony (Eroica)**,

Fifth Symphony, and **Ninth Symphony**, which contains the iconic **Ode to Joy**. These works pushed the boundaries of music, expanding the emotional and structural possibilities of symphonic composition. Beethoven's later compositions are filled with innovation—his use of dissonance, complex rhythms, and emotional depth challenged the conventions of the classical music of his time and laid the foundation for the Romantic era.

Despite his deafness, Beethoven continued to compose prolifically until his death in 1827. His final years were marked by illness, personal struggles, and isolation, yet his **Ninth Symphony**, completed in 1824, remains one of the most powerful testaments to human resilience and creativity. It is a triumph of the spirit over adversity, a work filled with joy, hope, and defiance. Beethoven died at the age of 56, but his influence endures, and his music continues to be celebrated for its emotional depth, complexity, and transformative power.

Lessons and Applications

Beethoven's life offers profound lessons in **resilience, innovation, and the pursuit of excellence**. His ability to overcome personal hardship, break new ground in his field, and remain true to his artistic vision provides valuable insights for anyone striving to achieve greatness. Let's explore three key lessons from Beethoven's life and how you can apply them to your own journey.

1. Embrace Adversity—Turn Challenges into Fuel for Your Growth

One of the most powerful lessons from Beethoven's life is his ability to **embrace adversity** and use it as fuel for his creativity. Beethoven didn't just endure his deafness—he channeled it into his work, pushing himself to create music that transcended the limitations of sound. Rather than allowing his disability to define or defeat him, Beethoven found a way to express himself even more fully, producing some of his greatest masterpieces after he became deaf.

The key takeaway here is that **adversity doesn't have to stop you—it can propel you forward.** Beethoven teaches us that challenges, no matter how overwhelming, can be transformed into opportunities for growth and innovation. Instead of viewing obstacles as roadblocks, we can choose to see them as **catalysts for creative solutions.**

For practical application, think about the challenges you're currently facing. Whether they are personal setbacks, professional difficulties, or emotional struggles, ask yourself: **How can I turn this adversity into an opportunity for growth?** Rather than viewing your challenges as limitations, look for ways to use them to fuel your progress. Just as Beethoven's deafness led him to innovate and push beyond traditional musical boundaries, your struggles can inspire new approaches, ideas, and breakthroughs in your own life.

One way to start embracing adversity is to **reframe how you think about challenges.** Instead of seeing them as things to avoid or overcome, view them as opportunities to learn, grow, and stretch your abilities. Remember, **greatness often emerges from hardship**, and the most meaningful achievements are often the result of perseverance in the face of difficulty.

2. Innovate Boldly—Don't Be Afraid to Break the Rules and Push Boundaries

Beethoven was an innovator, not just in music, but in the way he approached his work. He wasn't content to follow the conventions of the classical era; instead, he pushed boundaries and redefined what music could be. His **Symphony No. 3 (Eroica)**, for example, broke new ground with its emotional depth and length, marking a departure from the more restrained style of his predecessors. His later works, such as the **Ninth Symphony**, introduced a chorus and soloists into what had traditionally been instrumental-only compositions, transforming the symphonic form.

The lesson here is clear: **innovation requires boldness**. If you want to achieve greatness, you can't be afraid to break the rules, experiment, and push boundaries. Beethoven didn't become a legend by playing it safe—he took risks, and those risks paid off, changing the course of musical history.

For practical application, think about the areas in your life where you can **break away from tradition or convention**. Ask yourself: **Where can I take bold risks and innovate, rather than sticking to what's comfortable or expected?** Whether in your career, creative pursuits, or personal life, consider how you can push beyond the boundaries of what has already been done and explore new possibilities.

Innovation requires both **courage** and a willingness to face uncertainty. Just as Beethoven took the leap from classical conventions to create something entirely new, you too can forge your own path by embracing creative risk-taking. Don't be afraid to disrupt old ways of thinking or challenge established norms—**greatness often comes from daring to be different**.

3. Pursue Excellence Relentlessly—Commit to Mastery, No Matter the Obstacles

Beethoven's life was defined by his **relentless pursuit of excellence**. From a young age, he dedicated himself to mastering the piano and composition, even when it meant long hours of practice and intense personal sacrifice. As his hearing deteriorated, he didn't lower his standards or give up on his craft—he doubled down on his commitment to creating music that would stand the test of time. Beethoven wasn't just talented; he was relentless in his drive to achieve **artistic mastery**, no matter the obstacles.

The key lesson here is that **excellence requires commitment**. Greatness doesn't come from half-hearted efforts or occasional bursts of inspiration—it comes from a deep, sustained dedication to honing your craft and pushing yourself to new levels of mastery. Beethoven's success wasn't just the result of his natural talent—it was the product of years of hard work, discipline, and an uncompromising commitment to creating the best work possible.

For practical application, reflect on your own commitment to excellence. Ask yourself: **Am I fully dedicated to achieving mastery in my field, or am I settling for "good enough"?** Whether it's in your career, creative pursuits, or personal growth, make a conscious decision to pursue excellence with the same determination that Beethoven applied to his music.

To build this mindset, start by setting **high standards** for yourself and your work. Don't settle for mediocrity or let obstacles discourage you. Instead, commit to improving every day, whether through practice, learning, or seeking feedback. Remember, **excellence is a journey**, not a destination. The pursuit of mastery is a lifelong endeavor, and the most successful people are those who are willing to push themselves beyond their current limits.

Michelangelo

When you think of **Michelangelo**, the name alone conjures images of some of the greatest artistic masterpieces ever created. From the towering marble statue of **David** to the awe-inspiring frescoes of the **Sistine Chapel**, Michelangelo left an indelible mark on the world of art and architecture. But his brilliance wasn't just the result of raw talent; it was the product of relentless hard work, a grand vision, and an unyielding pursuit of mastery.

Michelangelo lived during the **Renaissance**, a time of explosive intellectual and artistic growth. Yet, even in an era filled with genius, he stood out, not only as a sculptor but also as a painter, architect, and poet. His works are celebrated for their technical precision, emotional depth, and sheer grandeur. But more than that, Michelangelo's life is a story of **visionary thinking** and **uncompromising dedication**—traits that transformed his immense talent into timeless greatness.

What sets Michelangelo apart isn't just the perfection of his work, but the **mindset and discipline** that drove him to create these masterpieces. His journey shows us that greatness comes from dedicating oneself entirely to a vision, pushing through obstacles, and mastering the finer details of one's craft. This chapter will explore Michelangelo's life and the valuable lessons we can take from his approach to life, work, and artistry. Michelangelo reminds us that with the right combination of **dedication, vision**, and **craftsmanship**, we can create something extraordinary, no matter the field we are in.

Autobiography

Michelangelo di Lodovico Buonarroti Simoni was born on **March 6, 1475**, in **Caprese, Italy**, into a family of modest means. His father,

Ludovico Buonarroti, was a minor government official, and although Michelangelo came from a noble family, their fortune had diminished. From an early age, Michelangelo showed a passion for the arts, but his father had other plans, wanting him to pursue a more conventional career in government. However, Michelangelo's passion for drawing was undeniable, and by the age of 13, he was apprenticed to **Domenico Ghirlandaio**, one of the most prominent painters in Florence.

At 15, Michelangelo's talent caught the attention of **Lorenzo de' Medici**, one of the most powerful patrons of the arts in Florence. Michelangelo joined the **Medici court**, where he had access to some of the greatest minds of the Renaissance, including philosophers, poets, and artists. His early exposure to both classical and contemporary thought profoundly influenced his later work, particularly his fascination with human anatomy, which became a hallmark of his sculptures and paintings.

Michelangelo's early works demonstrated an unparalleled ability to capture the human form. His first major commission, the **Pietà**, completed in 1499 when he was just 24, is still considered one of the finest sculptures ever created. Carved from a single block of marble, the Pietà depicts the Virgin Mary holding the body of Christ after the Crucifixion. It is celebrated for its technical precision and emotional depth, blending delicate beauty with profound sorrow.

However, it was the statue of **David** that catapulted Michelangelo into international fame. Completed in 1504, David became a symbol of the **Republic of Florence** and represented the Renaissance ideals of human potential and strength. The statue's muscularity, poised stance, and expressive detail remain one of the most admired sculptures in history.

Despite his success as a sculptor, Michelangelo is perhaps most famous for his work as a painter, particularly his monumental frescoes on the ceiling of the **Sistine Chapel** in the Vatican.

Commissioned by **Pope Julius II** in 1508, Michelangelo worked for four years on the project, lying on his back on scaffolding to create one of the most awe-inspiring works of art ever conceived. The Sistine Chapel ceiling features over 300 figures and tells the story of the creation of the world, the fall of man, and the promise of salvation. **The Creation of Adam**, in particular, has become one of the most iconic images in the history of art.

Michelangelo's career didn't stop there. Later in life, he took on architectural projects, including the design of **St. Peter's Basilica** in the Vatican, one of the most important architectural works of the Renaissance. Michelangelo continued to create, sketch, and innovate until his death on **February 18, 1564**, at the age of 88. His legacy as a **polymath**—someone who mastered multiple disciplines—endures, and his work continues to inspire not only artists but anyone striving for greatness in their field.

Lessons and Applications

Michelangelo's life offers profound lessons on **vision, mastery, and relentless dedication**. His ability to turn his ideas into reality, often against immense physical, financial, or personal challenges, provides valuable insights for anyone seeking to achieve greatness. Let's explore three key lessons from Michelangelo's life and how you can apply them to your own journey.

1. Commit to Mastery—The Path to Greatness Is Through Relentless Practice and Dedication

One of the most defining aspects of Michelangelo's life was his **unwavering commitment to mastery**. He was a man who obsessed over the smallest details, constantly striving to perfect his craft, whether it was sculpting marble, painting frescoes, or designing buildings. Michelangelo believed that there was no substitute for hard work, and his dedication to his art was unparalleled. He once famously said, "**If people knew how hard I worked to get my mastery, it wouldn't seem so wonderful at all.**"

Michelangelo wasn't born a master—he became one through decades of relentless practice, study, and refinement. He spent countless hours in his studio, sketching, sculpting, and experimenting with new techniques. He even dissected corpses to better understand human anatomy, which allowed him to create figures with an unparalleled sense of realism and dynamism. His quest for perfection meant that he never took shortcuts, and this dedication is what set him apart from his contemporaries.

The key lesson here is that **mastery requires relentless effort and dedication.** Whatever your field—whether it's art, business, or a personal passion—the path to greatness is paved with practice, persistence, and an obsession with getting better. Michelangelo didn't settle for "good enough"; he pushed himself to reach new levels of excellence every day.

For practical application, reflect on your own level of commitment to mastery. Ask yourself: **Am I truly dedicating myself to mastering my craft, or am I satisfied with mediocrity?** If you want to achieve greatness, you must be willing to put in the work. This means **practicing consistently**, seeking out opportunities for learning and improvement, and pushing yourself beyond your comfort zone. Set high standards for yourself, just as Michelangelo did, and never stop striving to improve, no matter how much you've already accomplished.

2. Think Big—Great Achievements Come From Bold Vision and Grand Ambition

Michelangelo wasn't afraid to **think big**. Whether it was carving a colossal statue like **David** or painting a ceiling that covered over 5,000 square feet, Michelangelo had a vision that went beyond the ordinary. He believed in the power of **grand ambition**, and he understood that to create something truly great, you had to aim high—even if the task seemed impossible. When Michelangelo took on the Sistine Chapel project, he had never painted frescoes before, yet he didn't let this inexperience stop him from creating one of the most magnificent works of art in history.

Michelangelo's willingness to tackle monumental projects came from his belief in his own potential and his refusal to let fear or doubt limit him. He didn't shy away from challenges—he embraced them as opportunities to showcase his skills and bring his artistic vision to life. This mindset allowed him to push the boundaries of what was possible, and it's the reason his work continues to inspire awe centuries later.

The key lesson here is that **great achievements come from bold vision**. If you want to leave a lasting impact, you need to be willing to think big and take on challenges that stretch your abilities. Michelangelo didn't settle for small or safe projects—he set his sights on creating masterpieces that would stand the test of time. You can do the same by **setting ambitious goals** and pursuing them with everything you've got.

For practical application, reflect on the goals you've set for yourself. Ask yourself: **Am I thinking big enough? Am I pushing myself to pursue ambitious projects, or am I playing it safe?** If you want to achieve something great, you need to be willing to take risks and pursue projects that may seem daunting. **Don't let fear hold you back**—like Michelangelo, embrace the challenge and trust in your ability to rise to the occasion.

3. Endure Through Obstacles—Persistence in the Face of Difficulty Leads to Masterpieces

Michelangelo's life was far from easy. Despite his genius, he faced countless obstacles, both personal and professional. He dealt with financial struggles, artistic rivalries, and the immense physical challenges of creating his monumental works. The Sistine Chapel, for example, was an overwhelming project—Michelangelo spent four years painting the ceiling, often lying on his back for hours at a time, suffering from physical pain and exhaustion. Yet, he **persisted**. He pushed through the difficulty and created one of the most celebrated artistic achievements in history.

Michelangelo's story teaches us that **obstacles are an inevitable part of any great endeavor**, but it's how you respond to them that defines your success. He didn't give up when things got hard—instead, he used the challenges as fuel to keep going. His ability to endure through difficulty, to keep pushing even when the task seemed impossible, is what made him great.

The key lesson here is that **persistence is the key to success**. No matter how talented or skilled you are, you will face obstacles on your path to greatness. What separates those who achieve greatness from those who don't is the ability to keep going when things get tough. Michelangelo's life shows us that the greatest works of art, the most significant achievements, are often the result of **pushing through adversity**.

For practical application, reflect on the obstacles you're facing in your own life. Ask yourself: **Am I letting difficulties stop me, or am I using them as fuel to keep moving forward?** When challenges arise, remind yourself of Michelangelo's persistence and commit to pushing through, even when it feels overwhelming. Remember, **greatness isn't about avoiding obstacles—it's about enduring through them.**

Frida Kahlo

When we think of **Frida Kahlo**, we think of more than just an artist—we think of a woman who used her creativity and her pain as fuel to create some of the most personal and emotionally charged works of art ever produced. Her vibrant colors, surreal symbolism, and often raw depictions of her physical and emotional suffering make Kahlo not only an icon of art but also a symbol of **resilience, authenticity**, and the courage to be unapologetically oneself.

Kahlo's life was marked by intense physical pain, emotional struggles, and societal obstacles, but rather than allowing these challenges to defeat her, she transformed them into art that continues to inspire millions. Her paintings explore the depths of identity, femininity, post-colonialism, and trauma. For Kahlo, art wasn't just a profession—it was a **means of survival**, a way to express the truth of her experience and connect with others on a deeply emotional level.

Her story teaches us that **greatness doesn't come from ease**. It comes from facing life's hardships with courage and turning those difficulties into something beautiful. Kahlo's life is a testament to the idea that **vulnerability is power**, and that embracing who we truly are, flaws and all, is the path to personal freedom. In this chapter, we'll explore the life of Frida Kahlo and how her resilience, authenticity, and ability to turn suffering into self-expression can inspire us to live more meaningful, creative, and empowered lives.

Autobiography

Frida Kahlo was born on **July 6, 1907**, in **Coyoacán, Mexico**, to a German father and a mestiza mother. Though she would later claim to be born in 1910 to align her identity with the start of the **Mexican Revolution**, Kahlo's early life was shaped by both her mixed heritage and her strong connection to Mexican culture. She was proud of her roots, and much of her artwork reflects this, incorporating traditional Mexican folk art, vibrant colors, and indigenous symbolism.

From an early age, Kahlo's life was marked by trauma. At the age of six, she contracted **polio**, which left her with a lifelong limp. Despite this, Kahlo was an active and intellectually curious child, known for her rebellious spirit and her desire to challenge societal norms. Her father, a photographer, encouraged her love for art, but it wasn't until tragedy struck in her late teens that Kahlo fully immersed herself in painting.

At the age of 18, Kahlo was involved in a horrific **bus accident** that left her with severe injuries, including a broken spine, pelvis, and ribs. She was bedridden for months, and her injuries would cause her chronic pain and health problems for the rest of her life. During her long recovery, she began to paint seriously, using her time in bed to explore her emotions, pain, and identity through her art. This accident would not only change the course of her life but would also shape the themes of her work, as she often depicted her physical suffering and her complicated relationship with her body.

In 1929, Kahlo married famed Mexican muralist **Diego Rivera**, a relationship that would be central to her life and work. Their marriage was passionate but tumultuous, filled with infidelities and periods of separation. Despite their personal struggles, Rivera had a profound influence on Kahlo's career, introducing her to prominent artists and intellectuals of the time and encouraging her to embrace Mexican culture in her art. However, Kahlo's work was distinctly her own—deeply personal, filled with symbolism, and reflective of her inner world.

Kahlo's paintings, such as **"The Two Fridas"**, **"The Broken Column"**, and **"Self-Portrait with Thorn Necklace and Hummingbird"**, are raw depictions of her emotional and physical turmoil. She often used herself as the central figure in her paintings, exploring themes of pain, identity, love, and loss. Her use of surrealist elements—though she rejected the label of a surrealist artist—allowed her to depict complex emotions and the inner workings of the mind in a way that was visually striking and deeply emotional.

Kahlo's work was not widely recognized during her lifetime, as she was often overshadowed by Rivera's success. However, her art gained significant recognition in the decades following her death, becoming a symbol of **feminism**, **Mexican national pride**, and **the resilience of the human spirit**. Today, Kahlo is celebrated as one of the most important and influential artists of the 20th century.

Frida Kahlo passed away on **July 13, 1954**, at the age of 47, after a life marked by pain, suffering, but also deep creativity and resilience. She left behind a legacy of art that continues to inspire people to embrace their truth, no matter how difficult or painful it may be.

Lessons and Applications

Frida Kahlo's life offers profound lessons in **resilience**, **authenticity**, and the power of **self-expression**. Her ability to turn her pain into art, to embrace her unique identity, and to remain true to herself despite personal and societal challenges provides valuable insights for anyone striving to live a more meaningful and empowered life. Let's explore three key lessons from Frida Kahlo's life and how you can apply them to your own journey.

1. Embrace Your Pain—Turn Adversity Into a Source of Strength

Frida Kahlo's life was filled with physical and emotional pain. From her childhood bout with polio to the devastating bus accident that left her in constant agony, Kahlo faced adversity that could have easily defeated her. Yet, rather than allowing her pain to hold her back, she used it as a source of **inspiration** and **strength**. Her paintings are a testament to her ability to transform her suffering into something beautiful and meaningful. She didn't shy away from her pain—she confronted it, explored it, and expressed it through her art.

The key lesson here is that **pain and adversity don't have to be barriers to success or happiness.** In fact, they can be powerful sources of growth and creativity. Like Kahlo, we all face challenges in life—whether physical, emotional, or circumstantial—but it's how we respond to those challenges that defines us. Kahlo's ability to channel her pain into her art teaches us that **adversity can be a source of strength**, and that by embracing and confronting our difficulties, we can turn them into opportunities for self-expression and personal growth.

For practical application, reflect on the challenges and difficulties you're currently facing. Ask yourself: **How can I use this pain as fuel for growth and creativity?** Rather than avoiding or suppressing your struggles, try to embrace them and use them as a source of inspiration. Whether it's through writing, art, physical movement, or any other form of self-expression, find a way to channel your pain into something constructive and meaningful. Remember, **the things that hurt you can also make you stronger**, and by embracing your pain, you can transform it into a source of power.

2. Be Unapologetically Authentic—Embrace Your True Self, Flaws and All

Frida Kahlo is celebrated not only for her art but also for her unapologetic authenticity. She was fiercely herself, embracing her identity as a **Mexican woman**, an **artist**, and a person with a disability. Kahlo didn't try to conform to societal expectations or hide her flaws—instead, she celebrated them. Her self-portraits, often depicting her physical scars and emotional turmoil, are raw, honest, and deeply personal. In a world that often pressures us to fit into boxes or present a polished version of ourselves, Kahlo's life and art remind us of the power of **authenticity**.

The lesson here is that **being true to yourself is one of the most powerful things you can do**. Kahlo's success wasn't because she conformed to the art world's standards or tried to fit in—it was because she embraced her uniqueness and expressed it fearlessly. Her authenticity resonated with people because it was real, raw, and honest. In your own life, embracing who you are, flaws and all, can lead to deeper connections with others and a greater sense of personal freedom.

For practical application, think about the areas in your life where you might be holding back or trying to fit into societal expectations. Ask yourself: **Am I being true to who I am, or am I trying to present a version of myself that others will approve of?** Take inspiration from Kahlo's courage to be herself, and commit to embracing your authentic identity. This might mean expressing your true feelings, embracing your imperfections, or pursuing a path that aligns with your true passions. **Authenticity is freedom**, and by being unapologetically yourself, you can create a life that feels true and fulfilling.

3. Use Creativity as a Tool for Healing—Artistic Expression Can Be a Path to Emotional Freedom

For Frida Kahlo, art wasn't just a career—it was a form of therapy, a way to process her emotions and heal from her trauma. Her paintings allowed her to explore the depths of her pain, her identity, and her experiences in a way that words alone couldn't express. Kahlo's life teaches us that **creativity can be a powerful tool for**

healing, a way to work through difficult emotions, confront our inner struggles, and find freedom in self-expression.

The lesson here is that **creativity is more than just a hobby or a pastime—it's a way to connect with your emotions and heal from the inside out**. Whether it's through painting, writing, music, or any other form of creative expression, tapping into your creativity can help you process your feelings and gain a deeper understanding of yourself. Kahlo's ability to turn her emotional and physical pain into art shows us that creative expression can be a powerful tool for personal transformation and healing.

For practical application, consider incorporating **creative activities** into your life as a way to connect with your emotions and promote healing. Ask yourself: **How can I use creativity to express my feelings and work through my challenges?** Whether it's through journaling, drawing, painting, or even just doodling, find a creative outlet that allows you to explore your inner world. You don't have to be an artist to benefit from creative expression—the process of creating, rather than the end result, is what matters. By making creativity a regular part of your life, you can use it as a tool for healing, self-discovery, and emotional freedom.

Maya Angelou

Few voices in modern literature and civil rights have had the impact of **Maya Angelou**. She was more than just a poet, writer, and activist—she was a **truth-teller**, a woman who understood the power of words and how they could transform the world. Angelou's life, filled with hardship and triumph, serves as a profound reminder that resilience, courage, and self-expression can change not only one's personal destiny but also the lives of others. Her journey from childhood trauma to global recognition as a literary and cultural icon is a testament to the human spirit's ability to rise, even in the most challenging circumstances.

Through her work—whether it was her poetry, autobiographies, or speeches—Angelou explored themes of **identity**, **freedom**, **racism**, and **womanhood**. But her message wasn't just about overcoming external struggles; it was about finding the strength within oneself to confront internal battles and emerge stronger. Her life teaches us that **our voice is our greatest weapon**—when we learn to use it with confidence, authenticity, and courage, we can transcend limitations and leave a lasting legacy.

This chapter will explore the life of Maya Angelou, the challenges she overcame, and the lessons we can draw from her remarkable journey. Angelou shows us that **no matter what life throws at us**, we have the power to rise, to speak, and to claim our truth. If you've ever faced adversity, struggled with your identity, or hesitated to express yourself, Angelou's life offers profound insights into how to find your voice and use it to inspire and lead.

Autobiography

Maya Angelou was born **Marguerite Annie Johnson** on **April 4, 1928**, in **St. Louis, Missouri**. Her early childhood was filled with instability, as her parents' troubled marriage led to her being sent to live with her grandmother in **Stamps, Arkansas**. It was there, in the segregated South, that Angelou first experienced the harsh realities of **racism**. These early years in Stamps deeply influenced her understanding of inequality, oppression, and the strength found in community and family.

Angelou's childhood took a devastating turn when, at the age of 8, she was sexually assaulted by her mother's boyfriend. After she told her brother about the assault, the man was arrested and later killed by members of her family. Overcome with guilt, Angelou fell into a self-imposed silence, refusing to speak for nearly five years. During this period of muteness, Angelou discovered the power of **literature**. She devoured books, finding solace in the words of Shakespeare, Edgar Allan Poe, and Black writers like **Langston Hughes** and **Paul Laurence Dunbar**. Though she did not speak, her inner world was vibrant and rich, and this period of silence would later shape her identity as a writer and thinker.

At the age of 15, Angelou moved to **San Francisco**, where she attended school and took on various jobs to support herself, including working as the city's first Black female streetcar conductor. It was here that Angelou began to find her voice again, and after becoming a single mother at the age of 17, she realized that she needed to create a better life for herself and her son, **Guy Johnson**.

Angelou's life was marked by a diversity of experiences. She worked as a **dancer**, **singer**, and **actress**, performing in clubs and even touring Europe with a production of **Porgy and Bess**. However, it was her writing that brought her true fulfillment. In 1969, she published her first autobiography, **"I Know Why the Caged Bird Sings"**, which recounted her early life and the trauma she endured. The book was a critical and commercial success, catapulting Angelou to literary fame. It remains one of the most celebrated autobiographies in American literature, praised for its raw honesty, emotional depth, and vivid storytelling.

In addition to her writing, Angelou was an influential figure in the **civil rights movement**, working alongside leaders like **Martin Luther King Jr.** and **Malcolm X**. Her activism, combined with her literary talent, made her a powerful voice for justice, equality, and empowerment. Over the course of her career, she published numerous volumes of poetry, essays, and memoirs, and became a respected public speaker, known for her wisdom, grace, and commanding presence.

Maya Angelou's influence extended beyond the written word. In 1993, she recited her poem **"On the Pulse of Morning"** at the inauguration of President **Bill Clinton**, becoming the first African American woman to do so. Her ability to inspire through her words and her presence made her a global icon of courage, resilience, and human dignity.

Angelou passed away on **May 28, 2014**, at the age of 86, but her legacy endures. Through her words, she continues to inspire millions to **speak their truth**, to **stand tall in the face of adversity**, and to **embrace their identity** without apology.

Lessons and Applications

Maya Angelou's life offers profound lessons in **resilience, finding your voice**, and **standing up in the face of adversity**. Her ability to transform personal trauma into art, her courage in using her voice to fight for justice, and her unwavering commitment to truth provide powerful insights for anyone seeking to live a more empowered and authentic life. Let's explore three key lessons from Maya Angelou's life and how you can apply them to your own journey.

1. Find Your Voice—Your Words Have the Power to Transform Your Life and the Lives of Others

One of Maya Angelou's greatest gifts was her ability to **find her voice** in a world that often tried to silence her. After her childhood trauma, Angelou spent five years in silence, but when she finally found the courage to speak again, she discovered the immense power of words. Her writing and speeches became vehicles for expressing her truth, and through them, she not only healed herself but also gave others the courage to speak their own truths.

Angelou teaches us that **our voice is our most powerful tool**. Whether we use it to share our stories, advocate for change, or express our emotions, speaking up allows us to claim our place in the world. In a society that often encourages conformity and silence, Angelou's life reminds us that **using our voice is an act of rebellion and empowerment**.

For practical application, reflect on how you can **use your voice more boldly and authentically**. Ask yourself: **Where in my life am I holding back from expressing myself fully?** Whether in your relationships, your career, or your creative pursuits, make a conscious decision to speak your truth. This might mean standing up for yourself in difficult situations, sharing your story with others, or using your platform—whether big or small—to advocate for what you believe in. Remember, **your voice has the power to inspire change**, both in your life and in the lives of others.

Don't wait for permission to speak. Angelou found her voice after years of silence, and once she did, she never looked back. **You have something important to say**, so trust in the value of your words and let them be heard.

2. Rise Above Adversity—Resilience is Built by Overcoming the Challenges Life Throws at You

Maya Angelou's life was filled with adversity—poverty, racism, trauma, and personal loss. Yet, despite these challenges, she refused to be defined by her hardships. Instead, she used them as **stepping stones** to greatness. Angelou's resilience wasn't about avoiding pain or hardship—it was about learning how to rise each time she was knocked down. Her famous quote, "**I can be changed by what happens to me, but I refuse to be reduced by it,**" perfectly encapsulates her ability to transform adversity into strength.

The lesson here is that **resilience is the key to success and fulfillment.** Life will inevitably throw obstacles in your path, but it's your ability to persevere through them that will define your journey. Angelou's life teaches us that we all have the capacity to rise, no matter how difficult our circumstances may be. Resilience is built through action—by confronting challenges head-on and refusing to let them break us.

For practical application, reflect on the challenges you're facing in your life right now. Ask yourself: **How can I rise above these obstacles, and what can I learn from them?** Rather than viewing adversity as a setback, see it as an opportunity to grow, adapt, and become stronger. Just as Angelou turned her personal trauma into art and activism, you can use your challenges as fuel for personal growth and success.

To build resilience, practice shifting your mindset from one of **victimhood** to one of **empowerment**. Instead of asking, "Why is this happening to me?" ask, "What can I learn from this, and how can I use it to grow?" Resilience isn't about avoiding pain—it's about developing the inner strength to overcome it and emerge stronger on the other side.

3. Stand for Something—Courage is Found in

Advocating for What You Believe In

Throughout her life, Maya Angelou was a passionate advocate for **justice, equality,** and **freedom**. Whether working alongside Martin Luther King Jr. during the civil rights movement or writing poetry that challenged societal norms, Angelou used her platform to **stand up for what she believed in**. Her courage wasn't just in her words—it was in her actions. She knew that change required both **courage and action**, and she embodied both throughout her life. Angelou didn't just talk about what needed to change—she actively participated in the fight for justice and equality. Her life reminds us that **true courage is found in standing for something**, even when it's difficult, even when it makes others uncomfortable.

The lesson here is that **we must stand for what we believe in**. It's easy to remain silent or passive in the face of injustice or when we witness something that goes against our values. But Angelou's life shows us that **silence is complicity**, and that real change happens when we have the courage to speak up and take action. Whether you're advocating for social change, standing up for yourself, or defending someone who can't defend themselves, courage is found in the willingness to **take a stand** for what's right.

For practical application, reflect on your core values and ask yourself: **What do I truly believe in, and where can I take a stronger stand?** Whether it's in your community, workplace, or personal life, identify one area where you can make a difference by advocating for what you believe in. This might involve volunteering for a cause you're passionate about, speaking up in a situation where others are being treated unfairly, or even just having difficult conversations with people in your life.

Remember, courage doesn't always mean grand gestures—it can be found in the everyday actions of standing by your principles. Angelou's courage came from her deep commitment to justice and equality, and your courage can come from your commitment to your own values. **Stand for something**, and you'll find strength and purpose in the process.

Pablo Picasso

Few artists in history have had the sheer influence and impact of **Pablo Picasso**. He didn't just leave a mark on the art world—he **revolutionized it**. Known for his ability to continuously reinvent himself and his art, Picasso was a pioneer, a rule-breaker, and a relentless creator. From **Cubism** to **Surrealism**, from sculptures to paintings, Picasso's work wasn't about following trends; it was about **creating them**. He once said, "**Every act of creation is first an act of destruction.**" This philosophy defined his life and his work, as he constantly challenged conventional ideas of beauty, structure, and meaning.

But Picasso's greatness wasn't just born from talent. It came from his willingness to take risks, to **push boundaries**, and to follow his own path, even when others didn't understand his vision. His life was a testament to the power of **innovation** and the freedom that comes from creating without limits. For Picasso, art was more than just a form of expression—it was a way to **challenge perceptions** and **reshape the world**.

In this chapter, we'll delve deep into the life of Pablo Picasso and uncover the lessons his creative journey offers to anyone looking to achieve greatness. Picasso teaches us that **innovation is born from daring to be different**, that **reinvention is necessary for growth**, and that **relentless creativity** is the key to leaving a lasting legacy. If you've ever felt confined by the expectations of others or struggled to push past your creative limits, Picasso's life provides a roadmap for how to break free and chart your own course.

Autobiography

Pablo Ruiz Picasso was born on **October 25, 1881**, in **Málaga, Spain**, to a family with a deep connection to the arts. His father,

Don José Ruiz, was a painter and art professor, and he recognized his son's immense talent from a young age. Picasso's early exposure to art gave him a foundation in **classical techniques**, but even as a child, he wasn't content with traditional methods. By the age of seven, Picasso was already studying figure drawing and oil painting under his father's tutelage, and by the time he was 13, his work had surpassed that of his father.

In 1895, Picasso's family moved to **Barcelona**, where he attended the **La Llotja** Academy of Fine Arts. Although he excelled in his studies, Picasso quickly became disillusioned with the rigid structures of academic art. He wanted more—he wanted to experiment, to break the rules that had governed art for centuries. By the time he moved to **Paris** in 1904, Picasso was immersed in the avant-garde art scene, surrounded by writers, poets, and artists who were all questioning the status quo. It was here that his **Blue Period** began, a somber phase that reflected his growing introspection and his focus on themes of poverty, alienation, and despair.

Picasso's ability to continually evolve as an artist was one of his greatest strengths. Following the Blue Period came his **Rose Period**, a lighter phase filled with themes of love, circus performers, and brighter color palettes. But Picasso's most radical shift came with his co-creation of **Cubism** in 1907, alongside fellow artist **Georges Braque**. Cubism shattered the traditional rules of perspective, allowing Picasso to depict objects from multiple viewpoints simultaneously. His groundbreaking painting, **Les Demoiselles d'Avignon**, was a turning point in modern art, challenging the very foundation of how space and form were depicted.

Over the course of his life, Picasso produced more than 50,000 works of art, spanning everything from **painting** to **sculpture**, **ceramics**, **drawings**, and **stage design**. He worked obsessively, often producing several pieces a day, and his relentless creative energy set him apart from his peers. Even in his later years, Picasso continued to experiment, embracing new styles and pushing the boundaries of what art could be.

One of Picasso's most famous works, **Guernica** (1937), remains a powerful anti-war statement. Depicting the bombing of the Spanish town of Guernica during the Spanish Civil War, the painting's abstract forms and haunting figures captured the horrors of war in a way that no realist painting could. It became a symbol of resistance and a testament to Picasso's belief in the power of art to provoke thought and action.

Picasso's personal life was as complex as his art. Known for his intense relationships with women and his larger-than-life personality, he was both revered and criticized. However, despite his flaws, Picasso's work ethic, innovation, and courage to continually reinvent himself are undeniable.

Pablo Picasso died on **April 8, 1973**, at the age of 91, leaving behind a legacy that continues to shape the world of art and creativity. His life was a constant exploration of what it meant to **see** and **create** in new ways, and his refusal to be constrained by traditional methods or expectations made him one of the most important artists in history.

Lessons and Applications

Pablo Picasso's life offers powerful lessons in **innovation**, **reinvention**, and **relentless creativity**. His ability to continuously evolve as an artist, his refusal to conform to traditional expectations, and his drive to create without limits provide valuable insights for anyone striving to achieve greatness in their own field. Let's explore three key lessons from Picasso's life and how you can apply them to your own journey.

1. Innovation Requires Breaking the Rules—Don't Be Afraid to Challenge Convention

One of Picasso's defining characteristics was his **willingness to break the rules**. From an early age, Picasso understood the classical techniques of painting, but he didn't stop there. He knew that to truly innovate, he had to push beyond what had already been done. This mindset led to the creation of **Cubism**, which shattered traditional ideas of perspective and form. Picasso wasn't content to paint what he saw—he wanted to **reimagine** how things could be seen.

The key lesson here is that **innovation requires breaking away from conventional thinking**. If you want to achieve greatness in any field, you can't simply follow the rules or do what's been done before. Picasso teaches us that **true innovation comes from questioning the status quo** and daring to think differently. Whether you're an artist, entrepreneur, or leader, the ability to challenge existing norms and push boundaries is what will set you apart.

For practical application, reflect on the areas in your life where you might be stuck in **conventional thinking**. Ask yourself: **What rules am I following that are holding me back from true innovation?** Whether it's in your career, creative pursuits, or personal growth, identify the boundaries that you can push. This might mean experimenting with new methods, questioning long-standing traditions, or even embracing failure as part of the creative process.

Remember, **breaking the rules doesn't mean being reckless**—it means having the courage to question whether the way things have always been done is the best way forward. Picasso's life shows us that the willingness to disrupt conventional thinking is the key to creating something revolutionary.

2. Reinvent Yourself Constantly—Growth Comes From

Evolution, Not Stagnation

One of the most remarkable aspects of Picasso's career was his ability to **constantly reinvent himself**. From the **Blue Period** to **Cubism**, from sculpture to ceramics, Picasso never allowed himself to be confined by a single style or medium. He was always evolving, always pushing himself to explore new ideas and forms of expression. This constant reinvention wasn't just about artistic growth—it was about **personal growth**. Picasso understood that **stagnation is the enemy of creativity**.

The lesson here is that **growth requires reinvention**. If you want to continue evolving in your career or personal life, you have to be willing to let go of what's comfortable and familiar. Picasso's life teaches us that **sticking to one path**—no matter how successful it might be—can limit your potential. Instead, be open to change, to trying new things, and to **redefining yourself** as you grow.

For practical application, reflect on the areas of your life where you might be resisting change. Ask yourself: **Am I clinging to a single identity or way of doing things because it feels safe?** Whether it's in your career, relationships, or creative projects, look for opportunities to reinvent yourself. This might mean learning a new skill, taking on a completely different role, or approaching a familiar challenge in a new way.

Reinvention isn't about abandoning who you are—it's about **expanding who you are**. Picasso never stopped being an artist, but he continuously found new ways to express that identity. In your own life, reinvention can help you unlock new potential and keep your journey exciting and fulfilling.

3. Create Relentlessly—Mastery Comes From Consistent Practice and Exploration

Picasso's work ethic was legendary. Over the course of his life, he produced tens of thousands of pieces of art—paintings, drawings, sculptures, and more. He worked relentlessly, often creating multiple pieces in a single day. But Picasso's prolific output wasn't just about quantity—it was about **constant exploration.** He didn't wait for inspiration to strike; he created every day, knowing that mastery comes from **consistent practice and exploration.**

The key lesson here is that **greatness is achieved through relentless effort.** Picasso didn't achieve mastery because he was a genius (though he was); he achieved it because he worked harder and created more than almost anyone else. His life teaches us that **talent alone isn't enough**—it's the daily practice, the willingness to create even when you don't feel inspired, that leads to true mastery.

For practical application, reflect on your own **creative or professional output.** Ask yourself: **Am I consistently putting in the work, or am I waiting for inspiration to strike?** Whether it's writing, designing, leading a team, or building a business, commit to showing up every day and doing the work. This might mean setting aside time for creative exploration, even when you don't feel motivated, or pushing through challenges when things don't go as planned.

Picasso's relentless creativity shows us that **mastery is a result of consistent effort,** not occasional bursts of brilliance. By committing to your craft and creating every day, you'll not only improve your skills but also open yourself up to new ideas and opportunities.

Explorers and Adventurers

Marco Polo

When we think of **Marco Polo**, we envision a legendary explorer whose travels opened up the world, not only geographically but culturally. Polo's journeys to the farthest corners of the earth during a time when much of the world was still uncharted set him apart as one of the greatest adventurers in history. Long before modern technology and global communication, Marco Polo crossed deserts, mountains, and seas, encountering civilizations vastly different from his own, and bringing back stories that would ignite the imaginations of generations.

But Marco Polo's greatness wasn't just in his **physical exploration**—it was in his **curiosity**, his **ability to adapt to new environments**, and his deep interest in learning from other cultures. At a time when much of Europe viewed foreign lands with suspicion, Polo embraced the unknown with an open mind, eager to learn and share. His life teaches us that **greatness comes from a willingness to step outside of our comfort zones**, to experience new things, and to **expand our understanding of the world**.

In this chapter, we will delve into the life of Marco Polo, exploring not only the thrilling details of his travels but also the lessons his journey offers to us in our modern lives. Whether you're striving to achieve success in business, looking to broaden your horizons, or seeking personal growth, Polo's story serves as a reminder that **adventure and discovery aren't limited to the past—they are opportunities we can still seize today.**

Autobiography

Marco Polo was born in **1254** into a wealthy family of Venetian merchants. From an early age, Polo's life was shaped by trade and travel, as his father, **Niccolò Polo**, and his uncle, **Maffeo Polo**, were experienced merchants who had already traveled to distant lands, including the court of the **Mongol Empire**. When Marco was just a teenager, his father and uncle returned to Venice after years of traveling, bringing with them incredible tales of the East, sparking the young Polo's imagination.

In **1271**, at the age of 17, Marco Polo set out with his father and uncle on an epic journey to the court of **Kublai Khan**, the ruler of the vast Mongol Empire, which stretched from Eastern Europe to China. Their goal was to establish trade relations and offer their services to Kublai Khan, who was eager to learn more about the West. It took the Polos three long years to reach Kublai Khan's court, crossing dangerous terrain such as the **Gobi Desert**, the **Hindu Kush mountains**, and treacherous seas along the way.

Once at Kublai Khan's court in **Beijing**, Marco Polo quickly became one of the Khan's most trusted advisers. He was given special privileges, rare for a foreigner, and was sent on various diplomatic and administrative missions throughout the empire. This gave Polo an unprecedented view of the Mongol Empire, from its bustling cities to its remote regions, and allowed him to gather invaluable knowledge about the customs, economy, and politics of one of the largest empires the world had ever seen.

For over 17 years, Polo remained in the service of Kublai Khan, traveling extensively throughout China, India, and Southeast Asia. During this time, he witnessed advanced technologies, such as **paper money** and **gunpowder**, that were virtually unknown in Europe. He marveled at the sophistication of Chinese cities like **Hangzhou**, which were far larger and more organized than any city in Europe at the time. Polo's travels also brought him into contact with new philosophies, religions, and cultures, expanding his understanding of the world far beyond what most Europeans of his era could imagine.

In **1295**, after nearly 24 years away from Venice, Marco Polo returned home with his father and uncle. However, his tales of the

East were met with skepticism. Many found it hard to believe the incredible stories he told of vast riches, strange customs, and foreign technologies. Polo's adventures might have faded into obscurity had it not been for his capture during a war between Venice and Genoa. While imprisoned, Polo dictated his travels to a fellow prisoner, **Rustichello da Pisa**, who compiled them into the book we know today as "**The Travels of Marco Polo**". This book became one of the most important travel accounts in history, influencing explorers like **Christopher Columbus** and broadening Europe's awareness of the East.

Marco Polo died in **1324**, but his legacy as one of the greatest explorers and cultural intermediaries lives on. Through his journeys, he connected the East and the West, breaking down barriers and expanding the horizons of what was possible for future generations.

Lessons and Applications

Marco Polo's life is filled with powerful lessons about **exploration**, **curiosity**, and the importance of understanding other cultures. His travels were not only a physical journey but also an intellectual and spiritual one, marked by his desire to learn and grow. Let's explore three key lessons from Polo's life and how you can apply them to your own journey.

1. Embrace Curiosity—Let Your Desire to Learn Drive Your Success

One of the defining traits of Marco Polo was his **insatiable curiosity**. Unlike many of his contemporaries, who viewed foreign lands and cultures with suspicion, Polo was driven by a deep desire to learn and understand the unknown. He wasn't content with what he already knew—he wanted to discover more, to experience more, and to see the world from new perspectives. His willingness to ask questions, explore unfamiliar places, and engage with people from different backgrounds was the key to his success as an explorer and diplomat.

The key lesson here is that **curiosity is a powerful tool for growth and success.** Whether in business, personal development, or relationships, the ability to remain curious and open-minded is what allows us to continuously learn and improve. Curiosity drives innovation, creativity, and problem-solving, as it pushes us to look beyond the surface and explore new possibilities. Polo's life shows us that **the world is full of opportunities**—but we can only seize them if we are willing to step outside of our comfort zones and learn.

For practical application, think about the areas in your life where you can cultivate more curiosity. Ask yourself: **Where am I limiting myself by sticking to what I already know? What new experiences, ideas, or perspectives could I explore to broaden my understanding?** Whether it's learning a new skill, exploring a different culture, or simply asking more questions, embracing curiosity can lead to new opportunities for growth.

Don't be afraid to venture into the unknown. Just as Marco Polo embarked on a journey across continents to satisfy his curiosity, you can seek out new experiences that challenge your assumptions and expand your worldview. **Curiosity is the engine of growth**, and by embracing it, you'll find yourself constantly learning and evolving.

2. Take Bold Risks—Great Rewards Come to Those Who Dare to Explore

Marco Polo's life was defined by his willingness to take **bold risks**. Traveling from Venice to China in the 13th century was no small feat—Polo and his family faced extreme conditions, treacherous terrain, and the constant threat of danger. Yet, despite these risks, Polo persisted, driven by the belief that the rewards of exploration were worth the challenges. His journey to Kublai Khan's court not only opened up new opportunities for trade and diplomacy but also expanded the boundaries of what was possible for future explorers.

The lesson here is that **great rewards come to those who dare to take risks**. Whether in your career, personal life, or creative pursuits, the willingness to step outside your comfort zone and face uncertainty is what leads to true success. Polo's journey teaches us that **playing it safe rarely leads to greatness**—it's the bold moves, the willingness to explore uncharted territory, that open up new doors.

For practical application, reflect on the risks you may be avoiding in your life. Ask yourself: **What bold steps can I take to push myself further and achieve my goals?** Whether it's pursuing a new career path, starting a business, or embarking on a personal challenge, don't let fear hold you back. Taking risks doesn't mean being reckless—it means having the courage to pursue opportunities even when the outcome is uncertain.

Like Marco Polo, embrace the mindset of an explorer. **Take calculated risks** that align with your values and goals, and trust that the rewards will come. The greatest achievements in life often come from daring to venture into the unknown.

3. Cultivate Cultural Understanding—Success Comes From Embracing Diversity

One of Marco Polo's most valuable traits was his ability to **understand and appreciate other cultures**. Rather than imposing his own views or judgments on the people he encountered, Polo approached each new culture with **respect and curiosity**. His time at Kublai Khan's court allowed him to immerse himself in a culture vastly different from his own, and his willingness to learn from others helped him build strong relationships and navigate complex political landscapes.

The key lesson here is that **cultural understanding is essential for success in a global world**. In today's interconnected society, the ability to communicate, collaborate, and empathize with people from different backgrounds is more important than ever. Polo's life teaches us that **embracing diversity**—whether it's in business, community, or personal relationships—leads to richer experiences and greater success.

For practical application, think about how you can cultivate greater **cultural awareness** in your life. Ask yourself: **How can I learn more about other cultures, perspectives, and ways of life? How can I build stronger connections with people who have different backgrounds or beliefs?** Whether through travel, reading, or engaging in conversations with people from different walks of life, expanding your cultural understanding can lead to new opportunities for collaboration and growth.

In today's globalized world, success often depends on your ability to navigate diverse environments and connect with people from all over the world. By following Marco Polo's example, you can cultivate the cultural understanding needed to thrive in a world that's more interconnected than ever before.

Ferdinand Magellan

When you think of the great explorers of history, **Ferdinand Magellan** stands out as a figure of **remarkable vision and daring**. He wasn't just an adventurer seeking fame or fortune—he was a man with a deep desire to **push the boundaries of what was known**, a person determined to chart new paths, even when the odds seemed overwhelmingly against him. Magellan's greatest achievement, leading the first expedition to **circumnavigate the globe**, changed the world forever. It opened the doors to global trade, reshaped geography, and proved that the Earth was indeed round, reinforcing the idea that **impossible goals could be reached through relentless determination.**

But Magellan's legacy isn't just about the discovery of new territories—it's about his ability to lead through **uncertainty**, to press forward when faced with mutinies, unknown seas, and the prospect of failure. His life offers lessons in the **courage to pursue a vision** that others might not understand, in the importance of resilience, and in the power of leadership when navigating uncharted waters—both literal and metaphorical.

In this chapter, we'll explore the life of Ferdinand Magellan, drawing out practical lessons from his story that we can apply to our own lives. Whether you're facing personal challenges, leading a team, or working toward a seemingly impossible goal, Magellan's journey will inspire you to **embrace risk, lead with courage**, and stay the course in the face of adversity. His story reminds us that **greatness doesn't come from comfort—it comes from pushing into the unknown with unwavering resolve.**

Autobiography

Ferdinand Magellan was born in **1480** in **Sabrosa, Portugal**, into a family of minor nobility. As a young man, Magellan served as a page in the Portuguese royal court, which gave him early exposure to the world of exploration. Portugal, at that time, was a leader in sea voyages, and Magellan was inspired by explorers like **Vasco da Gama**, whose journeys to India had opened up new trade routes and possibilities for European powers.

In his early twenties, Magellan joined the Portuguese fleet, participating in several voyages to the **East Indies** and gaining firsthand experience in navigating the seas. He fought in battles and navigated through dangerous waters, honing his skills as a sailor and leader. However, Magellan's ambitions stretched far beyond the conventional paths followed by his contemporaries. He began to believe that there was a westward route to the **Spice Islands** (modern-day Indonesia), a belief that directly contradicted the Portuguese strategy of sailing east around Africa to reach Asia.

Magellan proposed his bold plan to the Portuguese King, **Manuel I**, but was rejected. Undeterred, he turned to **Spain**, which had been engaged in its own age of exploration following **Christopher Columbus's** discovery of the New World. In **1518**, Magellan secured funding and support from **King Charles I** of Spain for his ambitious expedition. His mission? To find a westward sea passage to the Spice Islands, something no one had ever accomplished. He was given command of five ships—the **Trinidad**, **San Antonio**, **Concepción**, **Santiago**, and **Victoria**—and a crew of about 270 men.

Magellan set sail from **Seville** on **September 20, 1519**, and quickly encountered challenges that tested his leadership and resolve. His fleet endured **mutinies, storms,** and **shortages of supplies** as they navigated through the treacherous waters of the **Atlantic** and then down the coast of **South America**, searching for a passage through to the Pacific Ocean. That passage—later named the **Strait of Magellan**—was finally found in late 1520, after months of perilous exploration.

But even after successfully navigating through the strait, Magellan and his crew faced the vast, uncharted **Pacific Ocean**. The journey across the Pacific was grueling, with many of his men succumbing to starvation and disease. Magellan, however, remained determined to complete his mission, continuing to lead his men through hardship and uncertainty.

Tragically, Magellan did not live to see the full completion of his circumnavigation. In **April 1521**, he was killed in a skirmish with local warriors in the **Philippines**. Despite his death, his legacy was secured when one of his ships, the **Victoria**, under the command of **Juan Sebastián Elcano**, completed the voyage and returned to Spain on **September 6, 1522**, becoming the first ship to circumnavigate the globe.

Magellan's expedition proved that the Earth could be circumnavigated, opening up new trade routes and forever altering the course of history. His journey stands as one of the greatest achievements of the Age of Exploration, symbolizing the power of **vision, leadership,** and **unwavering determination.**

Lessons and Applications

Ferdinand Magellan's life offers profound lessons in **vision, determination,** and **leadership in the face of uncertainty.** His ability to lead an expedition into the unknown, his relentless pursuit of a seemingly impossible goal, and his capacity to inspire others through hardship provide valuable insights for anyone striving to achieve greatness. Let's explore three key lessons from Magellan's life and how you can apply them to your own journey.

1. Pursue a Vision Bigger Than Yourself—Great

Achievements Come From Bold Goals

One of the defining traits of Ferdinand Magellan was his **boldness of vision**. He didn't settle for what was known or comfortable. Instead, he pursued a goal that others considered impossible—to find a westward route to the Spice Islands and, in doing so, to sail around the world. His vision wasn't just about personal glory; it was about expanding the horizons of human knowledge and reshaping global trade.

The lesson here is that **great achievements require bold, visionary goals**. If you want to leave a lasting impact, you can't be satisfied with small, incremental steps—you need to pursue a vision that challenges the status quo and pushes the limits of what's possible. Magellan didn't achieve greatness by playing it safe. He aimed for something that no one had ever done before, and in doing so, he changed the world.

For practical application, reflect on the goals you've set for yourself. Ask yourself: **Am I aiming high enough? Is my vision bold enough to inspire others and make a lasting impact?** Whether in your career, personal life, or creative pursuits, don't be afraid to think big. Set goals that stretch your abilities and challenge you to grow. Remember, **bold goals inspire bold actions**, and by pursuing a vision that's bigger than yourself, you can achieve things that once seemed impossible.

It's important to note that pursuing a grand vision doesn't mean ignoring practical realities—it means being willing to take calculated risks, plan strategically, and stay the course even when challenges arise. Magellan's vision to circumnavigate the globe was grounded in meticulous preparation and a deep understanding of the seas. Likewise, your bold vision should be backed by thoughtful planning and a relentless commitment to achieving your goal.

2. Lead Through Uncertainty—True Leadership is

Tested in Times of Challenge

Magellan's leadership was tested repeatedly throughout his journey, from the **mutinies** that threatened to derail his expedition to the **unknown seas** that stretched endlessly before them. Yet, Magellan's ability to lead through uncertainty is one of the reasons his name endures in history. He maintained his focus, inspired loyalty among his men (despite the odds), and made decisive choices in moments of crisis. He wasn't immune to fear or doubt, but he refused to let uncertainty paralyze him or his mission.

The lesson here is that **true leadership shines in times of uncertainty and challenge**. It's easy to lead when everything is going smoothly, but real leaders are those who can navigate through chaos, make tough decisions, and keep their team motivated when the outcome is uncertain. Magellan's journey was full of unknowns, but his ability to stay focused and keep moving forward is what made his mission a success.

For practical application, think about how you handle uncertainty in your own life. Ask yourself: **How can I lead more effectively when faced with challenges or unknown outcomes?** Whether you're leading a team at work, navigating a personal crisis, or pursuing a difficult goal, remember that your ability to stay calm, make decisions, and inspire others will determine your success. Leadership isn't about always having the right answers—it's about having the confidence to move forward even when the path isn't clear.

One way to strengthen your leadership during times of uncertainty is to **focus on the bigger picture**. Like Magellan, keep your ultimate goal in mind, and use it as a guiding light when making tough choices. By keeping your vision front and center, you can maintain your sense of purpose and direction, even when the immediate future feels uncertain.

3. Persevere Through Hardship—Success Requires Relentless Determination

Magellan's expedition faced almost unimaginable hardships—**scurvy, starvation, storms**, and the loss of ships and crew members. Yet, through it all, Magellan remained determined to complete his mission. Even when his men doubted him, even when the sea stretched endlessly before them, Magellan pressed forward. His life teaches us that **greatness isn't achieved without enduring significant hardship**—and the ability to persevere in the face of adversity is what separates those who succeed from those who fall short.

The key lesson here is that **success requires relentless determination**. There will be times when everything seems to be going wrong, when the obstacles feel insurmountable, and when giving up seems like the easier option. But those who achieve greatness—like Magellan—are the ones who **keep going** even when the journey gets tough. They are the ones who understand that hardship is part of the process and that persistence is the key to overcoming any challenge.

For practical application, reflect on the challenges you're currently facing in your life or work. Ask yourself: **Am I allowing obstacles to derail me, or am I pushing through with relentless determination?** The next time you encounter a setback, instead of seeing it as a reason to give up, view it as a test of your perseverance. Like Magellan, commit to staying the course, even when the road ahead seems difficult. **Resilience and persistence are the true keys to success**, and by embracing these qualities, you can push past any barrier.

One way to strengthen your perseverance is to break down your larger goal into smaller, manageable tasks. This will help you focus on making steady progress, rather than becoming overwhelmed by the magnitude of the journey ahead. Remember, every small victory brings you one step closer to your ultimate goal.

Amelia Earhart

When you hear the name **Amelia Earhart**, what comes to mind? For most, she is the very definition of a **pioneer**, a woman who defied societal expectations and took to the skies at a time when few women would have even considered it. But beyond her status as an aviation icon, Earhart's legacy speaks to something much larger: the power of **fearless ambition** and the willingness to break barriers, no matter how impossible they may seem.

Amelia Earhart didn't just want to fly—she wanted to **push the limits of what was possible**. She sought to inspire not only herself but others to follow their dreams, to look beyond societal norms, and to see the world from a broader perspective—literally and figuratively. Her life and career were marked by a refusal to accept limitations, a theme that echoes through all of her accomplishments.

Earhart teaches us that **the greatest achievements come from having the courage to step into the unknown**. Her determination to challenge the status quo, coupled with her fearless nature, provides us with a roadmap for how we can approach our own goals. Whether you're looking to break free from the expectations others place on you, trying to push through personal challenges, or simply seeking inspiration, Earhart's story is one of relentless drive and **fearless pursuit of one's dreams**.

Autobiography

Amelia Earhart was born on **July 24, 1897**, in **Atchison, Kansas**. From an early age, she showed an adventurous spirit. While other girls her age played with dolls, Earhart spent her time climbing trees, collecting insects, and engaging in activities that were often reserved for boys in her era. Her parents, particularly her mother, encouraged her to embrace her independent nature, even as society tried to impose limitations on what a young girl should and shouldn't do.

Her childhood, however, was not without its struggles. Her father, **Edwin Earhart**, had a troubled relationship with alcohol, and his inability to maintain steady employment caused instability in the family. The Earharts moved frequently, and financial difficulties strained the family's dynamics. Despite these challenges, Amelia's independent streak remained strong. She excelled in school, particularly in science and mathematics, areas in which girls were rarely encouraged to pursue at the time.

Earhart's first experience with aviation came in **1920**, when she attended an airshow in **California**. It was here that she took her first ride in an airplane, a 10-minute flight that would change her life forever. From the moment the plane left the ground, Earhart knew that she wanted to fly. As she later recounted, **"As soon as we left the ground, I knew I myself had to fly."**

Determined to make her dream a reality, Earhart worked tirelessly to fund her flying lessons. She saved money from various jobs, including working as a photographer, truck driver, and even a stenographer, to pay for lessons with **Neta Snook**, one of the few female flight instructors at the time. In 1921, she bought her first airplane, a second-hand **Kinner Airster** that she nicknamed **The Canary**. This was just the beginning of a long and illustrious career in aviation.

Amelia Earhart quickly made a name for herself in the world of aviation. In **1922**, she set her first record, becoming the first woman to fly solo to an altitude of 14,000 feet. Her reputation continued to grow, and in **1928**, she was invited to be the first woman to fly across the Atlantic as part of a crew. Although she didn't pilot the plane, the feat made her an international celebrity, and she used her newfound fame to advocate for both aviation and women's rights.

In **1932**, Earhart made history once again, becoming the first woman to fly solo across the Atlantic Ocean. The flight was perilous—she encountered icy conditions, mechanical problems, and strong winds—but her successful journey from **Newfoundland** to **Ireland** solidified her place as one of the greatest aviators of her time. Following this achievement, she continued to set records, including being the first person to fly solo from **Hawaii** to **California**.

Despite her fame, Earhart remained committed to inspiring others, particularly women, to pursue their dreams and break through the barriers society imposed on them. She wasn't content with her own success; she wanted to open doors for others to follow.

In **1937**, Earhart embarked on her most ambitious flight yet—an attempt to become the first woman to circumnavigate the globe. However, after a series of delays and technical difficulties, tragedy struck. On **July 2, 1937**, during the last leg of her journey near **Howland Island** in the Pacific, Earhart's plane disappeared. Despite extensive search efforts, neither Earhart nor her navigator, **Fred Noonan**, were ever found. To this day, the mystery of her disappearance remains unsolved, but her legacy as a fearless pioneer endures.

Lessons and Applications

Amelia Earhart's life offers profound lessons in **ambition**, **breaking barriers**, and **relentless determination**. Her ability to push beyond societal expectations, take on immense challenges, and inspire others provides valuable insights for anyone striving to achieve greatness. Let's explore three key lessons from Earhart's life and how you can apply them to your own journey.

1. Break Through Barriers—Challenge the Limitations Imposed by Others and Society

One of Amelia Earhart's most defining qualities was her refusal to accept the limitations society placed on her. As a woman in the early 20th century, Earhart faced significant societal barriers, particularly in a male-dominated field like aviation. Women were often discouraged from pursuing careers in science, technology, and adventure, but Earhart ignored these expectations. Instead, she challenged the notion that women were limited to traditional roles, proving that gender should never dictate what one can achieve.

The key lesson here is that **society's expectations should never define your limits**. Whether it's family, culture, or societal norms, there will always be forces that try to impose restrictions on what you can or cannot do. Like Earhart, you must have the courage to **break through those barriers** and forge your own path. Earhart wasn't content to live within the narrow confines of what was expected of her; she pushed beyond them to create a legacy that transcends gender and time.

For practical application, reflect on the barriers—whether imposed by society or yourself—that are holding you back. Ask yourself: **What limitations am I accepting that I need to break through?** Whether it's in your career, personal life, or relationships, consider how you can challenge the expectations placed upon you. By refusing to accept arbitrary limits, you'll open up new opportunities and possibilities that others might have overlooked.

Earhart's life teaches us that **real progress happens when we step outside the boundaries of societal expectations**. Don't let fear or tradition hold you back—take that bold first step toward breaking through the barriers in your life.

2. Embrace Fearless Ambition—Dare to Dream Bigger Than Anyone Else

Amelia Earhart's ambitions were not small. From the moment she took her first flight, she envisioned herself pushing the limits of aviation, doing what had never been done before. Whether it was flying solo across the Atlantic or attempting to circumnavigate the globe, Earhart's goals were always ambitious and often considered impossible. Yet, it was her **fearless ambition** that made her stand out—not only in aviation but as a symbol of what's possible when you dare to dream big.

The lesson here is that **ambition is a powerful force for achievement**. To truly make an impact, you need to be willing to dream bigger than those around you. Earhart didn't just want to be a pilot—she wanted to make history. Her success was built on the foundation of constantly setting new, ambitious goals for herself. It's important to remember that **ambition isn't arrogance**—it's the belief that you are capable of achieving more, that there is always a higher goal to reach for.

For practical application, consider the goals you've set for yourself. Ask yourself: **Am I aiming high enough, or am I playing it safe?** Don't be afraid to set **ambitious goals** that push you beyond your current limits. Whether it's advancing your career, starting a new venture, or mastering a skill, embrace the power of dreaming big. By doing so, you'll not only motivate yourself to achieve more but also inspire those around you.

Earhart's life reminds us that **fearless ambition opens doors that others might not even see**. By setting your sights high, you can achieve things that once seemed impossible.

3. Persist Through Challenges—Relentless Determination is the Key to Success

Amelia Earhart's journey to success was not without its challenges. She faced **financial difficulties, criticism, technical problems**, and numerous other obstacles throughout her career. Yet, despite these setbacks, she remained **relentlessly determined** to achieve her goals. Earhart knew that greatness didn't come easily—every step toward her dream required perseverance, grit, and the ability to push through adversity.

The lesson here is that **persistence is the key to success**. No matter how ambitious your goals are, you will inevitably face challenges along the way. What separates those who achieve greatness from those who fall short is the ability to keep going when things get tough. Earhart's life teaches us that setbacks are not failures—they are simply part of the journey. The true failure would have been giving up.

For practical application, reflect on the challenges you've faced recently. Ask yourself: **Am I allowing these obstacles to derail me, or am I pushing through with relentless determination?** The next time you encounter a setback, instead of seeing it as a reason to stop, view it as an opportunity to prove your resilience. Like Earhart, commit to staying the course, even when the road ahead seems difficult. **Success is not about never failing—it's about persisting until you succeed.**

One practical way to cultivate persistence is by setting **incremental goals** that keep you focused and motivated, even in the face of setbacks. By breaking down your larger goal into smaller, manageable tasks, you can maintain momentum and celebrate small victories along the way. Remember, **every small step forward brings you closer to your ultimate goal.**

Ernest Shackleton

Few stories in the annals of exploration capture the human spirit's ability to endure and lead in times of crisis quite like that of **Ernest Shackleton**. In the early 20th century, as the world raced to claim the uncharted territories of Antarctica, Shackleton distinguished himself not only as an explorer but as a leader of unparalleled tenacity and compassion. While other expeditions sought glory through conquering new lands or racing to geographic milestones, Shackleton's most famous achievement was not reaching the South Pole—it was leading his crew through one of the greatest survival stories in history, despite monumental failure.

Shackleton's Antarctic expedition, aboard the ill-fated **Endurance**, became a testament to his leadership, his ability to remain calm in the face of unimaginable adversity, and his refusal to give up on his men when hope seemed lost. His story resonates far beyond exploration, providing timeless lessons in **leadership under pressure**, **resilience**, and the sheer power of **determination**. Shackleton didn't just endure the impossible—he showed the world what it meant to lead others through it.

This chapter will dive deep into the life of Ernest Shackleton, using his incredible journey to shed light on lessons we can apply to our own lives. Whether you're facing personal or professional challenges, Shackleton's story teaches us that **great leadership isn't about avoiding failure—it's about guiding others through it**. His courage, loyalty, and steadfast focus on survival offer invaluable insights for anyone striving to overcome obstacles and achieve lasting success.

Autobiography

Ernest Henry Shackleton was born on **February 15, 1874**, in **Kilkea, Ireland**. His family later moved to London, where he was educated. From an early age, Shackleton was fascinated by adventure and exploration, yet his path to greatness wasn't obvious from the start. He was known for his restless energy, his love for the outdoors, and a deep curiosity about the world. However, formal education did not appeal to him, and at 16, he left school to join the **merchant navy**, where he gained valuable seafaring experience.

By the time Shackleton was in his mid-twenties, the **Age of Antarctic Exploration** was in full swing. In 1901, he was selected to be part of **Robert Falcon Scott's** expedition to the **Antarctic** aboard the **Discovery**. This was Shackleton's first taste of the Antarctic, and although the expedition did not succeed in reaching the South Pole, it fueled his obsession with the icy continent. Shackleton's time on this expedition also exposed him to the challenges of extreme cold, physical exhaustion, and the mental strain that accompanies long periods of isolation.

In 1907, Shackleton launched his own expedition aboard the **Nimrod**, aiming to be the first man to reach the South Pole. Although he fell short by about 97 miles, Shackleton's decision to turn back before his crew succumbed to starvation or death earned him widespread admiration. It was during this expedition that Shackleton's priorities as a leader became clear—**the safety of his men would always come before personal glory**.

Shackleton's most famous and enduring story, however, began in **1914**, when he set out on his third Antarctic expedition aboard the **Endurance**. His goal was to cross the entire Antarctic continent, a feat never before achieved. The expedition quickly became a catastrophe when the Endurance was trapped in the pack ice of the **Weddell Sea** and eventually crushed, leaving Shackleton and his crew stranded on the ice with no hope of rescue.

What followed was one of the most incredible survival stories in history. Shackleton led his 27-man crew on a desperate journey across the ice, camping on unstable floes, navigating treacherous seas in lifeboats, and eventually reaching the remote **Elephant Island**. Realizing that Elephant Island offered no possibility of rescue, Shackleton and five of his men set out on an 800-mile journey across the **Southern Ocean** in a small lifeboat to reach **South Georgia Island**, where they knew a whaling station existed. After 16 days at sea, they miraculously reached land, but their ordeal was far from over—they had to traverse the island's mountainous interior, which had never been crossed, to reach the station.

In the end, Shackleton returned with a rescue team and, against all odds, every one of his men survived the ordeal. Shackleton's leadership in the face of overwhelming challenges became legendary, solidifying his place as one of history's greatest explorers and leaders.

Shackleton died in **1922** while preparing for another Antarctic expedition, but his legacy endures as a symbol of **courage, endurance**, and **leadership under pressure**. His ability to guide his crew through what seemed like certain death remains one of the most compelling stories of resilience in the face of impossible odds.

Lessons and Applications

Ernest Shackleton's life offers profound lessons in **leadership**, **resilience**, and the ability to maintain focus and morale through extreme challenges. His ability to keep his crew united and motivated, even when their situation seemed hopeless, provides valuable insights for anyone facing adversity or uncertainty in their own life. Let's explore three key lessons from Shackleton's life and how you can apply them to your own journey.

1. Lead with Empathy—Understand and Prioritize the Needs of Your Team

One of the most remarkable aspects of Shackleton's leadership was his deep sense of **empathy** for his men. Unlike many leaders of his time, Shackleton did not view his crew as expendable or merely instruments of his own ambition. Instead, he prioritized their well-being and survival above all else. This empathy built trust, loyalty, and an unshakable bond between Shackleton and his crew. His decision to turn back during his 1907 Nimrod expedition, just short of the South Pole, was a testament to his commitment to the safety of his men, even at the expense of personal glory.

During the Endurance expedition, Shackleton's empathy was evident in the way he managed his men's morale. Trapped on the ice for months, Shackleton knew that mental exhaustion and hopelessness were just as dangerous as the physical elements. He made sure to rotate responsibilities, ensuring no man felt useless, and he engaged his crew in routine activities to keep spirits up. Shackleton also shared the hardships of his men, sleeping in the same freezing conditions, eating the same rations, and never placing himself above them.

The lesson here is that **effective leadership starts with empathy**. Understanding the needs, fears, and strengths of those you lead allows you to make better decisions and build trust. People will follow a leader they believe genuinely cares for them, especially in difficult times. Shackleton's story shows that **leadership isn't about barking orders—it's about standing shoulder to shoulder with your team, listening to their concerns, and making their well-being a priority.**

For practical application, think about the teams or people you lead in your own life. Whether in your professional or personal spheres, ask yourself: **Am I truly listening to the people around me? Am I taking their needs into account when making

decisions? Leading with empathy means prioritizing the success and well-being of those you lead, ensuring they feel valued and heard. By doing so, you'll foster a deeper sense of trust and loyalty, and people will be more willing to follow you, even in challenging circumstances.

2. Maintain Unwavering Positivity—Set the Tone for How Your Team Handles Adversity

In any crisis, the **attitude** of the leader sets the tone for how the team responds. Shackleton was a master at maintaining a **positive, can-do attitude**, even when the situation seemed hopeless. When the Endurance was crushed by the ice, Shackleton didn't give in to despair or panic—he remained calm and optimistic, reinforcing to his men that **they would survive**. He knew that if he showed fear or doubt, his men would lose hope. By projecting **confidence and positivity**, Shackleton kept his crew focused on survival and ensured that they didn't fall into mental despair.

One of Shackleton's key leadership traits was his ability to instill **purpose** even in the most dire of circumstances. Whether it was establishing a daily routine on the ice, organizing lifeboat duties, or planning their escape, Shackleton ensured that his men always had something to focus on. He famously said, "**Difficulties are just things to overcome, after all.**" This mindset helped his men see challenges as obstacles to be conquered, not insurmountable barriers.

The lesson here is that **your mindset in the face of adversity directly impacts those around you.** As a leader, or even in your personal life, maintaining an attitude of **resilience and optimism** can keep you and your team moving forward, no matter the difficulty. Shackleton's story shows that in times of crisis, your attitude can make the difference between survival and collapse. When faced with setbacks, rather than dwelling on what has gone wrong, focus on solutions and keep a forward-thinking mindset.

For practical application, reflect on how you respond to challenges in your life. Ask yourself: **Am I reacting to adversity with positivity and confidence, or am I letting fear and doubt control my actions?** Cultivate a mindset that embraces challenges as opportunities for growth and solutions. This doesn't mean ignoring the reality of difficulties—it means refusing to let them define you or your team. By setting the right tone, you'll inspire those around you to persevere, just as Shackleton did with his crew.

3. Adapt to Changing Circumstances—Be Willing to Adjust Your Goals in the Face of New Realities

One of the greatest strengths of Shackleton's leadership was his ability to **adapt to changing circumstances**. When his original goal of crossing the Antarctic continent became impossible after the Endurance was trapped and destroyed, Shackleton quickly shifted his focus from exploration to **survival**. He didn't cling to the failed mission—he adjusted his strategy and prioritized what was most important: saving his men.

Shackleton was pragmatic in his approach, recognizing that **goals must evolve when the situation changes**. His adaptability allowed him to pivot and make decisions that kept his crew alive, even when they faced seemingly insurmountable odds. This flexibility in leadership is critical because rigid adherence to a plan in the face of shifting realities can lead to disaster. Shackleton's ability to change course when necessary is a key reason why his men survived.

The lesson here is that **success often depends on your ability to adapt to new challenges**. Whether in business, personal goals, or leadership, circumstances will inevitably change, and your ability to adjust your approach will determine your success. Shackleton teaches us that **rigid adherence to a failing plan is a recipe for disaster**—great leaders know when to adapt, change course, and focus on what truly matters in the moment.

For practical application, reflect on your own ability to adapt. Ask yourself: **When things don't go as planned, am I able to shift my goals and strategies to fit the new reality, or do I cling to outdated plans?** Cultivate a mindset of flexibility, recognizing that success isn't about sticking to a single path—it's about adjusting your course when necessary. By being open to change, you'll be better equipped to overcome obstacles and achieve long-term success.

Christopher Columbus

Few names in history are as synonymous with exploration and discovery as **Christopher Columbus**. He is often remembered as the man who "discovered" the Americas, a title that has sparked both admiration and controversy over the centuries. However, beyond the debates, Columbus's life offers powerful lessons in **vision**, **perseverance**, and the courage to **embrace the unknown**. Columbus set sail across the Atlantic at a time when much of the world believed that such a journey would end in disaster. He believed there was a way to reach the riches of Asia by sailing west, and even though his calculations were wrong, his spirit of exploration was unwavering.

Columbus's journeys changed the world forever, setting off a chain of events that would shape global history. But more importantly, his life speaks to the **importance of pursuing your vision**, even when faced with skepticism, setbacks, and seemingly insurmountable challenges. His belief in the possibility of something greater, his determination in the face of rejection, and his willingness to take the greatest of risks provide timeless insights for anyone seeking to push the limits of their potential.

In this chapter, we will explore the life of Christopher Columbus, delving into the practical lessons his journey offers to those looking to achieve greatness in their own lives. Whether you're striving to achieve a personal goal, lead others into uncharted territory, or simply build a legacy that lasts, Columbus's story offers valuable guidance on **how to turn dreams into reality**.

Autobiography

Christopher Columbus was born in **1451** in the Republic of **Genoa**, in present-day Italy. From an early age, Columbus developed a fascination with the sea and the idea of exploration. Genoa, being a bustling maritime city, gave young Columbus exposure to the world of trade and navigation. He grew up hearing tales of distant lands, vast oceans, and the riches of the East. However, like many others of his time, Columbus believed there was a quicker route to these riches by sailing west across the Atlantic Ocean, rather than the established route around Africa.

Columbus's early years were spent working as a seaman and navigator, learning the intricacies of sailing, ship management, and geography. He eventually became convinced that the world was much smaller than his contemporaries believed, and that **Asia could be reached by sailing directly west from Europe**. This idea was revolutionary at the time, but also highly controversial. Most scholars and sailors believed that the Atlantic was simply too vast to be crossed without encountering certain death.

Despite the widespread skepticism, Columbus was undeterred. He spent years petitioning European monarchs to fund his expedition, convinced that his vision was not only possible but would bring unimaginable wealth to whoever supported him. However, he was repeatedly rejected. **Portugal**, one of the leading maritime powers of the time, refused his proposal, as did **England** and **France**. Columbus's vision seemed to be fading into obscurity as monarch after monarch turned him away.

Finally, after years of lobbying, Columbus found support from **Queen Isabella** and **King Ferdinand** of **Spain**. In **1492**, they agreed to finance his voyage, providing him with three ships: the **Niña**, the **Pinta**, and the **Santa María**. With this backing, Columbus set out on a journey that would change the course of history.

On **August 3, 1492**, Columbus and his crew set sail from **Palos de la Frontera**, Spain, bound for the unknown waters of the Atlantic. For weeks, the voyage was fraught with uncertainty. The men began to lose hope, and Columbus struggled to keep them motivated. However, his relentless belief in his mission kept them going. On **October 12, 1492**, after 36 days at sea, land was finally sighted. Columbus and his crew had arrived in what they believed to be the East Indies, but was in fact the **Bahamas**, marking the first European encounter with the Americas.

Columbus would go on to make three more voyages across the Atlantic, exploring the Caribbean islands, parts of Central America, and South America. While he never reached his intended destination of Asia, his voyages opened up the New World to European exploration and colonization, forever changing the course of history. Columbus's legacy is complex—while his discoveries led to significant advances in trade and exploration, they also brought about the colonization and exploitation of indigenous peoples, a dark aspect of his legacy that is still discussed today.

Columbus died in **1506**, believing he had reached the outskirts of Asia. He never fully realized the magnitude of his discovery, but his determination to pursue his vision against all odds remains an enduring example of **bold ambition and perseverance.**

Lessons and Applications

Christopher Columbus's life offers profound lessons in **vision, perseverance**, and the **willingness to embrace the unknown**. His ability to push past rejection, lead his men into uncharted waters, and hold fast to his belief in the face of doubt provides invaluable insights for anyone striving to achieve greatness. Let's explore three key lessons from Columbus's journey and how you can apply them to your own life.

1. Pursue Your Vision Relentlessly—Even in the Face of Rejection

One of the defining traits of Christopher Columbus was his **unwavering belief in his vision**. For years, he knocked on doors, petitioned monarchs, and faced rejection after rejection. Portugal, the preeminent maritime power of the day, dismissed his proposal, as did the leaders of England and France. But Columbus didn't let these rejections deter him. He persisted, knowing that his idea had the potential to reshape the world.

The key lesson here is that **great visions are often met with resistance**. When you're pursuing something revolutionary, something that challenges the established norms, you will likely face skepticism and rejection. However, as Columbus's story shows, the ability to **persist in the face of doubt** is what separates those who succeed from those who give up. Columbus didn't take no for an answer—he continued to seek support until he found someone who believed in his vision.

For practical application, think about the goals and ideas you're pursuing in your life. Are you facing rejection or skepticism? Ask yourself: **Am I willing to keep pushing forward, even when others don't believe in my vision?** Whether you're working on a career goal, building a business, or striving for personal growth, recognize that **rejection is part of the journey**. Don't let it discourage you—use it as fuel to keep moving forward. Columbus didn't let the opinions of others define his success, and neither should you.

Persistence is a trait shared by all great achievers. Just because others don't see your vision doesn't mean it lacks value. Keep your focus, stay determined, and continue pursuing your goals with relentless passion.

2. Embrace the Unknown—Greatness is Found Beyond Your Comfort Zone

Columbus's decision to sail west into the vast, unknown Atlantic was an act of incredible **courage**. At the time, many people believed that such a journey was impossible and that the open ocean would lead to certain death. But Columbus was willing to take the risk, embracing the uncertainty of what lay ahead. His journey was not only about seeking riches or glory—it was about **pushing beyond the boundaries of the known world** and discovering something new.

The lesson here is that **true greatness is found outside of your comfort zone.** Columbus's willingness to venture into the unknown is a reminder that if you want to achieve something extraordinary, you can't stay in the safety of what's familiar. You have to be willing to take risks, to face the possibility of failure, and to **embrace uncertainty** as part of the process. Columbus didn't know what he would find when he set sail—but he knew that **staying where he was would lead to nothing new.**

For practical application, think about the areas in your life where you're playing it safe. Ask yourself: **Where am I holding back because I'm afraid of the unknown? What risks can I take to push myself beyond my current limits?** Whether it's pursuing a new career opportunity, starting a new project, or taking on a challenge you've been avoiding, recognize that the path to greatness is rarely clear or certain. Embrace the unknown, and you may discover opportunities you never imagined.

Like Columbus, you don't need to have all the answers before you start—you just need to have the courage to take the first step. By venturing into uncharted territory, you'll open yourself up to new possibilities for growth and success.

3. Lead with Conviction—Your Belief in Your Mission

Inspires Others to Follow

Columbus was not only an explorer—he was a **leader**. Throughout his journey, Columbus faced numerous challenges, including mutinies, bad weather, and the fear of the unknown. Many of his men wanted to turn back when weeks passed without sight of land. But Columbus's **unshakable belief in his mission** kept his crew motivated, even when hope seemed lost. He led with conviction, inspiring his men to follow him into uncharted waters.

The lesson here is that **great leaders inspire through conviction**. When you believe deeply in your mission, others will follow. Columbus didn't always have all the answers, but his confidence in the journey inspired trust and loyalty in his crew. As a leader—whether in your personal or professional life—it's not about knowing every detail of the path ahead. It's about **believing in the destination** and communicating that belief to those around you.

For practical application, reflect on your leadership style. Ask yourself: **Am I leading with conviction, or am I letting doubt influence my actions?** Whether you're leading a team at work, guiding your family, or inspiring others in your community, recognize that your belief in your mission is contagious. When others see your confidence and determination, they are more likely to follow your lead, even in difficult or uncertain situations.

Like Columbus, your ability to lead others through adversity will depend on your conviction in the mission. If you believe in what you're doing, others will believe in it too. By leading with confidence and purpose, you'll inspire those around you to push through challenges and stay focused on the goal.

James Cook

The name **James Cook** is synonymous with **exploration** and **discovery**. Known for his extraordinary voyages across the Pacific Ocean, Cook expanded the map of the world, uncovering vast new territories and making monumental contributions to science, navigation, and geography. But what sets Cook apart from other explorers is not only his capacity to venture into the unknown, but his **relentless pursuit of precision, his leadership in times of uncertainty**, and his **commitment to the greater good** of humanity through discovery and knowledge.

At a time when large portions of the world remained uncharted, Cook's voyages aboard the **Endeavour**, **Resolution**, and **Discovery** transformed the understanding of our planet. His explorations laid the foundation for modern scientific inquiry, navigational techniques, and an appreciation for the diverse cultures of the Pacific. Cook wasn't just a man who sailed across oceans—he was a man who pushed the boundaries of human potential, showing that **great exploration requires not just bravery, but meticulous planning, discipline, and a sharp intellect.**

In this chapter, we'll explore the life of James Cook, drawing practical lessons from his incredible journey. Whether you're navigating the challenges of your own life, aiming to lead others through uncertainty, or striving to break new ground in your field, Cook's life offers invaluable guidance. His relentless drive for precision, his ability to command respect and maintain order, and his unwavering commitment to discovery remind us that **success lies in combining bold ambition with strategic discipline.**

Autobiography

James Cook was born on **October 27, 1728**, in **Marton, England**, into a humble family. The son of a Scottish farm laborer, Cook's early life offered few opportunities for education or advancement. However, from a young age, he showed a deep fascination with the sea and a natural aptitude for mathematics and navigation. At 18, he was apprenticed to a shipowner in the coastal town of **Whitby**, where he learned the basics of seamanship and honed the skills that would later make him one of the greatest navigators in history.

After completing his apprenticeship, Cook joined the **British Royal Navy** in 1755. His timing was fortuitous, as England was embroiled in the **Seven Years' War**, providing Cook with the chance to distinguish himself as a navigator and cartographer. His ability to precisely chart coastlines and his keen understanding of the seas earned him recognition. By 1768, Cook was chosen to lead one of the most important scientific voyages of the era: an expedition to the Pacific to observe the **transit of Venus** across the sun, a celestial event that scientists believed would provide crucial data for measuring the distance between Earth and the sun.

Cook's first voyage aboard the **Endeavour** was transformative. While the official mission was scientific, Cook was also tasked with exploring and mapping new territories. His journey took him to **New Zealand** and the eastern coast of **Australia**, making him the first European to make detailed maps of these lands. Cook's precision in mapping and his careful leadership during the voyage earned him international fame. His ability to maintain the health of his crew through proper nutrition and strict discipline—at a time when scurvy was rampant among sailors—further cemented his reputation as an exceptional leader.

Cook embarked on two more voyages, each more ambitious than the last. His second voyage, aboard the **Resolution**, took him farther south than any European explorer had ever ventured, searching for the fabled **Great Southern Continent**. While the continent remained elusive, Cook's journey through the southern Pacific and Antarctic waters provided invaluable knowledge about the region's geography and climates. His third voyage, intended to discover the **Northwest Passage**—a hoped-for sea route connecting the Pacific and Atlantic oceans through the Arctic—ended in tragedy. Cook was killed in a conflict with native Hawaiians in **1779**, but his legacy as one of history's greatest explorers was already secured.

Cook's expeditions fundamentally changed the Western world's understanding of the globe. His detailed maps, his interactions with indigenous peoples, and his scientific contributions had a lasting impact on navigation, exploration, and science. He was a man who not only dared to explore the unknown but did so with **intellectual rigor, ethical leadership**, and **unwavering discipline**. His ability to combine **courage with precision**, **exploration with order**, and **ambition with scientific integrity** remains a model for anyone seeking to achieve greatness.

Lessons and Applications

James Cook's life offers timeless lessons in **exploration, precision, and leadership**. His ability to manage long and perilous voyages, to maintain the health and morale of his crew, and to explore with both curiosity and scientific rigor provides valuable insights for anyone striving to push beyond the ordinary. Let's dive into three key lessons from Cook's life and explore how they can be applied to your own journey.

1. Combine Bold Vision with Meticulous Preparation—Great Achievements Require Both Ambition and Discipline

James Cook was not simply a man of bold vision; he was a man of **meticulous preparation and precision**. His explorations were groundbreaking not just because he ventured into unknown waters, but because he did so with **careful planning** and an understanding of the need for precision in execution. Cook's voyages were defined by his attention to detail, whether it was in the meticulous mapping of coastlines, the careful preservation of his crew's health, or the scientific measurements he conducted along the way.

The lesson here is that **great achievements don't happen through ambition alone—they require disciplined preparation and execution**. It's one thing to dream big, but it's another to ensure that your dreams are grounded in **well-thought-out plans** and **strategic actions**. Cook's ability to merge **boldness with discipline** is what made him successful. He didn't leave anything to chance—he studied the seas, mastered navigation techniques, and ensured that his crew was prepared for every possible challenge.

For practical application, reflect on your own goals. Ask yourself: **Am I balancing my ambition with the discipline needed to achieve it?** Whether in your career, fitness, or personal projects, take time to plan and prepare. **Map out your path**, understand the challenges you may face, and ensure that you are taking concrete steps toward your goal. Bold visions are important, but without the groundwork, they are unlikely to come to fruition.

Think like Cook—prepare for every possibility, study the landscape, and execute with precision. By combining ambition with meticulous planning, you'll be in a stronger position to achieve your goals and overcome obstacles along the way.

2. Lead with Discipline and Compassion—Great

Leadership Requires Both Firmness and Empathy

James Cook was known for his ability to **lead with discipline** without sacrificing his **compassion for his crew**. At a time when naval expeditions were notorious for high mortality rates due to disease, particularly **scurvy**, Cook's strict but compassionate leadership style ensured the health and well-being of his men. He implemented rules that were ahead of his time—requiring his crew to eat fresh produce whenever possible, maintain strict cleanliness, and engage in daily exercise. As a result, Cook's crew remained healthier than most, even on the longest and most dangerous voyages.

The lesson here is that **effective leadership requires a balance of discipline and empathy**. Cook didn't lead through fear or intimidation, but through mutual respect and a shared sense of purpose. He demanded excellence from his crew, but he also understood their needs and took care of them. This balance of firmness and compassion earned him the loyalty of his men and ensured that his voyages were successful.

For practical application, think about how you lead in your own life, whether in your work, family, or community. Ask yourself: **Am I balancing my expectations of others with an understanding of their needs?** Leadership is about more than just issuing orders—it's about caring for those you lead, understanding their struggles, and finding ways to motivate them through both challenges and successes.

By leading with both discipline and empathy, you'll inspire trust and loyalty in those around you, just as Cook did with his crew. Great leaders demand excellence, but they also know when to provide support, encouragement, and understanding.

3. Embrace Exploration with Curiosity and Responsibility—New Discoveries Require Openness

and Accountability

One of the most impressive qualities of James Cook was his ability to **explore with a sense of responsibility**. His journeys were not just about claiming new lands or achieving personal fame—they were driven by a genuine desire to expand human knowledge and understanding. Cook approached each new land and culture he encountered with **curiosity**, a scientific mind, and an appreciation for the people he met. Although his encounters were not always peaceful or without conflict, Cook is remembered for his efforts to **learn from indigenous peoples** and respect their ways of life.

The lesson here is that **exploration—whether literal or metaphorical—requires curiosity, responsibility, and respect for others**. Cook's success as an explorer was due not only to his navigation skills but also to his approach to discovery. He sought to learn, to document, and to appreciate the diversity of the world around him. In our modern world, we often "explore" new ideas, new technologies, and new ways of thinking, and it's critical to do so with the same mindset—one that values **understanding and responsibility** rather than exploitation or domination.

For practical application, think about the new territories you are exploring in your life, whether they are new skills, relationships, or experiences. Ask yourself: **Am I approaching these new opportunities with curiosity and responsibility?** Exploration, in any form, should come with a commitment to **learn and grow**, not just for personal gain but for the benefit of others. By embracing curiosity and maintaining a sense of responsibility, you'll ensure that your discoveries lead to **positive outcomes** for both yourself and those around you.

Like Cook, approach the unknown with an open mind and a respect for the new knowledge you acquire. Exploration is a powerful force for change, but only when guided by responsibility and respect for the world and people around us.

Scientists and Pioneers

Albert Einstein

The name **Albert Einstein** is synonymous with **genius**. He was not only the most famous physicist of the 20th century but also one of the most revolutionary thinkers in human history. When we think of Einstein, images of a wild-haired, bespectacled man, deep in thought, come to mind. But beneath that iconic image was a man whose life exemplified **curiosity**, **persistence**, and a relentless desire to challenge the status quo. Einstein wasn't just a scientist—he was a **visionary** who changed our understanding of the universe, transforming physics with his theories of **relativity** and **quantum mechanics**.

Yet, Einstein's life wasn't one of effortless success. Behind his groundbreaking theories and Nobel Prize was a journey filled with **struggles, failures, and setbacks**. Despite facing personal and professional obstacles, Einstein's ability to persevere, question accepted truths, and embrace his curiosity made him one of the greatest minds of all time. He teaches us that **genius isn't about being born with extraordinary abilities—it's about an extraordinary attitude toward learning, thinking, and solving problems**.

In this chapter, we'll explore the life of Albert Einstein, diving deep into the key lessons that made him an icon of both scientific brilliance and personal persistence. Whether you're aiming to excel in your career, solve complex problems, or simply cultivate a more innovative mindset, Einstein's story serves as a roadmap for how to unlock your potential and **redefine what's possible**.

Autobiography

Albert Einstein was born on **March 14, 1879**, in **Ulm, Germany**. His family moved to Munich when he was a child, where his father,

Hermann Einstein, ran a small business manufacturing electrical equipment. From an early age, Einstein showed signs of intellectual curiosity, although his early academic life was far from exceptional. In fact, Einstein struggled in traditional schooling environments, finding the rigid structures of his teachers stifling. He often questioned authority, preferring to solve problems in his own way rather than follow the prescribed methods. His rebellious attitude toward rote learning would become a defining characteristic of his approach to science later in life.

Despite his struggles with formal education, Einstein had a natural affinity for mathematics and physics. He devoured scientific texts and taught himself advanced concepts from a young age. By the time he was a teenager, Einstein had become fascinated with **light** and **energy**, pondering the nature of space and time. These early interests would later culminate in his revolutionary work on the **theory of relativity**.

In 1896, Einstein enrolled at the **Swiss Federal Polytechnic School** in **Zurich**, where he pursued a teaching diploma in physics and mathematics. However, even here, he found himself at odds with the rigid educational system. Upon graduating, Einstein faced difficulties securing an academic position and took a job at the **Swiss Patent Office** in **Bern**. It was in this unassuming setting, working as a patent examiner, that Einstein developed some of his most groundbreaking ideas. During this period, he spent his free time working on theoretical physics, often late into the night.

In **1905**, Einstein experienced what is often called his "**Annus Mirabilis**" or "miracle year." In a span of just 12 months, Einstein published four pivotal papers that would forever change the field of physics. Among them was his **special theory of relativity**, which introduced the now-famous equation $E=mc^2$, demonstrating the relationship between energy and mass. This revolutionary idea not only reshaped how we understand the universe but also laid the foundation for modern quantum mechanics and nuclear physics.

Einstein's fame skyrocketed in 1915 when he published his **general theory of relativity**, which provided a new understanding of **gravity**. The theory predicted that massive objects, like stars and planets, could bend the fabric of space and time, an idea that was later confirmed by observations of solar eclipses. Einstein's ability to rethink the fundamentals of physics placed him among the greatest minds in history, and in **1921**, he was awarded the **Nobel Prize in Physics** for his work on the **photoelectric effect**, another pivotal contribution to quantum theory.

Despite his success, Einstein's life was far from easy. He faced personal challenges, including a troubled marriage and political persecution. As a Jewish intellectual in the years leading up to **World War II**, Einstein fled Nazi Germany in 1933 and settled in the United States, where he took a position at the **Institute for Advanced Study** in **Princeton, New Jersey**. While living in the U.S., Einstein became an advocate for **peace** and **civil rights**, using his fame to speak out against **war** and **nuclear weapons**.

Einstein continued his work in physics throughout his life, always maintaining his childlike sense of wonder and curiosity about the universe. He died on **April 18, 1955**, leaving behind a legacy of intellectual courage and boundless curiosity that continues to inspire generations of scientists, thinkers, and dreamers.

Lessons and Applications

Albert Einstein's life offers profound lessons in **curiosity**, **persistence**, and the ability to **challenge conventional thinking**. His journey from a young boy who questioned everything to a global icon of scientific thought provides invaluable insights for anyone striving to break new ground in their field. Let's explore three key lessons from Einstein's life and how they can be applied to your own journey.

1. Cultivate Relentless Curiosity—The Key to Innovation is to Keep Asking Questions

Albert Einstein's greatest strength was his **relentless curiosity**. From a young age, he was driven by a need to understand the world around him, constantly asking questions about the nature of light, time, and energy. Unlike many of his peers, Einstein wasn't content with simply accepting the established laws of physics—he wanted to **explore the mysteries that others overlooked**. His famous quote, "**I have no special talent. I am only passionately curious,**" reflects his belief that curiosity is at the heart of all great discoveries.

The key lesson here is that **curiosity is the engine of innovation**. Many people stop asking questions as they grow older, content to accept things as they are. But if you want to break new ground, whether in your career, personal life, or creative endeavors, you must continue to **question the status quo**. Curiosity drives us to explore new ideas, challenge old assumptions, and seek out new perspectives that can lead to breakthroughs.

For practical application, ask yourself: **Am I still asking questions, or am I accepting things as they are?** Look at your field, your work, or your personal life—are there areas where curiosity could lead to better solutions or new opportunities? By cultivating a mindset of **relentless curiosity**, you can unlock doors that others may not even know exist.

One practical way to develop your curiosity is to **pursue diverse interests**. Einstein was not only passionate about physics but also music, philosophy, and politics. His broad interests allowed him to approach problems from different angles, which fueled his creativity. Likewise, seek out new experiences, read widely, and engage with people from different backgrounds. The more you expose yourself to new ideas, the more questions you'll have—and the more innovative solutions you'll find.

2. Persevere Through Setbacks—Failure is a Stepping Stone to Success

Einstein's path to success was not smooth. He faced rejection after rejection when trying to secure an academic position after graduation. His ideas were often met with skepticism, and for years, he worked as a patent clerk, far removed from the academic world he aspired to be part of. Yet, Einstein didn't give up on his passion for physics. He used his time at the patent office to **develop his theories in private**, working late into the night to pursue the ideas that would eventually revolutionize science.

The lesson here is that **perseverance is crucial to achieving greatness**. Einstein's early setbacks did not define him; instead, they fueled his determination to push forward. **Failure is an inevitable part of the journey** to success, and those who achieve the most are often those who refuse to let setbacks deter them from their goals.

For practical application, think about the challenges or failures you've encountered in your own life. Ask yourself: **Am I letting setbacks hold me back, or am I using them as opportunities to learn and grow?** Like Einstein, view failure not as the end of the road, but as a stepping stone toward eventual success. **Persistence is the key to overcoming obstacles**, and the ability to keep moving forward despite adversity is what separates those who succeed from those who give up.

One way to cultivate perseverance is to **focus on small victories**. Instead of being discouraged by the enormity of the challenges ahead, break your goals into smaller, manageable tasks. Celebrate each step forward, no matter how small, and use those victories to build momentum. Einstein didn't develop his groundbreaking theories overnight—he worked on them piece by piece, often in isolation, until they were ready to be shared with the world.

3. Challenge Conventional Thinking—True Innovation Requires Breaking Away from the Norm

Albert Einstein's theories, particularly his **theory of relativity**, were revolutionary because they **challenged the conventional thinking** of the time. Most physicists accepted **Newtonian mechanics** as the final word on motion, time, and space. But Einstein questioned these long-held beliefs and wasn't afraid to propose ideas that seemed radical, even absurd, to his contemporaries. His willingness to **rethink the fundamentals** of physics is what allowed him to make discoveries that transformed the way we understand the universe.

The lesson here is that **true innovation requires challenging the status quo**. Many of the greatest breakthroughs in history have come from people who refused to accept the limitations of existing ideas and dared to think differently. If you want to create something new, whether in business, art, science, or personal development, you must be willing to **question the norms** and **take risks**.

For practical application, consider the areas of your life where you're sticking to conventional wisdom. Ask yourself: **Are there ideas or assumptions I've accepted without question? What if there's a better way?** By challenging conventional thinking, you open yourself up to new possibilities and innovative solutions. Don't be afraid to propose ideas that others might find unconventional—sometimes, it's the **craziest ideas that change the world**.

One practical way to challenge conventional thinking is to **surround yourself with diverse perspectives**. Engage with people who think differently from you, read books or articles from opposing viewpoints, and always be willing to question your own assumptions.

The more you expose yourself to alternative ways of thinking, the more likely you are to develop groundbreaking ideas of your own.

Charles Darwin

Few figures in history have shaken the foundations of human understanding quite like **Charles Darwin**. His groundbreaking work on the theory of **evolution** transformed not just the field of biology, but our view of humanity's place in the natural world. Darwin's theory of **natural selection**, detailed in his monumental work, *On the Origin of Species*, altered the course of science and fundamentally changed how we understand the development of life on Earth. But Darwin's contributions weren't born from sudden inspiration—they were the result of **decades of patient observation, careful study**, and an unshakable commitment to understanding the truth, no matter how controversial.

Darwin's life is a testament to the virtues of **persistence, adaptability**, and the power of **observation**. His journey wasn't just one of scientific discovery; it was one of personal growth, intellectual struggle, and moral courage. At a time when his ideas were seen as radical and even heretical, Darwin's determination to pursue the truth, despite opposition from society and the church, provides us with valuable lessons in **courage** and **conviction**.

In this chapter, we'll dive deep into the life of Charles Darwin and uncover the key lessons we can learn from his patient yet relentless quest for knowledge. Whether you're facing opposition, trying to overcome intellectual challenges, or simply seeking a deeper understanding of the world around you, Darwin's life offers powerful insights that can help you **adapt and thrive** in your own personal journey.

Autobiography

Charles Darwin was born on **February 12, 1809**, in **Shrewsbury, England**, into a wealthy and well-educated family. His father,

Robert Darwin, was a successful doctor, and his grandfather, **Erasmus Darwin**, was a renowned intellectual and naturalist. From a young age, Charles was expected to follow in the family tradition of medicine, but his passion for nature and exploration would eventually steer him in a very different direction.

As a child, Darwin was fascinated by the natural world, collecting beetles, stones, and shells with the enthusiasm of a budding scientist. However, his early academic life was far from promising. Darwin's father once famously remarked that Charles cared for nothing but **"shooting, dogs, and rat-catching**,**"** predicting he would amount to nothing. Sent to study medicine at **Edinburgh University**, Darwin struggled with the gruesome realities of surgery and quickly realized that becoming a doctor wasn't for him. He later enrolled at **Christ's College, Cambridge**, with the aim of becoming a clergyman. But it was during his time at Cambridge that Darwin found his true calling, thanks to his growing interest in natural history and a friendship with **John Henslow**, a botany professor who became Darwin's mentor.

In **1831**, Darwin received a life-changing opportunity when he was invited to join the **HMS Beagle** as a naturalist on a five-year survey voyage around the world. The Beagle's mission was to chart the coastlines of South America and the Pacific, but for Darwin, it became an unparalleled opportunity to study the natural world in its most diverse and untamed forms. During the voyage, Darwin collected thousands of specimens—plants, animals, fossils—and filled notebooks with observations on the geological formations, ecosystems, and species he encountered. The **Galápagos Islands**, in particular, left a profound impression on Darwin, as he noted subtle variations among species of finches and tortoises from one island to the next, planting the seeds for his later theories.

Upon his return to England in **1836**, Darwin spent the next 20 years refining his ideas, meticulously analyzing his findings, and developing what would eventually become the theory of **natural selection**. He struggled with the implications of his work, knowing that it would challenge the prevailing views of **creationism** and the established religious doctrines of the time. Darwin's reluctance to publish his findings stemmed not from doubt about his conclusions, but from the fear of the societal and personal consequences.

In **1859**, after years of hesitation, Darwin finally published *On the Origin of Species*, laying out his theory that species evolve over time through a process of natural selection, where the organisms best adapted to their environment are more likely to survive and reproduce. The book was both celebrated and condemned, igniting fierce debate across scientific, religious, and philosophical communities. Despite the controversy, Darwin's ideas gained acceptance, and over time, they became the cornerstone of modern biology.

Throughout his life, Darwin remained committed to his research, continuing to publish works on topics ranging from orchids to earthworms. He died on **April 19, 1882**, leaving behind a legacy of intellectual courage and scientific discovery that has shaped our understanding of life itself.

Lessons and Applications

Charles Darwin's life offers profound lessons in **patience, adaptability**, and the power of **relentless observation**. His ability to take his time, to adapt his ideas in the face of new evidence, and to remain steadfast in his pursuit of the truth provides valuable insights for anyone striving to achieve greatness. Let's explore three key lessons from Darwin's journey and how they can be applied to your own life.

1. Be Patient in Your Pursuit of Knowledge—True Understanding Takes Time

One of Darwin's most remarkable traits was his **patience**. While he made groundbreaking discoveries during his voyage on the Beagle, he didn't rush to publish his findings. Instead, Darwin spent over two decades carefully developing his ideas, refining his theories, and ensuring that his conclusions were supported by rigorous evidence. This level of patience allowed Darwin to avoid hasty conclusions and gave him the time to build a theory that would stand the test of time.

The lesson here is that **true understanding takes time**. In a world that often values quick results, Darwin's life reminds us of the importance of **slow, deliberate thinking**. Whether you're developing a skill, solving a problem, or pursuing a personal goal, the best results come when you allow yourself the time to fully explore, refine, and understand what you're working on. Rushing to conclusions can lead to mistakes, missed opportunities, or incomplete solutions.

For practical application, ask yourself: **Am I allowing myself the time I need to truly understand and grow in the areas I'm focusing on?** Whether you're learning a new skill, building a career, or working through a personal challenge, take a page from Darwin's book and allow yourself the patience to fully immerse in the process. Understand that mastery and clarity come with time, and that the best results are often the product of slow, deliberate effort.

One way to cultivate patience is to set **long-term goals** and focus on incremental progress. Just as Darwin spent years collecting data and refining his theories, break your goals into smaller, manageable steps, and focus on making steady progress. Patience doesn't mean waiting idly—it means **actively working toward a goal**, knowing that the journey may take longer than you expect.

2. Adapt to New Information—Flexibility is Key to

Growth

Darwin's theory of natural selection is fundamentally about **adaptation**—the idea that species evolve by adapting to their environment. But this principle of adaptation wasn't just a scientific discovery for Darwin; it was a reflection of his own intellectual approach. Darwin's willingness to **adapt his ideas** in light of new evidence was key to his success. He didn't cling to rigid beliefs—he allowed his thinking to evolve as he gathered more data, always open to changing his mind if the facts supported it.

The lesson here is that **adaptability is essential for growth**. Too often, we get stuck in our ways, clinging to outdated ideas or habits that no longer serve us. Darwin's life teaches us the importance of being flexible—of being open to new information and willing to change our approach when the situation calls for it. Whether in your career, relationships, or personal development, the ability to adapt is what allows you to keep evolving and improving.

For practical application, ask yourself: **Am I open to adapting my approach in the face of new information or changing circumstances?** Whether you're working on a project, pursuing a goal, or navigating life's challenges, be willing to reassess your strategies and make adjustments as needed. **Growth requires flexibility**, and the more adaptable you are, the better equipped you'll be to handle the inevitable changes and obstacles that come your way.

One practical way to develop adaptability is to regularly **evaluate your progress** and be honest with yourself about what's working and what's not. Just as Darwin continuously evaluated his data and adjusted his theories, take time to reflect on your own path and make changes when necessary. Don't be afraid to try new approaches or abandon old habits that no longer serve you.

3. Observe Relentlessly—The Power of Careful

Observation and Attention to Detail

Charles Darwin's success as a scientist wasn't just due to his groundbreaking theories—it was his ability to **observe the world with incredible detail and precision** that made him great. During his voyage on the Beagle, Darwin collected thousands of specimens, carefully noting even the smallest variations between species. His ability to see connections where others saw randomness was what ultimately led to his theory of natural selection. Darwin's relentless observation allowed him to piece together a puzzle that had eluded scientists for centuries.

The lesson here is that **careful observation is the foundation of insight**. Whether in science, business, or personal development, the ability to observe patterns, details, and subtle differences can lead to breakthroughs that others might miss. By training yourself to pay closer attention—to people, to situations, to your own thoughts and behaviors—you can uncover opportunities for improvement and growth that would otherwise go unnoticed.

For practical application, ask yourself: **Am I truly observing the world around me, or am I missing important details?** Whether in your personal life or professional pursuits, take the time to observe more closely. Pay attention to the small details, and you may discover patterns or insights that can lead to significant breakthroughs. The ability to **see what others overlook** is often the difference between success and stagnation.

One way to improve your observational skills is to **practice mindfulness**—being fully present and engaged in the moment. Whether you're in a meeting, working on a project, or having a conversation, make a conscious effort to focus on the details. By sharpening your observational skills, you'll be better equipped to identify opportunities for growth and improvement.

Galileo Galilei

If ever there was a figure who embodied the boldness of **intellectual rebellion**, it would be **Galileo Galilei**. Often referred to as the **"father of modern science,"** Galileo dared to challenge the long-established views of his time, despite overwhelming opposition from the church and academic authorities. He revolutionized astronomy, laid the groundwork for physics, and perhaps most importantly, taught the world the value of **questioning authority** in the pursuit of truth.

Galileo's life is a story of **relentless inquiry, unwavering perseverance**, and the willingness to **stand alone against the masses** for what he knew to be true. His astronomical discoveries—particularly his support for the **heliocentric model** of the solar system—were not just groundbreaking; they were **dangerous**. In an era when the dominant belief was that Earth stood immovable at the center of the universe, Galileo's assertion that the **Earth revolved around the Sun** shook the foundations of both science and religion. For this, he was persecuted, tried by the **Inquisition**, and placed under house arrest for the remainder of his life.

But Galileo's defiance and intellectual courage teach us that **progress often requires rebellion**—the willingness to go against the grain, to push beyond established limits, and to fight for the truth even when it's uncomfortable. Whether you're striving to challenge conventional thinking in your own life, standing firm in your beliefs against opposition, or simply aiming to see beyond the surface of things, Galileo's story offers profound lessons on how to do so with conviction, integrity, and bravery.

Autobiography

Galileo Galilei was born on **February 15, 1564**, in **Pisa, Italy**, into a family of musicians and scholars. His father, **Vincenzo Galilei**, was a musician and music theorist, which instilled in young Galileo an appreciation for critical thinking and skepticism of established knowledge. Though originally destined for the clergy, Galileo's early interests in mathematics and physics quickly diverted him from a life of theology toward one of scientific exploration.

At the age of 17, Galileo enrolled at the **University of Pisa** to study medicine, but it wasn't long before he found himself drawn more to mathematics and physics. He left the university without a degree, returning to Florence to pursue his own studies in physics and the natural sciences. His first major work, published in **1586**, was on the center of gravity in solids, and soon after, he was offered a position as a professor of mathematics at **Pisa**.

One of Galileo's earliest experiments involved testing the Aristotelian belief that heavier objects fall faster than lighter ones. Using the **Leaning Tower of Pisa** as his laboratory, Galileo is said to have dropped two spheres of different masses, proving that they hit the ground simultaneously. This was one of his first major challenges to the accepted scientific "truths" of the time. His findings laid the groundwork for his later work on **kinematics** and the laws of motion.

Galileo's contributions to astronomy, however, would make him one of the most famous and controversial figures of his time. In **1609**, Galileo heard of a new invention from the Netherlands—a device that magnified distant objects. Improving upon this invention, Galileo built his own **telescope** and pointed it at the night sky. What he saw would forever alter humanity's view of the cosmos. His observations revealed **mountains and craters on the moon**, the four largest moons of **Jupiter**, and countless stars previously invisible to the naked eye.

But perhaps Galileo's most significant and controversial discovery came when he observed the **phases of Venus**, a phenomenon that could only be explained if Venus orbited the Sun, not the Earth. This directly contradicted the long-held **geocentric** model, which placed Earth at the center of the universe, a belief supported by the **Catholic Church**. Galileo's findings supported the **Copernican theory**, which posited that the Earth and other planets revolved around the Sun.

In **1616**, Galileo was called before the Roman **Inquisition** and warned not to defend the Copernican system. He complied for a time, but his passion for scientific truth could not be contained. In **1632**, he published his most famous work, *Dialogue Concerning the Two Chief World Systems*, in which he compared the geocentric and heliocentric models of the universe. Though written as a dialogue, the book clearly favored the heliocentric model, reigniting the ire of the church.

Galileo was tried by the Inquisition in **1633**, found guilty of heresy, and forced to recant his support for heliocentrism. He was sentenced to life under house arrest, where he continued to work on his theories of motion and mechanics until his death in **1642**. Despite his persecution, Galileo's contributions to science continued to inspire future generations, and his work laid the foundation for the **scientific revolution**.

Lessons and Applications

Galileo's life offers timeless lessons in **intellectual courage**, **persistence against opposition**, and the importance of **questioning established beliefs**. His willingness to challenge the most powerful institution of his time and his relentless pursuit of truth provide valuable insights for anyone striving to break through barriers, stand firm in their convictions, or explore uncharted intellectual territory.

Let's explore three key lessons from Galileo's journey and how they can be applied to your own life.

1. Question Authority—The Path to Progress Lies in Challenging Established Norms

Galileo's greatest contribution to science wasn't just his discoveries—it was his willingness to **question authority**. In a time when the **Church** held immense power over intellectual thought, Galileo dared to challenge the dominant worldview that placed Earth at the center of the universe. He didn't accept the established wisdom simply because it came from respected institutions. Instead, he trusted his observations and his intellect, even when doing so put him at odds with the most powerful forces in society.

The key lesson here is that **progress often requires challenging the status quo**. Whether in science, business, or personal development, **blindly accepting established norms** can prevent you from making new discoveries or advancing your goals. Galileo teaches us the importance of **critical thinking**—the ability to question assumptions, examine evidence, and trust our own reasoning, even when it contradicts what others believe.

For practical application, ask yourself: **Am I questioning the assumptions that govern my life or work? Am I willing to challenge established norms if the evidence points in a different direction?** Whether you're working on a personal project, pursuing a career goal, or simply seeking truth in your own life, take a lesson from Galileo and don't be afraid to challenge the dominant narratives. **Critical thinking is the key to innovation**, and by questioning the status quo, you open yourself up to new possibilities for growth and discovery.

One way to develop this skill is to **regularly examine your beliefs** and ask: **Why do I believe this? Is there evidence to support it, or am I accepting it because it's widely held?** By training yourself to think critically, you'll be better equipped to spot opportunities for improvement and innovation in your life, just as Galileo did in his.

2. Persevere in the Face of Opposition—Courage and Conviction Lead to True Breakthroughs

Galileo faced tremendous opposition throughout his life, not just from the church, but from fellow academics who were deeply invested in the geocentric model. Despite this, Galileo remained steadfast in his pursuit of scientific truth. Even after being convicted of heresy and forced to live under house arrest, Galileo continued his work on physics and mechanics, advancing the field of motion. His perseverance in the face of overwhelming opposition is a reminder that **true breakthroughs often come at a cost**, and that courage is required to see your vision through.

The lesson here is that **perseverance is essential to achieving greatness**. When you push the boundaries of what's possible, you will inevitably face resistance—whether from societal norms, personal doubts, or external critics. Galileo's story teaches us that **if you believe in your vision**, you must be willing to endure opposition and stand firm in your convictions, even when it feels like the world is against you.

For practical application, think about the challenges you're currently facing. Ask yourself: **Am I letting opposition or criticism hold me back from pursuing my goals?** Like Galileo, recognize that resistance is part of the process, and use it as fuel to keep moving forward. The ability to **persevere through difficulty** is what separates those who achieve their dreams from those who abandon them.

One practical way to develop perseverance is to **focus on your long-term goals** rather than immediate setbacks. Galileo's vision extended far beyond the confines of his time—he wasn't deterred by short-term obstacles because he knew his discoveries would impact future generations. Similarly, keep your eye on the bigger picture, and remind yourself that the path to success is often filled with challenges, but those who persist are the ones who ultimately succeed.

3. See Beyond the Surface—Great Insight Comes from Looking Deeper into the Details

Galileo's greatest discoveries came not from accepting things at face value but from looking **beyond the surface**. With his telescope, he saw craters on the moon where others saw a perfect sphere; he saw moons orbiting Jupiter, shattering the belief that all celestial bodies orbited the Earth. Galileo's ability to observe and analyze what others overlooked led to insights that would change the course of science forever.

The lesson here is that **true insight often comes from looking deeper** than others are willing to go. Whether in science, business, or personal life, the ability to **see beyond the obvious** allows you to uncover hidden opportunities, solve complex problems, and make discoveries that others miss. Galileo's curiosity and attention to detail show us that **great insight requires deep observation and analysis**.

For practical application, consider how you approach problems or challenges in your life. Ask yourself: **Am I looking deeply enough into the details, or am I accepting things at face value?** Take the time to examine situations more closely, look for patterns that others might miss, and question whether there's more to the story than what's immediately apparent. By doing so, you'll develop a deeper understanding and be better equipped to make breakthroughs, just as Galileo did with his observations of the cosmos.

One way to cultivate this skill is to practice **mindful observation**. Whether you're analyzing data at work, solving a personal challenge, or even observing the world around you, train yourself to look deeper. Ask more questions, seek out hidden connections, and be willing to see things differently than those around you. The more you practice, the more likely you are to discover insights that lead to meaningful change.

Isaac Newton

Isaac Newton is one of the most monumental figures in the history of science. His contributions were nothing short of world-changing. From the invention of **calculus** to his groundbreaking laws of **motion and gravitation**, Newton didn't just observe the world—he redefined it. His work laid the foundation for modern physics, shaping everything from how we build bridges to how we launch rockets into space. But what makes Newton's legacy particularly remarkable isn't just his genius; it's his **unmatched focus, relentless discipline**, and **uncompromising pursuit of truth** that turned him into a towering intellectual force.

Newton's story teaches us that while genius is valuable, it's **persistence** and **deep focus** that bring extraordinary results. Often working in isolation, Newton's ability to immerse himself in problems and his refusal to accept anything less than absolute precision set him apart. His discoveries didn't happen overnight; they came from years of sustained, disciplined work, often in the face of personal and professional challenges.

In this chapter, we will explore the life of Isaac Newton, drawing powerful lessons from his journey—lessons that we can apply to our own lives, regardless of the challenges or ambitions we face. Whether you're striving to solve complex problems, build a lasting legacy, or simply improve yourself, Newton's life provides the **ultimate roadmap for discipline, intellectual mastery**, and an **unwavering commitment to personal growth**.

Autobiography

Isaac Newton was born on **January 4, 1643**, in **Woolsthorpe, England**. His early life was marked by hardship. His father died before he was born, and he was raised by his grandmother after his mother remarried and left him behind. This early period of abandonment and isolation would shape Newton's introverted and fiercely independent character. While he excelled academically from a young age, Newton was not a natural leader or socialite. Instead, he found solace in books and learning.

At the age of 18, Newton entered **Trinity College, Cambridge**, where his interest in mathematics and natural philosophy flourished. It was during these early years that he first encountered the works of **Galileo, Kepler,** and **Descartes**. These thinkers inspired him to delve deeper into the mysteries of mathematics, physics, and astronomy. However, Newton's education was interrupted by the **Great Plague of London** in 1665, which forced him to return home.

This two-year period away from formal education became one of the most productive in Newton's life. In isolation at **Woolsthorpe Manor**, he developed the foundational ideas for what would later become his **three laws of motion** and the **law of universal gravitation**. It was during this time that, according to legend, Newton observed an apple falling from a tree, which inspired him to think about the forces that govern the motion of objects on Earth and in the heavens. Though the story of the apple has been romanticized, the essence of his discovery remains: Newton realized that the same force pulling the apple to the ground also governed the motion of the planets.

In **1667**, Newton returned to Cambridge, where his work in mathematics and physics continued to evolve. In **1669**, at the age of just 27, he was appointed the **Lucasian Professor of Mathematics**, one of the most prestigious academic positions in the world. Over the next several years, Newton developed his **theory of calculus**, explored the nature of **light and optics**, and continued refining his ideas about gravity and motion.

In **1687**, Newton published his magnum opus, *Philosophiæ Naturalis Principia Mathematica*, commonly known as the *Principia*. This work laid out his laws of motion and his theory of universal gravitation, providing a mathematical framework that explained both celestial and terrestrial motion. The *Principia* is widely regarded as one of the most important scientific works ever written, and it cemented Newton's place as one of the greatest scientists in history.

But Newton's life wasn't without its struggles. He often clashed with other scientists, most notably **Robert Hooke** and **Gottfried Wilhelm Leibniz**, with whom he had a bitter dispute over the invention of calculus. Newton could be deeply competitive and secretive, traits that both helped and hindered him throughout his career. His intense focus sometimes led him to periods of deep isolation, during which he would work relentlessly on his projects, often forgetting to eat or sleep.

Newton's later years were marked by his move away from academia. In **1696**, he was appointed Warden of the **Royal Mint**, a role that involved overseeing the nation's currency. He took this position extremely seriously, leading a crusade against counterfeiters, some of whom were executed for their crimes. Newton's precision and discipline in his work at the Mint mirrored the exacting standards he had applied to his scientific pursuits.

Newton died in **1727**, leaving behind a legacy that reshaped science and our understanding of the universe. His contributions continue to influence modern physics, mathematics, and engineering to this day. But perhaps more important than his individual discoveries was his approach to life—his relentless **focus**, his **discipline**, and his **uncompromising pursuit of truth**, which made him one of the greatest minds in history.

Lessons and Applications

Isaac Newton's life offers timeless lessons in **focus, discipline,** and the relentless pursuit of **intellectual and personal mastery**. His ability to immerse himself in complex problems, his tireless work ethic, and his refusal to accept easy answers provide powerful insights for anyone striving to achieve greatness in their own life. Let's explore three key lessons from Newton's journey and how they can be applied to your own life.

1. Master the Art of Focus—True Greatness Comes from Deep Work and Total Immersion

Isaac Newton's most impressive quality was his **unmatched ability to focus**. Whether it was during his two years of self-imposed isolation at Woolsthorpe Manor or his intense periods of work on the *Principia*, Newton's ability to immerse himself fully in his work allowed him to make groundbreaking discoveries. He wasn't distracted by the noise of the outside world or by the pursuit of fame. Instead, he dedicated himself fully to solving the problems he was most passionate about, often losing himself in his work for days or weeks at a time.

The lesson here is that **true greatness requires deep focus**. In today's world, where distractions are endless, it's easy to be pulled in multiple directions, but to achieve anything truly significant, you need to cultivate the ability to immerse yourself in the task at hand. Whether you're working on a major project, learning a new skill, or solving a complex problem, **shallow work** will only take you so far. **Deep work**—the kind of focused, uninterrupted effort that Newton excelled at—leads to breakthroughs.

For practical application, think about how often you allow distractions to pull you away from your goals. Ask yourself: **Am I giving my full attention to the things that matter most?** Whether you're trying to build a business, achieve a fitness goal, or advance your career, carve out time for **uninterrupted, deep work**. Eliminate distractions, set clear goals for each work session, and commit to focusing solely on the task at hand.

One way to develop this skill is to **schedule blocks of time** where you focus entirely on your most important tasks. Set clear boundaries—turn off your phone, close unnecessary tabs on your computer, and let others know that you're unavailable. By consistently practicing deep work, you'll develop the focus necessary to achieve extraordinary results, just as Newton did.

2. Discipline is the Foundation of Mastery—Success Comes from Consistent Effort Over Time

Newton's success wasn't just a product of his genius; it was the result of **discipline and relentless effort**. He worked tirelessly on his theories, often spending years refining his ideas before sharing them with the world. Whether he was developing the theory of gravitation, studying optics, or inventing calculus, Newton's approach was marked by his ability to consistently **apply himself to the problem**. He didn't shy away from the difficult work required to solve complex problems—he embraced it.

The lesson here is that **discipline is the foundation of mastery**. Genius, talent, and inspiration can only take you so far. To truly excel, you need the discipline to show up every day and put in the work, even when it's difficult or frustrating. Newton's ability to maintain a disciplined approach to his work, day in and day out, is what enabled him to make the monumental discoveries for which he is remembered.

For practical application, reflect on your current level of discipline. Ask yourself: **Am I consistently putting in the effort required to achieve my goals?** Whether it's in your fitness routine, your career, or your personal life, success doesn't come from occasional bursts of motivation—it comes from **consistent, sustained effort** over time. Newton didn't become the father of modern physics overnight; he did it through decades of focused, disciplined work.

One way to build discipline is to **develop a daily routine** that aligns with your goals. Set clear, specific goals for what you want to achieve each day, and commit to working on them, regardless of how you feel. Over time, this consistency will compound, leading to significant progress. As Newton himself said, "If I have ever made any valuable discoveries, it has been owing more to patient attention than to any other talent."

3. Pursue the Truth Relentlessly—Be Uncompromising in Your Search for Knowledge and Clarity

Newton's life was defined by his **uncompromising pursuit of truth**. He wasn't satisfied with vague or incomplete answers—he wanted to understand the world with absolute clarity. Whether it was his work on motion, gravity, or optics, Newton's commitment to **intellectual rigor** and **precision** set him apart. He didn't accept easy explanations or stop when things got difficult; he pushed himself to uncover the deepest truths about the universe.

The lesson here is that **the pursuit of truth requires relentless dedication**. In your own life, whether you're seeking to solve a problem, achieve a personal goal, or understand yourself better, be **uncompromising in your search for clarity and knowledge**. Don't settle for surface-level understanding or half-truths—dig deeper, ask tougher questions, and be willing to put in the effort required to find the truth.

For practical application, consider how committed you are to truly understanding the challenges you face. Ask yourself: **Am I pursuing the truth with the same dedication that Newton did, or am I settling for incomplete answers?** Whether in your career, relationships, or personal growth, the more you push yourself to understand the deeper truths, the better equipped you'll be to make meaningful progress.

One practical way to apply this is to **cultivate a habit of critical thinking**. Don't take things at face value—whether it's information, advice, or even your own assumptions. Question everything, seek evidence, and be willing to challenge your own beliefs. By pursuing the truth with rigor and dedication, you'll gain a clearer understanding of the world and make better decisions in every aspect of your life.

Gregor Mendel

While names like **Darwin** and **Newton** may conjure images of groundbreaking discoveries that immediately shifted the trajectory of science, **Gregor Mendel** is a figure who worked largely in obscurity, his monumental contributions going unrecognized until after his death. But Mendel's work would forever alter the way we understand **genetics**, inheritance, and biological diversity. In a small monastery garden, this quiet, methodical man uncovered the **fundamental principles of heredity**, earning him the title "father of modern genetics."

Mendel's story teaches us that you don't need to be in the spotlight to make a lasting impact. His life is a testament to the power of **patience, meticulous observation**, and **unwavering curiosity**. Mendel wasn't driven by a desire for fame or recognition. Instead, he was motivated by a deep-seated passion for knowledge and a relentless pursuit of answers to the mysteries of life. Mendel's greatness lies not just in his discoveries, but in his willingness to work quietly and persistently, even when no one seemed to notice.

In this chapter, we will explore the life of Gregor Mendel, diving deep into the lessons his story offers us. Whether you're working behind the scenes, developing your own skills, or striving to make an impact without immediate recognition, Mendel's journey will show you the value of **patience, quiet perseverance**, and how small actions can lead to massive change in the long run.

Autobiography

Gregor Johann Mendel was born on **July 20, 1822**, in a small village called **Heinzendorf** (now in the Czech Republic), into a farming family. From an early age, Mendel showed a strong aptitude for academics, excelling in subjects like mathematics, physics, and biology. Despite his natural intelligence, Mendel's family was poor, and paying for an education was a constant struggle. Recognizing his academic talents, Mendel's family supported his decision to join the **Augustinian Abbey of St. Thomas** in **Brno**. This decision not only gave Mendel access to further education but also relieved his family of the financial burden of his schooling.

In **1843**, Mendel entered the monastery, where he took on the name **Gregor** and committed himself to both religious life and intellectual pursuits. The monastic life offered him not only spiritual solace but also the time and resources to study science. The monastery's extensive library and connection with academia provided Mendel with the tools to dive deep into his curiosity about the natural world, particularly in the areas of **botany and mathematics**.

During his time as a friar, Mendel studied at the **University of Vienna** from **1851 to 1853**, where he was introduced to advanced concepts in mathematics, statistics, and biology. This education equipped him with the knowledge and methodologies that would later help him in his famous experiments. Mendel's academic background was not that of a traditional scientist, but his interdisciplinary approach—a combination of religious life, mathematics, and science—gave him a unique perspective on the problems he would later tackle.

Upon his return to the monastery, Mendel began the work that would secure his place in history. Over a period of **eight years** (from 1856 to 1863), Mendel meticulously bred **pea plants** in the monastery garden. He observed and recorded how certain traits—such as flower color, seed shape, and pod texture—were passed down from one generation to the next. Through careful crossbreeding and statistical analysis, Mendel identified patterns of inheritance that contradicted the prevailing theories of the time.

His experiments led to the formulation of what are now known as **Mendel's Laws of Inheritance**: the **Law of Segregation** and the **Law of Independent Assortment**. These laws explained how traits are inherited in predictable ways, revolutionizing our understanding of genetics and heredity.

Mendel presented his findings in **1865** to the **Natural History Society of Brno**, but his work received little attention. The scientific community of the time was not ready to accept Mendel's ideas, and his groundbreaking discoveries went largely unnoticed for decades. Undeterred, Mendel continued his work, eventually becoming the **abbot** of his monastery, a position that demanded much of his time and forced him to put his scientific research on hold.

It wasn't until **1900**, 16 years after Mendel's death, that his work was rediscovered by three independent scientists—**Hugo de Vries**, **Carl Correns**, and **Erich von Tschermak**—who confirmed the accuracy of his findings. Mendel's work laid the foundation for the field of genetics, influencing everything from **modern biology** to **medicine** and **agriculture**.

Mendel died in **1884**, largely unaware of the profound impact his experiments would have on science. Though he worked in relative obscurity for most of his life, his patience, discipline, and curiosity have since earned him a place among the greatest scientific minds in history.

Lessons and Applications

Gregor Mendel's life offers powerful lessons in **patience**, **methodical work**, and **the importance of pursuing your passion even when the world isn't watching**. His dedication to his experiments, despite a lack of recognition during his lifetime, provides valuable insights for anyone striving to make a difference in their own life or field of work. Let's explore three key lessons from Mendel's journey and how they can be applied to your own life.

1. Patience is a Superpower—Great Results Take Time and Quiet Persistence

Mendel's experiments with pea plants took **eight long years** of meticulous work. He didn't rush his conclusions or seek immediate gratification. Instead, he approached his research with **patience**, allowing time for careful observation, experimentation, and analysis. While many people would have given up after a few months of slow progress, Mendel understood that **true breakthroughs take time** and require persistent effort over the long haul.

The key lesson here is that **patience is a superpower** in any endeavor. In a world that demands instant results and quick fixes, Mendel's life reminds us that the most impactful achievements are often the result of **consistent, patient work**. Whether you're trying to build a business, develop a new skill, or achieve a personal goal, patience is the virtue that will allow you to **outlast setbacks and disappointments**.

For practical application, ask yourself: **Am I being patient with my own progress? Am I willing to commit to long-term effort without immediate results?** Whether you're pursuing a professional or personal ambition, recognize that **slow progress is still progress**. Like Mendel, stay committed to your goals, even when they seem far off. Patience will enable you to build something enduring and meaningful.

One way to cultivate patience is to **focus on small, consistent actions** rather than large, immediate outcomes. Mendel didn't change the world in a single day—he changed it through thousands of small, repeated experiments over many years. By breaking down your goals into smaller, manageable tasks, and focusing on daily or weekly progress, you'll find it easier to stay patient and maintain momentum.

2. Pursue Curiosity Relentlessly—The Most Important

Discoveries Come from Asking the Right Questions

Mendel's success as a scientist came not from simply following established knowledge, but from his **relentless curiosity**. He wanted to know why and how traits were passed from one generation to the next, and he didn't stop until he found answers. This curiosity drove him to conduct experiments that were far ahead of his time, and even though no one seemed to care about his findings during his lifetime, he continued to push forward because he was passionate about the questions he was asking.

The lesson here is that **curiosity is the engine of discovery**. Whether in science, business, or personal development, the ability to **ask the right questions** and seek answers is what leads to breakthroughs. Mendel didn't let the opinions of others dictate his path—he followed his curiosity, even when it led him down roads that others weren't exploring.

For practical application, reflect on your own sense of curiosity. Ask yourself: **Am I asking the right questions? Am I exploring my interests with genuine curiosity, or am I limiting myself to what's already known?** The more you cultivate curiosity, the more likely you are to make discoveries or find solutions that others may overlook. Don't be afraid to ask unconventional questions or dive deep into topics that intrigue you. Curiosity is what drives growth and innovation.

One way to cultivate curiosity is to **challenge assumptions**. Look at the world around you—your work, your relationships, your habits—and ask, **Why is this the way it is? Could it be different?** By constantly questioning and exploring, you'll discover new insights and opportunities for improvement, just as Mendel did with his pea plants.

3. Impact Doesn't Require Immediate Recognition—Work Quietly, and Let Your Results

Speak for Themselves

Perhaps the most powerful lesson from Mendel's life is that **impact doesn't require immediate recognition**. Mendel's work went largely unnoticed for decades, and he never saw the full impact of his discoveries during his lifetime. Yet, today, his contributions to science are universally acknowledged. Mendel teaches us that it's possible to make a profound impact, even if the world isn't watching or acknowledging your efforts right away.

The lesson here is that **you don't need validation to make a difference**. If you believe in the value of what you're doing, keep pushing forward, even when recognition feels distant. **True impact** often takes time to manifest, and it may take years—or even decades—for your work to be fully appreciated. But that doesn't mean it's not worth doing. Mendel's story reminds us that it's not about being in the spotlight—it's about doing the work, quietly and diligently, knowing that it will make a difference in the long run.

For practical application, ask yourself: **Am I driven by a need for immediate recognition, or am I willing to do the work even if no one is watching?** Whether you're building a career, developing a project, or pursuing a personal goal, remember that **recognition is often delayed**. Focus on doing the best work you can, trusting that the results will speak for themselves over time.

One way to stay motivated without immediate recognition is to **set internal benchmarks for success**. Instead of relying on external validation, find satisfaction in the progress you're making and the knowledge that you're moving closer to your goals. By developing this internal compass, you'll be less dependent on the opinions of others and more focused on the value of your own efforts.

Rachel Carson

Imagine standing against powerful industries, entrenched governments, and widespread public complacency, all while carrying the weight of your own personal battles. This is exactly what **Rachel Carson** did in the 1960s when she wrote *Silent Spring*, a book that sparked the modern environmental movement. With **courage, vision**, and an unshakable commitment to truth, Carson exposed the dangers of unchecked pesticide use, particularly **DDT**, to both the environment and human health. She wasn't a politician, a wealthy industrialist, or a celebrity—she was a marine biologist and a writer. Yet, through her passion for science and love for the natural world, she changed the course of environmental policy and public awareness forever.

Rachel Carson's journey is a lesson in **persistence, conviction**, and **leadership**. She teaches us that even when the odds seem overwhelmingly against you, even when powerful interests are determined to silence your voice, it's possible to stand firm in your truth and make a lasting impact. Carson was not just a scientist—she was a **visionary**, someone who looked at the bigger picture and saw the consequences of human actions on the environment long before most people even considered it a concern. Her work reminds us of the power of one individual's voice and the profound impact it can have when backed by integrity and purpose.

In this chapter, we'll explore the life of Rachel Carson, diving into the key lessons she offers on **courage, truth**, and **persistence**. Her legacy isn't just for environmentalists—it's for anyone who wants to create meaningful change, pursue their passions, and stand firm in their values even in the face of overwhelming adversity.

Autobiography

Rachel Louise Carson was born on **May 27, 1907**, in **Springdale, Pennsylvania**, into a modest farming family. From a young age, Carson had a deep love for nature and spent much of her childhood exploring the woods and streams near her home. This early exposure to the natural world would become the foundation for her life's work.

Carson excelled academically and went on to study at **Pennsylvania College for Women** (now Chatham University), where she initially pursued a degree in English with dreams of becoming a writer. However, a required biology course reignited her passion for science, and she switched her major to biology. After graduating in 1929, Carson earned a master's degree in **zoology** from **Johns Hopkins University** in 1932, a remarkable achievement at a time when few women pursued advanced degrees in science.

Despite her academic qualifications, Carson struggled to find work as a scientist due to the **gender biases** of the era. Eventually, she landed a job with the **U.S. Bureau of Fisheries** (later the **U.S. Fish and Wildlife Service**), where she wrote radio scripts and educational materials about marine life. It was during this time that Carson honed her ability to communicate complex scientific ideas in a way that was accessible and engaging to the public—a skill that would later define her career.

Carson's first major literary success came in **1941** with the publication of *Under the Sea-Wind*, a beautifully written exploration of marine life. This was followed by *The Sea Around Us* (1951) and *The Edge of the Sea* (1955), both of which became bestsellers. Her lyrical prose and deep understanding of the natural world captivated readers, making her one of the most respected nature writers of her time.

However, it was her fourth and most controversial book, *Silent Spring*, published in **1962**, that would secure her place in history.

Carson had become increasingly alarmed by the widespread use of **synthetic pesticides**, particularly **DDT**, in agriculture and pest control. She saw firsthand the devastating effects these chemicals were having on wildlife, especially birds, and the potential dangers to human health. *Silent Spring* documented these dangers in painstaking detail, backed by meticulous research, and called for a reevaluation of humanity's relationship with nature.

The publication of *Silent Spring* was met with fierce opposition from the chemical industry, government agencies, and even some members of the scientific community. Carson was vilified, accused of being an alarmist, and faced intense personal attacks on her character and scientific credibility. Despite this, she stood her ground, continuing to advocate for the regulation of harmful chemicals and the protection of the environment.

Tragically, Carson's battle against cancer, which had been ongoing during the writing of *Silent Spring*, took her life on **April 14, 1964**, less than two years after the book's publication. However, her work lived on, and the public outcry following *Silent Spring* led to the eventual ban of DDT in the United States and the creation of the **Environmental Protection Agency** (EPA) in **1970**.

Rachel Carson's legacy is one of **courage**, **truth**, and **passion**. She fought not just for the environment, but for the very principles of **responsible science**, and she showed that even in the face of immense opposition, one person can make a profound difference.

Lessons and Applications

Rachel Carson's life and work offer powerful lessons in **courage**, **vision**, and the **relentless pursuit of truth**. Her ability to stand firm in her convictions, her perseverance in the face of adversity, and her commitment to protecting what she loved provide valuable insights for anyone striving to make a difference in the world. Let's explore three key lessons from Carson's journey and how they can be applied to your own life.

1. Have the Courage to Speak the Truth—Even When It's Unpopular

One of the most striking aspects of Rachel Carson's life was her **unwavering courage** in speaking the truth, even when it was deeply unpopular and dangerous to do so. When she published *Silent Spring*, Carson knew she would face significant backlash. The chemical industry was incredibly powerful, and many government agencies were invested in the continued use of pesticides like DDT. Despite this, Carson chose to speak out because she believed in the **importance of truth** and the necessity of protecting both the environment and public health.

The lesson here is that **courage is essential to making meaningful change**. Whether in your career, personal life, or any area where you want to have an impact, there will be times when speaking the truth is difficult or uncomfortable. But if you truly believe in something, if you see a wrong that needs to be righted, you must find the courage to stand up and speak out—even when it's unpopular or even when it feels like the whole world is against you.

For practical application, reflect on where you need more courage in your life. Ask yourself: **Am I avoiding speaking the truth because I'm afraid of the consequences?** Whether it's in your workplace, your personal relationships, or your community, there will be times when you need to **stand up for what's right**, even if it comes with risks. Carson teaches us that the cost of staying silent is far greater than the cost of speaking out.

One way to develop this courage is to **start small**. Begin by standing firm in smaller situations where you need to assert the truth, and gradually build up to bigger challenges. Over time, as you gain confidence in your ability to speak the truth, you'll find it easier to tackle the larger, more intimidating issues in your life.

2. Vision is Everything—Look Beyond the Immediate to See the Bigger Picture

Carson's greatness lay not only in her courage but also in her **vision**. She didn't just see the immediate effects of pesticide use—she understood the **long-term consequences** for ecosystems, wildlife, and human health. She had the foresight to recognize that unchecked industrial practices would lead to widespread environmental destruction, and she used her scientific knowledge and writing skills to paint a compelling picture of what that future could look like.

The lesson here is that **vision is essential for leadership and change**. It's easy to get caught up in the day-to-day tasks and challenges of life, but if you want to make a lasting impact, you need to be able to see the **bigger picture**—to understand how today's actions will shape the future. Carson's ability to step back and look at the broader consequences of pesticide use allowed her to make a case that resonated with millions of people and sparked real change.

For practical application, ask yourself: **Am I only focusing on the short-term, or am I considering the bigger picture?** Whether you're working on a project, making decisions about your career, or navigating personal challenges, take the time to consider the **long-term impact** of your choices. Vision requires you to step outside of the immediate concerns and see how your actions will ripple outward into the future.

One way to develop your vision is to **regularly reflect on your long-term goals** and values. What kind of life do you want to build? What kind of impact do you want to have on the world? By keeping these bigger questions in mind, you'll be better able to navigate short-term challenges and make decisions that align with your overall vision.

3. Persistence Pays Off—Change Takes Time, But the Results are Worth the Fight

Rachel Carson faced immense opposition throughout her life, particularly after the publication of *Silent Spring*. The chemical industry launched an aggressive campaign to discredit her, and even some of her scientific peers were reluctant to support her findings. Yet, despite this opposition, Carson persisted. She continued to advocate for environmental protection, she stood by her research, and she fought for the public to understand the truth about pesticide use. Her persistence paid off—not immediately, but over time. *Silent Spring* became a catalyst for environmental reform, leading to the banning of DDT and the eventual creation of the EPA.

The lesson here is that **persistence is crucial to making meaningful change**. Whether you're working toward a personal goal, trying to advance in your career, or fighting for a cause you believe in, there will be obstacles along the way. You'll face opposition, setbacks, and moments of doubt. But if you truly believe in what you're doing, persistence is what will carry you through.

For practical application, consider where you're encountering resistance or setbacks in your life. Ask yourself: **Am I giving up too easily when things get tough?** Persistence doesn't mean pushing blindly forward—it means being willing to adapt, adjust your approach, and keep moving forward, even when the path isn't easy. Carson's life shows us that meaningful change takes time, and the most important battles often require the most persistence.

One way to build persistence is to **break your goals into smaller, manageable tasks** and celebrate each step of progress. By focusing on small victories along the way, you'll maintain your motivation and build the resilience needed to push through challenges. Remember, it wasn't Carson's overnight success that changed the world—it was her **years of dedication** and perseverance in the face of adversity.

Social Influencers and Icons

Mother Teresa

In a world that often celebrates power, wealth, and influence, few figures stand out for their **selflessness** and **unwavering commitment to serving others** like Mother Teresa. Born as **Anjezë Gonxhe Bojaxhiu**, this humble nun dedicated her life to helping the poorest of the poor, the abandoned, and the forgotten in the slums of **Calcutta** (now Kolkata), India. Her work was not glamorous, nor was it celebrated initially, but it transformed the lives of countless individuals, and in doing so, left a permanent mark on the world.

Mother Teresa's life is a testament to the power of **compassion** and the ability to bring about meaningful change not through grand gestures, but through small, consistent acts of kindness. She was a figure who led by example, showing that even in the most difficult circumstances, it is possible to find **purpose** and **dignity** in service to others. In a world where people often focus on their own success and ambitions, Mother Teresa reminds us of the importance of looking beyond ourselves, seeking out those who need help, and offering love without expecting anything in return.

Her legacy provides us with invaluable lessons on **compassion**, **sacrifice**, and the deep satisfaction that comes from making a difference in the lives of others. Whether you're looking to improve your relationships, find more purpose in your work, or simply become a more compassionate human being, the life of Mother Teresa offers guidance on how to do so with humility and dedication.

Autobiography

Anjezë Gonxhe Bojaxhiu, later known as Mother Teresa, was born on **August 26, 1910**, in **Skopje**, then part of the Ottoman Empire (now North Macedonia). Her family was of Albanian descent, and she was raised in a devoutly Catholic household. From a young age,

Anjezë was known for her piety, but she was also marked by an intense curiosity about the world around her and a profound sense of empathy for the suffering of others.

At the age of **18**, Anjezë left home to join the **Sisters of Loreto**, an Irish order of nuns with missions in India. She never saw her family again after that fateful decision. After training in **Dublin**, she was sent to **Calcutta**, where she spent years teaching at a convent school for girls. Though she was dedicated to her students, it was during this time that she first encountered the extreme poverty of the city's slums. She could not ignore the sight of the poor, the sick, and the destitute who lived in the streets with little hope of relief.

In **1946**, during a train journey to the Himalayan foothills for a retreat, Mother Teresa experienced what she later described as her **"call within a call."** She felt deeply that God was calling her to leave the convent and devote herself entirely to helping the poor. This was no small decision—leaving the convent meant giving up the security and structure of the religious life she had known, but Mother Teresa was undeterred. She sought and received permission from her superiors to begin this new mission, and in **1948**, she left the convent to live among the poor in the slums of Calcutta.

With no resources and little support, Mother Teresa began her work by opening a school for slum children and tending to the sick. She soon attracted followers, and in **1950**, she founded the **Missionaries of Charity**, a religious congregation dedicated to serving "the poorest of the poor." The Missionaries of Charity grew rapidly, and their work expanded from providing basic education and healthcare to operating orphanages, hospices, and leprosy clinics around the world. What started as one woman's mission to help the needy became a global movement of compassion.

Despite her growing international recognition—culminating in her receiving the **Nobel Peace Prize** in **1979**—Mother Teresa remained humble and focused on her work. She famously rejected luxury and accolades, living simply and spending her days among those she sought to help. She believed that **"small things done with great love"** were the key to making a difference, and this philosophy permeated every aspect of her work.

Mother Teresa passed away on **September 5, 1997**, but her legacy lives on through the thousands of sisters, brothers, and volunteers who continue her mission around the world. Her life serves as a powerful reminder that **one person's dedication and love for others can change the world**, no matter how humble the beginning.

Lessons and Applications

Mother Teresa's life offers profound lessons in **compassion, selflessness**, and the importance of **serving others**. Her ability to dedicate herself entirely to the care of those most in need, without seeking recognition or reward, provides powerful insights for anyone looking to lead a more meaningful and impactful life. Let's explore three key lessons from Mother Teresa's journey and how they can be applied to your own life.

1. Practice Compassion—True Impact Comes from Empathy and Connection

At the heart of Mother Teresa's life was her **compassion for others**. She saw people not as statistics or problems to be solved, but as individuals deserving of love and dignity, regardless of their circumstances. Her work wasn't about grand gestures or sweeping reforms—it was about **individual acts of kindness** that made a profound difference in the lives of those she helped. She often said, **"If you can't feed a hundred people, then feed just one,"** reminding us that we don't have to solve every problem to make an impact.

The lesson here is that **true impact begins with compassion**. In a world that often encourages us to focus on our own success, Mother Teresa teaches us the value of **empathy** and **human connection**. Whether in your personal relationships, at work, or in your community, taking the time to understand and care for the people around you can make all the difference.

For practical application, ask yourself: **Am I showing enough compassion to the people in my life?** Whether it's your colleagues, family, or even strangers, make an effort to **listen** and **empathize**. True compassion requires that you see the world from someone else's perspective and offer your support in meaningful ways. You don't have to take on monumental tasks—small acts of kindness, done consistently, are often the most powerful.

One way to build compassion is to **practice active listening**. The next time someone shares a concern or problem with you, resist the urge to offer solutions right away. Instead, listen fully to what they have to say, validate their feelings, and offer your presence. In doing so, you'll not only strengthen your relationships but also develop a deeper sense of empathy and understanding.

2. Serve Without Expecting Recognition—The Most Meaningful Work Often Goes Unseen

Mother Teresa's work was defined by her **selflessness** and her ability to serve without seeking recognition or reward. While she eventually became a world-renowned figure, she never sought fame or accolades. Instead, she focused entirely on those she served, believing that the **act of service itself** was its own reward. She was not driven by ego or the desire for approval; her mission was purely to help those in need, regardless of whether anyone noticed or praised her for it.

The lesson here is that **true fulfillment comes from serving others without expecting anything in return**. In today's world, where social media often places a premium on public recognition and praise, Mother Teresa's life reminds us that the most meaningful work often happens quietly, behind the scenes. Whether it's in your career, your family life, or your community, the value of what you do is not measured by how many people recognize your efforts but by the impact you make on the lives of others.

For practical application, reflect on your motivations. Ask yourself: **Am I serving others because I truly want to help, or am I seeking recognition?** There's nothing wrong with being appreciated for your efforts, but true service comes from a place of **selflessness**. Whether you're helping a colleague, volunteering in your community, or supporting a loved one, focus on the act of giving itself, rather than the response you receive.

One practical way to practice selfless service is to **perform random acts of kindness** without expecting anything in return. Help someone in need, offer assistance, or simply show kindness to those around you without seeking recognition or acknowledgment. By doing this, you'll cultivate a sense of fulfillment that comes from knowing you're making a difference, regardless of whether anyone else knows about it.

3. Dedication to a Higher Purpose—Find Meaning Through Service

Mother Teresa's life was centered around her **dedication to a higher purpose**. Her work was driven by her faith and her belief that she was called to serve the poorest of the poor. This sense of **purpose** gave her the strength to endure the many challenges she faced, from the physical demands of working in the slums to the emotional toll of seeing so much suffering. Her life shows us the importance of **finding meaning** in what we do, especially when that meaning is rooted in something greater than ourselves.

The lesson here is that **finding purpose through service** can lead to deep fulfillment. Mother Teresa's life reminds us that when we dedicate ourselves to something larger than our own ambitions—whether it's a cause, a community, or even the well-being of others—we tap into a source of strength and motivation that can carry us through the hardest times.

For practical application, ask yourself: **What higher purpose am I serving?** Whether in your work, personal life, or community, seek out ways to contribute to something bigger than yourself. This doesn't necessarily mean quitting your job and moving to a distant land—it could be as simple as supporting a cause you believe in, mentoring someone in need, or working to improve the lives of those around you.

One way to develop a sense of purpose is to **identify your core values** and find ways to align your actions with those values. For example, if compassion is important to you, look for ways to serve others in your daily life. If justice is a core value, seek opportunities to stand up for fairness and equality in your workplace or community. By living in alignment with your values and serving a higher purpose, you'll find greater fulfillment in everything you do.

Oprah Winfrey

Few people embody the concept of **personal transformation** and **self-made success** quite like **Oprah Winfrey**. Rising from extreme poverty, abuse, and adversity, Oprah did not just survive—she thrived. Her journey from a troubled childhood to becoming one of the world's most influential media moguls is a story of **resilience, vision**, and the **unshakable belief** that you have the power to shape your own future. Oprah's life is a masterclass in overcoming obstacles and creating opportunities where none seemed to exist.

But Oprah's success isn't just about the billions of dollars she's earned, or the media empire she's built—it's about her ability to **own her story**, embrace vulnerability, and use her platform to empower others. Oprah taught us that **your past does not define your future**. She showed the world the power of **authenticity** and the importance of living in alignment with your purpose. Through her own experiences, she crafted a new narrative for millions of people: one of **self-worth, inner strength**, and **personal freedom**.

In this chapter, we will explore Oprah's extraordinary life, distill the lessons she offers, and see how you can apply these insights to your own journey. Whether you're seeking success in business, striving to overcome personal struggles, or simply looking for deeper meaning in your life, Oprah's story holds invaluable lessons in **resilience, self-empowerment**, and the courage to shape your destiny.

Autobiography

Oprah Gail Winfrey was born on **January 29, 1954**, in **Kosciusko, Mississippi**. Her early life was marked by poverty and instability. Oprah was raised primarily by her grandmother in rural Mississippi during her early years, and it was here, in a modest farmhouse with no running water, that she developed her love for storytelling and public speaking. Even as a child, Oprah was known for her charismatic personality, often reciting Bible verses in church and captivating audiences with her natural presence.

However, Oprah's childhood was far from idyllic. At the age of six, she moved to **Milwaukee, Wisconsin**, to live with her mother, Vernita Lee. It was during this time that Oprah endured horrific abuse, both sexual and physical, at the hands of family members and friends. These traumatic experiences left deep scars, and by the age of 14, Oprah had run away from home. Her early teenage years were filled with pain, confusion, and a search for stability.

Things took a positive turn when Oprah was sent to live with her father, **Vernon Winfrey**, in **Nashville, Tennessee**. Vernon was a strict but supportive figure in Oprah's life, providing the discipline and encouragement she needed to excel academically. Under his guidance, Oprah began to flourish. She became an honors student, earned a full scholarship to **Tennessee State University**, and began working at a local radio station, which kick-started her career in broadcasting.

In **1976**, Oprah moved to **Baltimore**, where she co-anchored the evening news. However, it was her transition to hosting **talk shows** that would change her life. Her genuine curiosity, ability to connect with people on a personal level, and candid interview style made her a natural for television. In **1983**, she was offered the opportunity to host a morning show in **Chicago**, which was later rebranded as *The Oprah Winfrey Show*. The show went national in **1986**, and within a few short years, Oprah became a household name.

The Oprah Winfrey Show revolutionized daytime television. Rather than focusing solely on celebrity gossip or sensationalism, Oprah's show tackled deep, often emotional issues, ranging from **mental health** to **personal development**, **spirituality**, and

relationships. Oprah's transparency about her own struggles, including her weight, her history of abuse, and her quest for self-improvement, resonated deeply with millions of viewers.

But Oprah wasn't content to just host a talk show—she wanted to create something bigger. In **1986**, she founded **Harpo Productions**, her own production company, becoming one of the first women in Hollywood to own her content. Over the years, Oprah built an empire that includes television, film, magazines, and even her own television network, **OWN (Oprah Winfrey Network)**.

Her influence extends far beyond entertainment. Oprah is a **philanthropist**, having donated hundreds of millions of dollars to education, disaster relief, and social causes. She established the **Oprah Winfrey Leadership Academy for Girls** in South Africa, providing educational opportunities to young women from disadvantaged backgrounds. Her book club, magazine, and spiritual teachings have helped millions of people transform their lives.

Oprah's life is a journey of **self-discovery**, **perseverance**, and **transformation**. From the pain of her childhood to her reign as a media queen, Oprah has used her voice to **uplift others**, inspire action, and remind us all that we hold the power to create the lives we desire.

Lessons and Applications

Oprah Winfrey's life provides profound lessons in **resilience**, **self-empowerment**, and **the courage to own your story**. Her ability to rise from unimaginable hardship to build an empire of compassion and personal growth offers valuable insights for anyone striving to achieve their own version of success. Let's explore three key lessons from Oprah's journey and how they can be applied to your life.

1. Own Your Story—Your Past Does Not Define Your Future

One of Oprah's most powerful lessons is her willingness to **own her story**. She never shied away from discussing her difficult past—her experiences of abuse, poverty, and trauma. But rather than letting these experiences define her negatively, she used them as a source of strength and inspiration. By being vulnerable and sharing her journey openly, Oprah empowered others to confront their own struggles and to see their past as a stepping stone, not a stumbling block.

The lesson here is that **your past does not dictate your future**. Everyone has faced hardships, but it's how you choose to respond to those challenges that shapes your destiny. Oprah teaches us that the key to empowerment is owning your story—acknowledging the pain, learning from it, and moving forward with a sense of purpose.

For practical application, ask yourself: **Am I letting my past hold me back?** Whether you've experienced failure, trauma, or setbacks, recognize that those experiences do not define who you are today. Take time to reflect on your story and how you can **reframe it** to serve you, rather than limit you. Oprah's life shows that by owning your story and sharing it with authenticity, you can turn even the darkest moments into sources of strength.

One way to apply this is to **embrace vulnerability**. Start by being honest with yourself about your past and the challenges you've faced. Then, take small steps to share your story with others—whether with friends, family, or even in professional settings. By embracing vulnerability, you'll find that your story can inspire and uplift others, just as Oprah's did.

2. Resilience is Key—Overcome Adversity and Keep Moving Forward

Oprah's life is a testament to **resilience**. She faced unimaginable hardships growing up—abuse, poverty, and instability—but she never gave up. Even when faced with professional setbacks, such as being fired from her first television anchor job, Oprah used every obstacle as an opportunity to grow. Rather than seeing adversity as a reason to quit, she saw it as a challenge to be overcome, a mindset that allowed her to continue striving for success even when the odds were stacked against her.

The lesson here is that **resilience is essential to achieving long-term success**. Life will throw obstacles in your path—sometimes big ones—but it's your ability to **keep moving forward** that will determine your outcome. Oprah's story teaches us that setbacks are not permanent; they're simply part of the journey.

For practical application, consider the challenges you're currently facing. Ask yourself: **Am I letting setbacks stop me, or am I using them as opportunities to grow?** Whether you're dealing with personal struggles, professional challenges, or failures, remember that resilience isn't about never facing difficulty—it's about your ability to rise each time you fall. Oprah's life shows that success comes not from avoiding failure, but from **bouncing back stronger** each time.

One way to build resilience is to **reframe your setbacks**. Instead of seeing failure as the end of the road, look at it as feedback—a way to learn what doesn't work and to improve. Oprah faced many setbacks throughout her career, but by staying committed to her vision and adapting along the way, she turned those setbacks into stepping stones toward success.

3. Find and Follow Your Purpose—Success Comes from Alignment with Your True Self

Oprah's career wasn't just built on talent or ambition—it was built on her deep **alignment with her purpose**. From the beginning, Oprah's success was rooted in her ability to **connect** with people on a personal level. She didn't just want to entertain—she wanted to **uplift, inspire**, and **help people transform their lives**. Every decision she made, from starting her talk show to building her media empire, was driven by this core purpose. And it's this sense of purpose that allowed Oprah to build such a lasting and impactful legacy.

The lesson here is that **true success comes from finding and following your purpose**. It's not enough to chase money, fame, or external validation—lasting fulfillment comes from living in alignment with your **true self** and doing work that feels meaningful to you. Oprah's life shows us that when you connect with your purpose, everything else—success, wealth, recognition—will follow.

For practical application, take a moment to reflect on your own sense of purpose. Ask yourself: **Am I living in alignment with my true self, or am I chasing someone else's definition of success?** Whether you're building a career, starting a new project, or navigating personal growth, the key to long-term fulfillment is finding work and goals that resonate with who you truly are.

One way to align with your purpose is to **explore your passions** and **values**. What activities or causes make you feel alive? What issues do you care about deeply? By aligning your goals with your passions and values, you'll find that your work becomes more meaningful and your success more fulfilling. Like Oprah, when you lead from a place of authenticity, you unlock your true potential.

Malala Yousafzai

In a world filled with powerful and influential figures, few stand out for their courage and resilience quite like **Malala Yousafzai**. Shot in the head by the Taliban at the age of 15 for simply advocating for girls' education, Malala's incredible journey from a rural village in Pakistan to becoming the youngest-ever **Nobel Prize laureate** is nothing short of inspiring. Her story is one of **unwavering determination, bravery**, and a commitment to a cause that transcends her own personal safety.

What sets Malala apart is not just the attack she survived, but how she responded to it. Many people would have retreated, but she chose to fight back—not with violence, but with **her voice**. Through her advocacy, Malala has raised global awareness about the importance of **education**, particularly for girls, and has become a symbol of hope and empowerment for millions of people worldwide. Her life is a testament to the fact that **one person, armed with nothing but their voice and conviction**, can change the world.

Malala's story is about **courage in the face of fear**, but it's also about understanding the power of **education** as a tool for personal and societal transformation. In this chapter, we will explore Malala's extraordinary journey, drawing lessons from her resilience, her commitment to education, and how she has used her platform to advocate for change. These lessons are not just for those interested in activism—they are universal principles that can guide anyone seeking to overcome adversity, find their purpose, and stand up for what they believe in.

Autobiography

Malala Yousafzai was born on **July 12, 1997**, in the Swat District of northwest Pakistan. Raised in the small town of **Mingora**, Malala grew up in a region that, for much of her early life, was relatively peaceful. Her father, **Ziauddin Yousafzai**, was an educator and the owner of a local school. He was deeply committed to education and gender equality, and he encouraged Malala to pursue her studies from a young age. It was Ziauddin's belief in the power of education that instilled in Malala the passion for learning and the drive to ensure that other girls in her community had the same opportunities she did.

However, the peace in Swat did not last. In **2007**, the **Taliban** began to take control of the region, enforcing a harsh interpretation of **Sharia law**. Among their many oppressive policies, they banned girls from attending school, a direct attack on Malala's dreams and those of many other young women. Despite the growing danger, Malala, with the encouragement of her father, began to speak out publicly against the Taliban's restrictions. She was only 11 years old when she started writing a **BBC blog** under a pseudonym, chronicling life under Taliban rule and her struggle to continue her education.

As her public profile grew, so did the risks. The Taliban issued threats against her and her family, but Malala remained undeterred. In **2012**, as she was returning home from school, a Taliban gunman boarded her school bus and shot her in the head. The attack was meant to silence her forever, but instead, it had the opposite effect. Malala survived the attack, though she was critically injured, and was flown to the **United Kingdom** for medical treatment.

The attack on Malala sent shockwaves around the world, and her story gained international attention. Following her recovery, Malala became a global advocate for **girls' education**. She co-authored the memoir *I Am Malala*, which details her journey, and in **2014**, at the age of 17, she became the **youngest recipient of the Nobel Peace Prize**. Rather than let the attack define her, Malala used it as fuel to amplify her voice, founding the **Malala Fund**, an organization dedicated to ensuring that every girl has access to 12 years of free, safe, and quality education.

Despite her global fame, Malala remains grounded, continuing her own education while advocating for others. She attended **Oxford University**, graduating with a degree in **Philosophy, Politics, and Economics**. Today, she continues to fight for the rights of girls worldwide, using her platform to raise awareness about issues ranging from education to gender equality and human rights.

Malala Yousafzai's story is one of incredible resilience and a reminder that even in the face of extreme violence and oppression, **the human spirit**—when fueled by purpose—can triumph. Her life offers lessons in **courage, determination**, and the **transformative power of education**.

Lessons and Applications

Malala Yousafzai's journey offers profound lessons for anyone striving to overcome adversity, find their voice, and make a difference in the world. Her resilience, her belief in the power of education, and her commitment to standing up for what is right provide valuable insights that can be applied to your own life. Let's explore three key lessons from Malala's story and how they can be put into practice.

1. Stand Up for What You Believe In—Courage in the Face of Fear

Malala's life is a testament to **courage in the face of overwhelming fear**. Despite living under the constant threat of violence from the Taliban, she refused to back down from her belief that **every girl deserves the right to education**. When many others chose to remain silent, Malala chose to speak up, knowing full well the potential consequences. Her bravery in the face of such danger shows that true courage isn't the absence of fear, but the decision to act despite it.

The lesson here is that **standing up for what you believe in**—whether in the workplace, your personal life, or within your community—requires courage. It's easy to stay silent, to avoid conflict, and to accept the status quo, but real change only happens when someone is willing to speak out. Malala's story teaches us that even when the stakes are high, standing up for your values and beliefs is worth the risk.

For practical application, reflect on the areas of your life where you might be staying silent out of fear. Ask yourself: **Am I avoiding speaking up because I'm afraid of the consequences?** Whether it's advocating for yourself at work, standing up for a cause you believe in, or confronting injustice in your community, now is the time to find your voice. The world needs more people willing to **speak up for what is right**, and by doing so, you can inspire others to do the same.

One way to build this courage is to **start small**. You don't have to take on a massive cause immediately—begin by speaking up in smaller situations. Over time, as you build confidence in your voice, you'll find it easier to tackle larger challenges. Remember, courage is a muscle that grows stronger the more you use it.

2. Education is Power—Invest in Learning, No Matter the Obstacles

Malala's unwavering commitment to education is central to her story. She risked her life to ensure that girls in her community, and around the world, had the opportunity to learn. She recognized that education is not just about acquiring knowledge; it's about **empowerment**, **freedom**, and the ability to shape your future. Education, for Malala, was the key to breaking the cycle of oppression and poverty.

The lesson here is that **education is one of the most powerful tools you can possess.** Whether it's formal education, self-learning, or developing new skills, investing in your own knowledge is crucial for personal and professional growth. Malala's story teaches us that no matter the obstacles, whether financial, social, or personal, the pursuit of learning is always worth the effort.

For practical application, consider your current level of commitment to your own education. Ask yourself: **Am I investing enough in my learning and development?** Whether you're already well-established in your career or just starting out, continuous learning is essential for growth. Make time to learn new skills, read books, attend workshops, or take courses that challenge you to think differently and expand your horizons.

One way to apply this is to **set learning goals** for yourself. Identify specific areas where you want to grow, whether in your career, personal interests, or intellectual pursuits. By making education a lifelong priority, you'll unlock new opportunities and gain the confidence to tackle challenges just as Malala did.

3. Resilience in the Face of Adversity—Use Setbacks as Fuel for Growth

Malala's life was marked by incredible adversity, but rather than allowing these challenges to break her, she used them as fuel to propel her forward. After the Taliban's attempt on her life, Malala didn't retreat—she came back stronger, using the global attention from the attack to amplify her voice and fight for girls' education with even more determination. Her resilience in the face of unimaginable hardship shows us that **setbacks** can be transformed into opportunities for growth and change.

The lesson here is that **resilience is essential** when facing challenges, both large and small. Life will inevitably throw obstacles in your path, but it's your ability to bounce back that defines your success. Malala's journey teaches us that even the most difficult experiences can be used as stepping stones toward something greater.

For practical application, reflect on the challenges you've faced or are currently facing. Ask yourself: **Am I letting setbacks hold me back, or am I using them to grow stronger?** Whether it's a professional setback, a personal loss, or a difficult situation in your life, see it as an opportunity to build resilience. Learn from the experience, adapt, and move forward with even more determination.

One way to build resilience is to **reframe challenges as opportunities**. Instead of focusing on the negative aspects of a setback, look for the lessons you can take from the experience. By shifting your mindset, you'll be better equipped to overcome obstacles and turn them into catalysts for growth, just as Malala did.

Conclusion

As we come to the end of this book, we've traveled through the lives of some of the most extraordinary individuals in history. From ancient philosophers to modern-day trailblazers, from warriors and kings to scientists and artists, the figures we've explored all shared one crucial trait: **a relentless commitment to becoming their best selves.** They were flawed, they faced hardships, and they encountered countless obstacles, but they persevered. The essence of greatness lies not in perfection but in **the continual pursuit of improvement.**

What we've uncovered throughout these pages is that **self-improvement isn't a destination—it's a lifelong journey.** The people we've examined didn't wake up one day as the icons we remember. They struggled, made mistakes, and failed repeatedly. But what set them apart was their refusal to let those failures define them. Whether it was **Abraham Lincoln's persistence through political failure, Marie Curie's tireless dedication to science,** or **Malala Yousafzai's courage in the face of violent oppression,** these figures remind us that greatness is born from struggle and sustained through resilience.

Let's now reflect on the core lessons we've drawn from these historical figures, as they form the foundation of a life committed to **personal growth, strength,** and **the betterment of self and society.** As you continue on your own path of self-improvement, take these final lessons to heart.

1. Self-Awareness: The Beginning of All Growth

From the very first chapters of this book, it became evident that **self-awareness is the foundation of personal growth.** Figures like **Socrates** taught us the importance of questioning ourselves, of understanding who we are, what drives us, and what values we stand for. Without a deep understanding of our own strengths, weaknesses, motivations, and desires, any effort to improve will be superficial at best.

For example, **Marcus Aurelius**, the stoic Roman emperor, constantly practiced self-reflection, journaling his thoughts to better understand his own mind. His **Meditations** were not written for the public—they were written for himself, as a guide for living with wisdom and integrity. He understood that self-awareness is a continuous process, one that requires ongoing effort to stay grounded in our principles and avoid being swayed by fleeting emotions or external pressures.

Practical Takeaway: Make time for self-reflection. Whether it's through journaling, meditation, or simply taking a few minutes at the end of each day to assess your actions, thoughts, and decisions, build the habit of checking in with yourself. This will give you the clarity needed to make conscious, intentional choices, rather than reacting blindly to life's challenges.

2. Resilience: Embrace the Struggles, Learn from Failures

One of the most consistent themes throughout history, as seen through the lives of people like **Oprah Winfrey**, **Nelson Mandela**, and **Thomas Edison**, is that **resilience is a key factor in achieving anything meaningful**. Every person we've explored faced moments of doubt, rejection, and defeat. What made them remarkable was their ability to rise after every fall.

Oprah Winfrey, for instance, was born into poverty and faced significant personal hardships, yet she turned these experiences into a source of strength, transforming herself into one of the most influential figures of modern times. **Nelson Mandela** spent 27 years in prison, yet he emerged with a spirit unbroken, becoming a symbol of reconciliation and peace for an entire nation. **Thomas Edison**

failed thousands of times in his quest to invent the electric light bulb, yet he famously said, "I have not failed. I've just found 10,000 ways that won't work."

Practical Takeaway: Embrace failure as a stepping stone to success. When faced with setbacks, resist the temptation to give up or let the experience define you. Instead, ask yourself what you can learn from the failure. **Use it as fuel** to come back stronger and smarter. Resilience doesn't mean avoiding failure—it means building the strength to keep going in the face of it.

3. Courage: Stand for Something Greater Than Yourself

The greatest figures in history weren't just great because of what they accomplished—they were great because they stood for something larger than themselves. Figures like **Mahatma Gandhi**, **Mother Teresa**, and **Malala Yousafzai** are revered not only for their personal courage but because their courage was rooted in a mission to serve others and fight for justice.

Mahatma Gandhi led a movement of non-violent resistance that inspired millions and reshaped the course of history. He was not seeking power for himself—his courage came from his commitment to freedom and justice for all. Similarly, **Malala Yousafzai** stood up for the education of girls in the face of brutal oppression. Even after being attacked by the Taliban, she didn't waver. Her courage wasn't about personal glory—it was about the fight for the rights of millions of girls around the world.

Practical Takeaway: Find a cause that is bigger than yourself. Whether it's within your career, your community, or a global movement, aligning yourself with a mission gives you the strength to overcome challenges that would otherwise feel insurmountable. When you are fighting for something larger than yourself, you tap into a **deeper well of motivation** and courage.

4. Vision and Purpose: Be Guided by Your North Star

Many of the figures we studied in this book had a clear **vision and purpose** that guided their actions, even when the odds seemed insurmountable. **Alexander the Great, Steve Jobs,** and **Leonardo da Vinci** all shared a deep sense of purpose that allowed them to push beyond their limits. They saw the world not as it was, but as it could be, and they devoted their lives to turning their visions into reality.

Steve Jobs, in particular, revolutionized the technology industry not because he was just good at making computers, but because he had a vision of how technology could change the way people live, work, and create. His purpose was not just to build a successful company but to **change the world** through innovation. Similarly, **Leonardo da Vinci's** curiosity and imagination drove him to explore new frontiers in art, science, and engineering, always seeking to merge beauty with functionality.

Practical Takeaway: Define your purpose. What is your personal vision for your life? What motivates you at a deeper level? Without a clear purpose, it's easy to lose direction or become overwhelmed by daily distractions. Take the time to reflect on what matters most to you, and use that as your **North Star**—the guiding principle that will help you stay on course, no matter what obstacles arise.

5. Discipline: Consistency Builds Greatness

Throughout the lives of great historical figures like **Isaac Newton, Marie Curie,** and **Friedrich Nietzsche**, we saw the importance of **discipline and consistency**. These individuals didn't just achieve greatness through brief bursts of inspiration or luck—they worked relentlessly, often in solitude, for years, perfecting their craft and pushing the boundaries of knowledge.

Isaac Newton spent decades immersed in his studies, and it was this intense focus that led to some of the most groundbreaking discoveries in physics and mathematics. Similarly, **Marie Curie** dedicated years to her work on radioactivity, often working under incredibly dangerous conditions, driven by her passion for science and the desire to contribute to humanity's understanding of the natural world.

Practical Takeaway: Success is built on small, consistent actions over time. Discipline is what separates those who achieve their goals from those who give up at the first sign of difficulty. Whether it's your fitness goals, career ambitions, or personal development, focus on **showing up every day** and doing the work. The path to greatness isn't about grand gestures—it's about being consistent, even when the work feels mundane or difficult.

Moving Forward: Becoming Your Best Self

As we conclude this book, remember that **greatness is not reserved for a select few**. Each of the historical figures we explored started somewhere, often facing insurmountable odds. What set them apart wasn't natural talent or luck—it was their mindset, their habits, and their unwavering belief in their capacity to grow and make a difference.

The message here is clear: **you, too, can become your best self**. Whether you're facing personal challenges, striving to achieve a long-held goal, or simply looking to improve day by day, the lessons from these figures can serve as your guide. **Self-improvement is a journey**, and while the road may be long, it is one worth traveling.

As you move forward, keep these final thoughts in mind:

- **Embrace self-awareness**: Know who you are and who you want to become.
- **Cultivate resilience**: Don't let failure stop you—let it

shape you.
- **Find courage**: Stand for something bigger than yourself.
- **Pursue your purpose**: Let your vision guide your actions.
- **Practice discipline**: Greatness is built through consistency.

The figures in this book lived their lives with purpose, courage, and determination. Now it's your turn. **Learn from the best. Become your best.**

Your journey is just beginning.

Acknowledgments

Writing this book has been an incredible journey, and it wouldn't have been possible without the support and inspiration of many people along the way.

First, I want to express my deepest gratitude to **my family and close friends**, who have stood by me through countless late nights and early mornings spent writing. Your encouragement and belief in me have been the backbone of this project.

A special thanks to **the historical figures whose lives shaped this book**—though they are no longer with us, their legacies continue to inspire and guide people toward greatness. Their stories have taught me as much as I hope they will teach the readers of this book.

To **my editor**, whose keen eye and relentless dedication helped refine and sharpen this work, thank you for pushing me to deliver my best. Your feedback has been invaluable in shaping this book into something I am truly proud of.

I also want to extend my appreciation to the countless **mentors, teachers, and writers** who have inspired me over the years. This book is a product of not only my effort but the collective wisdom of those who have influenced my thinking and encouraged me to chase my dreams.

Lastly, thank you to **the readers**—without you, this book would simply be a collection of words. It's your desire for self-improvement, your hunger for knowledge, and your willingness to learn from the greats of history that makes this work meaningful. I hope these pages serve as a guide, a companion, and a source of inspiration for your own journey toward becoming your best self.

Milton Keynes UK
Ingram Content Group UK Ltd.
UKHW040258181024
449757UK00001B/105